DRUGS AND DRUG DEPENDENCE

Drugs and drug dependence

Edited by
GRIFFITH EDWARDS
M. A. H. RUSSELL
DAVID HAWKS
MAXINE MacCAFFERTY
on behalf of
The Addiction Research Unit,
Institute of Psychiatry,
University of London

SAXON HOUSE | LEXINGTON BOOKS

23,434

Published by
SAXON HOUSE, D. C. Heath Ltd.
Westmead, Farnborough, Hants., England.

Jointly with
LEXINGTON BOOKS, D. C. Heath & Co.
Lexington, Mass. USA.

ISBN 0 347 01126 8
Library of Congress Catalog Card Number 75-30136
Printed in Great Britain by Butler and Tanner, Frome and London.

Contents

Acknowledgements vii

Preface x

RESEARCH STUDIES

1 Introduction 3

Part I *Epidemiological studies*

2 The dimensions of drug dependence in the United Kingdom 5
3 Cannabis use amongst British university students 30
4 Abuse of methylamphetamine 52
5 Sedative abuse by heroin addicts 68
6 Heroin users in a provincial town and their follow-up over a three year period 73
7 Appraisal 87

Part II *Treatment populations and treatment organisation*

8 The British approach to the treatment of heroin addiction 93
9 Patterns of behaviour of heroin addicts 104
10 British opiate users: I People approaching London drug treatment centres 118
11 British opiate users: II Differences between those given an opiate script and those not given one 134
12 A comparison of Canadian narcotic addicts in Great Britain and in Canada 146
13 Treatment of methylamphetamine users during the 1968 epidemic 155
14 The evaluation of measures to deal with drug dependence in the United Kingdom 163
15 Appraisal 176

THEORETICAL CONSIDERATIONS

16 Introduction 181
17 What is dependence? 182
18 The alcohologist's addiction: some implications of having lost control over the disease concept of alcoholism 188
19 Aspects of the relationship between alcohol and drug abuse 199
20 Towards a social psychology of dependence 214
21 Appraisal 222

List of Contributors 224

References 225

Bibliography of the Addiction Research Unit 235

Index 246

Acknowledgements

We wish to thank Sir Denis Hill, who as Head of the Department of Psychiatry of the Institute of Psychiatry, has given the Unit absolutely crucial support. Dr Philip Connell (Director of the Bethlem–Maudsley Drug Dependence Clinical Research and Treatment Unit), has been a constant source of wise and generous counsel. The contribution of Dr A. N. Oppenheim (Reader in Social Psychology, London School of Economics) to the building of an inter-disciplinary Unit has been in many ways indispensible. Since the Unit received a consolidated DHSS/MRC programme grant useful guidance has been given by an Advisory Committee under the Chairmanship of Sir Martin Roth: we would thank Sir Martin and his colleagues not only in their formal role, but also for tangible friendship.

The major financial support for the research has come from the Medical Research Council and the Department of Health and Social Security. To these funding bodies who have so generously financed studies on often very sensitive questions, while allowing the research team autonomy of judgement, special gratitude is owed.

We acknowledge with gratitude advice and assistance given us by Dr H. David Archibald, Dr Michael Ashley-Miller, Dr A. A. Baker, Dr Keith Ball, Mr Peter Beedle, Mr D. H. Beese, Dr Douglas Bennett, Dr J. L. T. Birley, Dr E. R. Bransby, Dr Monamy Buckle, Dr Denis Cahal, Dr Peter Chapple, Mr D. Cordy, Dr T. A. Dibby, Dr Joan Faulkner, Dr S. L. Gauntlett, Dr M. M. Glatt, Dr Roy Goulding, Dr Malcolm Lader, Dr Isaac Marks, Dr Alan Mawson, Miss Joy Mott, Professor M. A. Preston, Professor Michael Shepherd, Dr Alan Sippert, Mr H. B. Spear, Professor Hannah Steinberg, Mr G. F. Todd, Professor Nigel Walker, and Professor John Wing. We have in various studies relied on use of DHSS and Home Office records, and we would particularly acknowledge the protection of subject anonymity which has been afforded. The assistance of the Central Statistical Office and of the Home Office Research Unit is gratefully noted.

For access to research populations we have to thank many persons and organisations. We would particularly mention consultants in charge of Drug Treatment Clinics and their staff: Dr T. H. Bewley, Dr H. Dale Beckett, Dr P. Boyd, Dr J. Buchanan, Dr I. G. Christie, Dr Philip Connell, Dr E. Curry, Dr P. J. Dally, Dr S. Das Gupta, Dr J. Denham, Dr G. Garmany, Dr M. M. Glatt, Dr E. P. Haldane, Dr D. E. N. Hassall, Professor J. Hinton, Dr L. K. V. Howell, Dr K. H. Lotinga, Dr J. Lyon, Dr J. W. Mack, Dr W. Massey, Dr

M. Mitcheson, Dr G. B. Oppenheim, Dr J. L. Reed, Dr R. F. Tredgold, Dr M. Tripp, Dr J. G. Wier, and Dr J. H. Willis. Generous co-operation in mounting a variety of surveys has been given by magistrates and court officials, prison authorities and staff, probation officers, college authorities, student unions, medical committees and governing bodies of hospitals, and general practitioners. Voluntary agencies which have borne our questioning include, among many others, CARE, the Community Drug Project, Phoenix House and St. Martin's-in-the-Fields Social Service Centre.

Research of the sort we report in this book relies fundamentally on the generosity and trust of people who owe the research workers nothing, and who answer what must often seem intrusive questions. In this regard our thanks must by now be due to many thousands of individuals – we will not attempt here to categorise them, but to each and every such person we express our gratitude for their helpfulness and tolerance.

Expert statistical advice and help with data processing has been given at different times by Miss Jane Chandler, Miss Margaret Elliott, Miss Carole Hewlett, Professor A. E. Maxwell, Mr Peter Nicholls, Mr Upendra Patel, Mr Julian Peto, Dr Patrick Slater, Mr Colin Taylor, and staff of the Department of Biometrics of the Institute of Psychiatry, and the University College Computer Centre.

The secretarial staff of the Unit have always been full members of the research team, and we wish to acknowledge their skills, energy, patience and unstinting loyalty. The following gave help in the original preparation of published papers: Miss Nadine Butler, Miss E. Cross, Mrs S. Ghosh, Miss Christine Guest, Miss Pauline Hampson, Mrs S. Heaven, Mrs Laura Hitchins, Mrs Joy Hodge, Miss Marion Horton, Mrs Gaynor Impanni, Mrs Joyce Oliphant, Mrs Julia Polglaze, Miss Sue Rees, Mrs Jean Crutch, Miss Pat Bevan, Miss Serena Dalrymple, Miss Jacqueline May and Miss Beryl Skinner. Mrs Sylvia Ghosh has played a central part in preparing the present book for publication.

Certain authors and co-authors who have not at any time been staff members of the Research Unit have generously allowed their work to be published in a book emanating from the Unit. In this regard we would thank Dr K. Myers, and Dr M. Webb.

We would thank the Editors of the following journals for permission to reprint material which appears in this book: *British Journal of Addiction, British Medical Journal, Bulletin on Narcotics, International Journal of Addictions, Lancet, Psychological Medicine* and *Quarterly Journal of Studies on Alcohol.* To the publishers of the following conference proceedings, Butterworths (Sydney), our thanks are also due.

We thank the journals concerned and the authors for waiving copyright fees. All royalties from the sale of this book will be paid to the funds of the Addiction Research Unit.

To our publishers thanks are due for unfailing helpfulness and much patience.

Preface

The purpose of this book is to present some view of the manner in which research methods have over recent years been applied to socio-medical aspects of illicit drug taking. To this end a selection of research papers from the Addiction Research Unit are put together. The work of this particular Unit obviously represents only a part of this country's recent scientific writings on drug dependence and a very small part indeed of the world's output. The papers are taken simply as text around which to arrange a debate on how the difficult business may be tackled of applying the scientific method to these problems and it is very much as material for critical discussion rather than as presentation of given truths that this selection of papers is essentially intended.

The second part of the book moves on from a consideration of research and research methods to a debate on underlying theoretical issues such as the meanings to be given to the concept of 'dependence'.

Each group of papers is preceded by a brief introduction which signposts what is to come, and at the end of each section a short critical appraisal is given which seeks to identify the crucial issues and the questions for further debate.

In a companion volume some of the Unit's work on drinking and on cigarette smoking is presented, together with a discussion of what has been termed 'the research position'. By that phrase is meant the position of the research worker in relation to the community which surrounds him and the policy makers who are the potential consumers of his product.

RESEARCH STUDIES

1 Introduction

This section of the book is itself divided into two parts. The first group of papers deals with epidemiological studies, while the second group has as its theme treatment populations and aspects of treatment organisation. Such a segmentation is employed only as a matter of convenience. Epidemiological studies speak to treatment issues, and equally the study of treatment populations provides an element of epidemiological insight.

The section on epidemiology starts with a review by David Hawks of 'the dimensions of drug dependence'. A particular year's statistics on any aspect of the drug problem are in a changing scene likely to be more or less out of date by the time they are published, and the intention of Hawk's paper is to provide a text for debate on the central issues of monitoring and description rather than to present an up-to-date compendium of all the facts. Another paper in the epidemiology section is a study of heroin users in a provincial town, and provides an illustration of the strengths and limitations of a research method which utilises network tracing rather than formal sampling.

Papers on methylamphetamine and sedative abuse describe studies based on a sampling technique which might fairly be described as the method of catch-as-catch-can: the method in each instance was to go out into the field and contact a number of agencies where people using these drugs were known to present themselves. Yet other sampling approaches lie behind the paper on cannabis users (Adele Kosviner and her colleagues).

The section on treatment is inevitably rather dominated by concern with what seems internationally to be known as 'the British system' of prescribing for opiate addicts. The system designation continues to enjoy currency despite the frequent British disclaimer as to there actually being any system in existence. It all no doubt depends on what meaning one chooses to give to the particular word, and despite the disclaimers it seems obvious that there are now certain ground rules which operate. The first paper in this section has therefore been chosen as one which outlines 'the British approach'.

The examination of the nature of this clinic operation then continues with a paper (Stimson and Ogborne), which reports on a sample survey of subjects attending London drug treatment centres. The orientation here is that of social psychology. There then follow two recent papers (Blumberg and his colleagues), which describe not only those people who are given prescriptions by the clinics but also the characteristics of those who are refused such maintenance treatment. Between them these three research reports provide for discussion a quite considerable body of material on who comes to the clinics and the manner in which the clinics operate.

Such a focus on clinic populations would be unfortunate if it accidentally carried the implied message that opiates and opiate takers are properly the only social concern. This would be far from a correct conclusion. The data overwhelmingly illustrate the arbitrariness of the 'opiate taker' label: nearly all young people who are self-damagingly involved in drug taking have acquaintance with a whole spectrum of drugs. Making any drug the central element of definition can also have the adverse consequence of putting too heavy an emphasis on typology by drug, rather than analysis in terms of person and social circumstance. The fact remains however that the treatment centres at present only very exceptionally take on for support people other than those who have been recently using narcotics, and there is no official system of care or well worked out strategy for, say, the person who is largely injecting barbiturates. A treatment orientation which has drug maintenance as more or less central to the approach, is somewhat stymied when as with barbiturates there is no obvious maintenance treatment to hand. The short paper which recounts experience with treatment of methylamphetamine users illustrates the dilemma.

The two papers which conclude this treatment section bear on the large question of whether the British approach to the nation's drug problems has been successful. The paper by Jim Zacune examines the light which may be thrown on the matter by analysing the implications of an 'experiment of nature' – the social adjustment of Canadian addicts in their home country as compared with their adjustment during sojourn in England. The essay by David Hawks seeks to determine what might be the several criteria of a policy's success, and then lists the available information against those criteria.

Part I Epidemiological studies

2 The dimensions of drug dependence in the United Kingdom*

DAVID HAWKS

Summary

The development and dimensions of drug dependency in the United Kingdom are reviewed. While pre-eminence is given to the development of opiate abuse it is emphasised that multiple drug use is the much more prevalent pattern. In addition to tracing the historical development of the present heroin 'epidemic', the age, ethnic, geographic, socio-economic and delinquent associations of opiate dependence are described. Evidence relating to mortality, morbidity and prognosis is also reviewed. While the abuse of other drugs is less adequately documented, sections are included on amphetamines, barbiturates/hypnotics, cannabis and LSD.

A number of very tentative conclusions are drawn relating to treatment measures, illicit sources, initiation and causation. The paucity of studies which examine the relationship between variables is commented on together with the methodological problems which beset research in this field. It is argued that these methodological problems are unlikely to be met except by prospective studies which, if they are to be economical, must identify 'at risk' groups. Such studies by their very nature require a degree of co-ordination and continuity of research effort which is unlikely to be realised by individual research workers.

---

* Condensed from a paper originally published in *International Journal of the Addictions*, vol. 6, 1971, pp. 135–60.

Introduction

Any account of the epidemiology of drug dependence in the United Kingdom inclines to give emphasis to the narcotic problem. That this should be so is hardly surprising given the recency of this phenomenon, its rapid escalation, and its associated high morbidity and mortality. Even so it needs to be recognised that the 'drug problem' in the United Kingdom involves multiple drug abuse and that the curtailment of a particular epidemic is likely to be attended by the increased abuse of another drug.

Narcotic abuse

The history of recent changes in the pattern of narcotic abuse in the United Kingdom has been documented in a number of sources. Bewley (1968) has pointed out that in the past ten years there has been a marked change in the incidence and the characteristics of those known to be dependent. Before 1950 the number known to be abusing narcotic drugs was relatively stable, varying between 400 and 600. Those involved tended to be middle-aged and a disproportionate number were drawn from the medical and paramedical professions. In most cases addiction had a therapeutic origin and the drug involved was usually morphine.

Almost coincidental with the publication of the first report of the Inter-Departmental Committee on Drug Addiction (the Brain Committee) there originated a series of changes which have continued in the same direction until the present day. There appeared both an increase in the number of people known to be dependent on narcotic drugs and an increasing tendency for their addiction to have nontherapeutic origins. The persons concerned also tended to be younger and predominantly male. There was evidence that the drug preferred was heroin rather than morphine and indications were that other drugs were being increasingly abused. Whereas the misuse of illicitly obtained drugs was originally confined to London the problem also spread to other parts of the country (see Tables 2.1, 2.2 and 2.3).

It needs to be emphasised that the figures on which these observations are based have not, until recently, been comprehensive. Prior to the introduction of the Dangerous Drugs (Notification of Addicts) Regulations in 1968, it was not obligatory for doctors treating dependent patients to notify their dependence, and the figures published by the Home Office were largely derived from the routine examination of pharmacists' records. The annual statistics published by the Home Office until 1968 showed only those addicts known to have been taking drugs during the previous year; they excluded

Table 2.1

Number of addicts known to the Home Office[a]
sex, origin and drugs used 1935–73

				Origin			Drugs Used[b]					
Year	No. of known addicts	Sex M	Sex F	Therapeutic[c]	Non-therapeutic	Unknown	Morphine[d]	Heroin[e]	Cocaine[f]	Pethidine[g]	Methadone[h]	Professional addicts
1935	approx. 700											approx. 120
1936	616	313	300									147
1937	620	300	320									140
1938	519	246	273									143
1939	534	269	265									131
1940	505	251	254									90
1941	503	252	251									91
1942	524	275	249									98
1943	541	280	261									94
1944	559	185	274									93
1945	367	144	223									80
1946	369	144	225									79
1947	383	164	219									87
1948	395	198	197									119
1949	326	164	162									100
1950	306	158	148									95
1951	301	153	148									77
1952	297	153	144									75
1953	290	149	141									71
1954	317	148	169									72
1955	335	159	176				179	57	6	64	21	86[i]
1956	333	163	170				176	54	6	64	20	99
1957	359	174	185				178	66	16	92	31	88
1958	442	245	349	349	68	25	205	62	25	117	47	74
1959	454	196	258	344	98	12	204	68	30	116	60	68
1960	437	195	242	309	122	6	177	94	52	98	68	63
1961	470	223	247	293	159	18	168	132	84	105	59	61
1962	532	262	270	312	212	8	157	175	112	112	54	57
1963	635	339	296	355	270	10	172	237	171	128	59	56
1964	753	409	344	368	372	13	171	342	211	128	62	58
1965	927	558	369	344	580	3	160	521	311	102	72	45
1966	1349	886	463	351	982	16	157	899	441	123	156	54
1967	1729	1262	467	313	1385	31	158	1299	462	112	243	56
1968	2782	2161	621	306	2420	56	198	2240	564	120	486	43
1969	2881	2295	586	289	2533	59	345	1417	311	128	1687	43
1970	2661	2071	590	295	2321	45	346	914	198	122	1820	38
1971	2769	2134	635	265	2457	47	346	959	178	135	1927	44
1972	2944	2272	672	244	2659	41	292	868	178	98	2171	33
1973	3025	2345	680	207	2631	187	268	866	194	81	2247	29

(For notes see p.8).

Table 2.1

[a] The sharp decrease in 1945 in number of addicts is due to the fact that until that year cases were included up to ten years after the Home Office had received the last information. From 1958 only those notified as using in a specific year are included in that year's figures. It is thus almost certain that the annual figures after 1958 give a conservative picture of drug dependence in any one year. On the other hand it is impossible to say whether all those notified would be covered by a definition of addiction or dependence. Only from 1968 was it imperative for a medical opinion to be given before a person was notified as addicted. After H. B. Spear (1969).

[b] Alone or in combination with other drugs.

[c] This information was not collected prior to 1958 (except for heroin addicts).

[d] Exact numbers not available but the proportion of addicts using morphine has varied from approximately 90% in 1935 to 60–67% in 1950–54.

[e] Exact numbers not available but the proportion of addicts using heroin has varied from 5% in 1935 to 19% in 1952.

[f] Exact numbers not available but less than 10% of the addicts used cocaine.

[g] From 1948 to 1954 the proportion of addicts using pethidine varied between 12% and 19%.

[h] Exact numbers not available except in 1949 and 1951 when there were 2 and 3 respectively.

[i] Nurses included in 'professional' for the first time; hitherto they had been included in 'other'.

[j] The increase in the number of known addicts which appears in the 1968 figures is spurious. During 1968 treatment centres were set up and many who were previously unknown, but nevertheless addicted, came forward and were incorporated into the 1968 total.

---

those who were not known to be currently taking drugs – for example, those addicts in prison or abroad or those who obtained their drugs entirely from illicit sources. While the total number of opiate addicts in the United Kingdom is still by international standards small – estimated by Bewley (1968) to be of the order of four to eight per 100,000 – the rate at which new cases have been notified leaves no cause for complacency. Thirty-six times as many addicts were known in 1968 as were known in 1958, a difference which partly reflects the introduction of the Notification of Addicts regulations in April 1968. One hundred and nineteen times as many new addicts were notified in 1968 as were first known in 1958.

Spear (1969) has attempted to analyse the events of the 1950s which

Table 2.2
Ages of addicts known to the Home Office[a]

	Under 20		20–34		35–49		50 and over		Age unknown
Age[b]	all drugs	heroin	all drugs	heroin	all drugs	heroin	all drugs	heroin	heroin
1959	–	–	50	35	92	7	278	26	34
1960	1	1	62	52	91	14	267	27	16
1961	2	2	94	87	95	19	272	24	7
1962	3	3	132	126	107	24	274	22	16
1963	17	17	184	162	128	38	298	20	8
1964	40	40	257	219	138	61	311	22	7
1965	145	134	347	319	134	52	291	16	10
1966	329	317	558	479	162	83	286	20	14
1967	395	381	906	827	142	66	279	24	7
1968	764	709	1530	1390	146	78	260	20	82
1969	637	598	1789	1709	174	101	241	46	40
1970	405	365	1813	1705	158	95	253	50	32
1971	338	304	2010	1912	156	94	226	47	39
1972	279	260	2262	2178	178	126	204	42	21
1973	253	226	2368	2262	185	129	214	49	5

[a] After H. B. Spear (1969).
[b] Precise details of age groupings were not included in Annual Reports until 1959.

heralded the present epidemic. He observes that the first significant change in the situation occurred after the Second World War, when there was an increase in the number of seizures of cannabis made by HM Customs and Excise. The first post-war annual report (1946) acknowledged that there was a small traffic in cannabis, largely confined to two black groups with black seamen being the principal importers. A further 'considerable increase' was noted in the following year, and the same source was implicated. By 1950 it was clear that the traffic in cannabis was of greater importance than the traffic in opium, and the total number of persons prosecuted for offences involving cannabis has risen ever since (Table 2.4).

While the use of this drug continued to be linked mostly with the non-white population, in 1950 it became apparent that cannabis was also being used by the indigenous population. A major case of drug trafficking occurred soon after when approximately 1,200 grains of morphine, mostly in tablet form,

Table 2.3
Number and origin of all heroin addicts and of new heroin addicts 1945–68[a]

Year	Total no. of heroin addicts	Therapeutic	Non-therapeutic	Unknown	No. of new heroin addicts in year	Therapeutic	Non-therapeutic	Unknown
1945					1	1	–	–
1946					1	–	1	–
1947					3	–	3	–
1948					4	1	3	–
1949		Not available			3	1	2	–
1950					3	1	1	1
1951					1	–	1	–
1952					8	3	5	–
1953					4	–	4	–
1954	57	20	36	–	16	2	14	–
1955	54	18	36	–	10	1	9	–
1956	53	17	36	–	10	1	9	–
1957	66	21	45	–	7	2	5	–
1958	62	19	43	–	11	3	8	–
1959	68	21	47	–	11	2	9	–
1960	94	22	72	–	24	1	23	–
1961	132	20	112	–	56	2	54	–
1962	175	18	157	–	72	–	72	–
1963	237	18	222	–	90	–	90	–
1964	342	13	329	–	162	2	160	–
1965	521	12	509	–	259	1	258	–
1966	899	13	885	1	522	3	518	1
1967	1299	9	1290	–	745	–	745	–
1968	2240	8	2232	–	1306	2	1304	–

[a] After H.B. Spear (1969).

and 14 ounces of cocaine were stolen from a firm of wholesale chemists. While the drugs had been stolen by one of the firm's employees, it transpired that the instigator was a person having contact with drug addicts in the West End of London. However, the persons to whom he supplied the drugs were already known addicts and there was no evidence that others were recruited to the habit by his activities. A further major case of trafficking occurred in 1951 when the dispensary of a hospital was broken into and considerable quantities of morphine, heroin and cocaine were stolen. The person involved was a former employee of the hospital. Although the full extent of his activities cannot be charted, it appears that a majority of those supplied drugs by him had no previous experience of heroin addiction. All of those of whom it could be ascertained that they had received their initial supplies from this source subsequently came to the notice of the Home Office as heroin addicts. While Spear does not attempt to explain the change in the pattern of drug abuse in the United Kingdom, he does observe that the appearance of a pusher in the West End of London and the scarcity of cannabis following increased police activity appear to have played a significant part.

Sex

In 1958 the ratio of male to female addicts (including narcotic addicts) known to the Home Office was 1:1.2. Prior to 1958 the ratio had been, with minor and inconsistent deviations, 1:1. In 1968 the ratio was 3.5:1, reflecting the consistent trend over the previous five years for males to increasingly predominate (Table 2.1).

As the average age of known addicts has declined and the number of cases of non-therapeutic addiction increased, the ratio of males to females has increased until it approximates that reported for American juvenile addicts. A number of other studies (Hawks et al. 1969; O'Connell, 1970; Murphy et al., 1969) have confirmed this tendency in adolescent non-narcotic users.

Age

Whereas in 1959 there were no heroin addicts under the age of 20, in 1968 they constituted 32 per cent of the total. A similar increase occurred in the 20–24 age group while those over 35 have stayed numerically the same (Table 2.2).

Origin

The number of heroin addicts whose dependence had a therapeutic origin has stayed remarkably stable over the entire period for which information is available (1954–69), while those whose addiction was nontherapeutic have shown a marked increase (Table 2.3). Of the 1,306 new addicts notified in 1968, all but two were of non-therapeutic origin. This tendency has paralleled the decreasing significance of the 'professional' addict, the medical and paramedical addict. Whereas professional addicts constituted 31 per cent of the total known addicts in 1950 and 14 per cent in 1960, they represented less than two per cent of the total in 1968.

Drug of choice[1]

Changes in the patterns of drugs used have largely followed changes in the origin and composition of the addict population. Whereas in 1958 only 14 per cent (62) of known addicts used heroin compared to 46 per cent (205) who used morphine and 26 per cent (117) who used pethidine, in 1968 the percentages were 80 per cent (2,240) heroin, seven per cent (198) morphine and four per cent (120) pethidine. This marked change reflects the younger, nontherapeutic addict's preference for heroin. Even in 1965 only 39 per cent (52) of the 35–49 age group were dependent on heroin; for those aged 50+ the percentage was five per cent (16).
Of current concern is the increasing tendency for methadone to be the principal drug of addiction. In 1958 only 11 per cent (47) were dependent on methadone; in 1968 the comparable percentage was 17 per cent (486). Preliminary figures for 1969 indicate a further percentage increase.

Nationality

The great majority of heroin addicts in the United Kingdom have been of British nationality. Of all new cases of heroin addiction notified over the years 1955–64, 77 per cent (348) were British, 20 per cent (88) Canadian, Australian, American or New Zealander and three per cent (14) were of other nationalities. Canadians have always constituted the single largest non-British group. Ninety-one are known to have arrived in the United Kingdom between 1959 and 1969. The peculiar characteristics of the Canadian group, their status in the United Kingdom, and the history of their migration has been analysed by Zacune (1971).

A study of those 519 persons known to the Home Office as dependent on narcotics in 1965 (Gobius and Hawks, 1970) showed that 83 per cent (433) were of British nationality, while in a representative sample of 111 patients prescribed heroin in London treatment centres in 1969 the percentage was 86 per cent (95) (Stimson and Ogborne, 1970[b]). A number of studies of largely unnotified heroin users (Kosviner, et al., 1968; Alarcon and Rathod, 1968; Zacune, et al., 1969[b]) have confirmed the view that the heroin problem in the United Kingdom largely concerns the indigenous population and that minority ethnic groups are not, as yet, disproportionately represented as is the case in the United States of America.

Table 2.4

Drug Offences[a b]

Year	Opium	Cannabis	Manufactured drugs
1921	184	Not	67
1922	94	controlled	110
1923	167	in the	128
1924	48	United	50
1925	35	Kingdom	33
1926	50		45
1927	27		33
1928	41		21
1929	39	3	31
1930	16	1	48
1931	26	3	40
1932	37	6	43
1933	17	6	32
1934	39	14	33
1935	13	15	33
1936	17	8	35
1937	9	3	27
1938	6	18	35
1939	13	1	36
1940	14	3	37
1941	201	–	25
1942	199	–	27
1943	147	2	40
1944	256	6	32
1945	206	4	20
1946	65	11	27
1947	76	46	65
1948	78	51	48
1949	52	60	56
1950	41	86	42
1951	64	132	47
1952	62	98	48

Table continued over page

Table 2.4 (continued)

Year	Opium	Cannabis	Manufactured drugs
1953	47	88	44
1954	28	144	47
1955	17	115	37
1956	12	103	37
1957	9	51	30
1958	8	99	41
1959	18	185	26
1960	15	235	28
1961	15	288	61
1962	16	588	71
1963	20	663	63
1964	14	544	101
1965	13	626	128
1966	36	1119	242
1967	58	2393	573
1968	73	3071	1099
1969	53	4683	1359
1970	66	7520	1214
1971	55	9219	1570
1972	98	12611	2068
1973	244[b]	14119	8497[c]

[a] From 1921–53 inclusive figures relate to prosecutions; from 1954 figures relate to convictions.

[b] After H. B. Spear (1969).

[b] Includes medicinal opium

[c] Includes offences under the Dangerous Drugs Act 1965, The Drugs (Prevention of Misuse) Act 1964, and the Misuse of Drugs Act 1971 which came into effect on 1 July 1973 and which repeated the 1965 and 1964 Acts.

Geographical distribution

While the misuse of illicitly obtained narcotics has spread beyond London, it remains the case that London is the main source of supply and the majority of known addicts are accommodated within its boundaries. In 1969, 80 per cent (904) of known addicts were registered with London Treatment centres.

A number of other urban centres have received publicity (Jones, 1968; Alarcon, 1969a; Owens, 1967) as having 'drug problems', but they tend to be readily accessible to London; to be supplied by London contacts; and when local restrictive measures are taken, 'lose' some of their addicts to London (Zacune, et al., 1969[a]). This is not to suggest, of course, that the vast majority of United Kingdom addicts are born in London or that where local centres are established they do not attract addicts from other areas, but only that addicts tend to congregate in London where illicit supplies are more plentiful and where the society of other drug users guarantees the continued fulfilment of their needs and the support which the 'junkie' subculture supplies.

Poverty

There have been very few systematic attempts to inquire into the actual material circumstances of those addicted, though, as has been previously stated, minority groups are not disproportionately represented. Most investigators have contented themselves with recording the addicts' best and present employment status. But given the youthfulness of the addict population, both provide unreliable indices. Consideration of their father's socio-economic status shows that this approximates the norm. Some studies (Kosviner et al., 1968) actually show a better than average socio-economic background. Comparison of fathers' and addicts' occupational status tends to show a disparity in favour of the father. This can hardly be unexpected given the age differential and present status of the addict.

It is to be expected that roughly half of any sample studied will be living with their parents and, thus, to some extent supported by them, and that the remainder are at least eligible to receive welfare benefits (though fewer than those eligible actually take advantage of these benefits). There is little evidence of heroin addiction in the United Kingdom being nurtured by material poverty on the one hand or producing it on the other. On the contrary, those notified in the 1960s were often construed as 'middle-class dropouts' whose addiction, far from being explicable in terms of some material disadvantage, appears to have been motivated by the deliberate rejection of middle-class norms and opportunities. While there is little factual information either to support or refute this view, there is some recent evidence that this 'exclusiveness' no longer characterises the addict population.

The older and typically more stable addicts characteristic of the 1950s tended to continue in employment. Of the 25 Canadians interviewed by Zacune (1971), 68 per cent (17) were currently employed and only 28 per cent (7) had any history of prolonged unemployment since arriving in England.

Table 2.5

Socio-economic grouping (Registrar General) of users, users' parents and economically active males (Greater London Area Census 1966)[a]

Classification	Socio-economic group	Users' occupation N	Users' occupation %	Users' parents' occupation N	Users' parents' occupation %	Population statistics %
Professional workers	3, 4	2	1.6	10	7.8	5.6
Employers and managers	1, 2, 13	10	7.8	23	18.0	12.0
Foremen, skilled manual and own account workers (other than professional)	8, 9, 12, 14	12	9.4	36	28.1	35.0
Non-manual workers	5, 6	43	33.6	20	15.6	23.5
Personal service workers, semi-skilled manual workers, and agricultural workers	7, 10, 15	33	25.8	10	7.8	14.5
Unskilled manual workers	11	23	18.0	15	11.7	8.0
Members of armed forces and persons with inadequately described occupation	16, 17	1	0.8	3	2.4	1.3
Not known	–	4	3.1	11	8.6	–

[a] After Stimson and Ogborne (1970[b]).

Delinquency and criminality

A basic tenet of the British 'solution' has been the assumption that by providing addicts with a licit supply of narcotics one avoids the growth of an illegal market such as has occurred in the United States and Canada. It is often inferred from this that, as a consequence, United Kingdom addicts have not engaged in delinquent activities before they became dependent nor do they embark on a criminal career once they are in receipt of a regular prescription. The evidence, however, does not wholly accord with this view. While the incidence of pre-drug delinquency in the various groups studied tends to reflect the mode of their selection and to show considerable variation from one group to another, approximately one-half of known addicts commit criminal offences before they are registered. While it is extremely difficult to distinguish between drug-related and unrelated offences after addiction has been notified, a significant proportion of registered addicts continue to commit criminal offences which are not obviously related either to obtaining or being in possession of drugs (Zacune, et al., 1969 ; Stimson and Ogborne, 1970 ; Mitcheson et al., 1970; Willis, 1969[a]; Kosviner et al., 1968; Hawks et al., 1969; James and D'Orban, 1970).

These statements represent generalisations and as such are open to exception. The majority of heroin addicts have used other drugs for periods of one to four years before they are notified and at least some of their pre-heroin delinquency may be precipitated by their pre-heroin drug use. Similarly, criminal offences committed after a person has become registered, while not involving possession of illegal drugs, may nevertheless be directly related to the individual's drug-dependent status.

The varying estimates deriving from different studies, as well as reflecting methodological differences and ambiguities, suggest that in some cases narcotic dependence is an extension of previous delinquent behaviour, whereas in others it occurs without there being evidence of previous criminality. However, even in those cases in which drug dependence is closely associated with pre-existing delinquency, delinquency in itself does not provide a sufficient explanation of drug dependence since the latter continues to be a minority manifestation.

Mortality (including suicide)

The mortality among United Kingdom addicts is extremely high, estimated to be 28 times in excess of the comparable age group in the general population (Bewley, et al., 1968 . James, 1967). Bewley et al. have calculated the mean age of death among nontherapeutic addicts during the periods 1955–64 and 1965–66 and found them to be 30.3 and 24.8 years, respectively. They conclude that while the declining age of death reflects the decreasing age of those addicted, mortality tends to be higher among younger addicts. Of the 12 cases of 'natural' death occurring in this sample almost all were indirectly due to the consequences of drug dependence; in the remaining 38 cases the relationship was unambiguous.

While the death rate among female addicts tends to be less than that among males it is, even so, five times in excess of the expected mortality rate. Bewley has suggested that this extremely high mortality, over twice that of heroin addicts in New York, possibly reflects the higher doses taken by United Kingdom addicts and their use of other drugs in combination. James concludes from similar evidence that the practice of maintaining narcotic addicts on a permanent allowance of legally supplied drugs is attended by such substantially increased mortality risks that it is not a satisfactory substitute for an abstinence-oriented programme.

In his study of 436 new nontherapeutic addicts who became known to the Home Office between 1955 and 1964, James (1967) found a suicide rate among the males 50 times in excess of that of the general population corrected for age. While it is extremely difficult to discern intention in cases of drug overdose, the circumstances in a sufficient number of cases suggest that suicide is a significant accompaniment of narcotic dependence.

The increasing tendency for narcotic addicts to inject barbiturates (Mitcheson et al., 1970; Stimson and Ogborne, 1970[b]) can be expected to result in an even higher mortality risk.

Morbidity

Admission to hospital for reasons related to drug dependence (excluding withdrawal) is extremely common among United Kingdom heroin addicts. In their study of 100 consecutive male heroin addicts discharged from a London hospital, Bewley and Ben-Arie (1968) found that in the two and one quarter years over which patients were followed-up there were a further 155 admissions, including readmissions, to the same hospital. There were in addition 148 admissions to other hospitals including 95 to other mental hospitals. Zacune, et al., (1969[a]) followed up 37 heroin users over 12 months and found that 11 of them had been admitted to hospitals a total of 23 times. Apart from drug withdrawal the most frequent reasons for hospitalisation are the treatment of abscesses, overdoses, hepatitis and septicaemia.

Liver function tests carried out on addicts show that 60–80 per cent have evidence of hepatocellular damage (Bewley, et al., 1968[b]; Marks and Chapple, 1967). Where jaundice occurs it is most often attributable to sharing someone else's needle. Stimson and Ogborne (1970[b]) found that only 11 per cent (12) of their sample could be said to use sterile injection procedures.

It may be concluded that despite the provision in the English system for the legal prescription of unadulterated heroin and the opportunity to supply disposable syringes and teach sterile injection practices which frequent clinic attendance allows, complications resulting from dependence are numerous and the resultant load placed on hospitals onerous. Recent correspondence in the medical press suggests that the number of complications treated in the casualty departments of general hospitals is increasing.

Prognosis

The current epidemic of narcotic dependence in the United Kingdom is of too recent origin for its long-term prognosis to be ascertained and any assessment of its short-term outcome is likely to reflect the relative lack of adequate treatment facilities as much as the course of the condition.

There are, however, some statistics available. Bewley et al., (1968[a]) in a study of 1,272 heroin addicts who first became known to the Home Office between 1947 and 1966, found that 70 per cent (890) were still taking opiates in 1966 and, of those 293 not known to be taking opiates, 64 per cent (189) were either in hospital, prison or some similar institution. There had in addition been 89 deaths where the principal causes of death were sepsis, overdose and suicide.

In their study of the 519 narcotic addicts known to the Home Office in 1965, Gobius and Hawks (1970) found that 56 per cent (292) were still known to be dependent in 1968. The distribution over the period 1965–68 is given in Table 2.6. Nor does the short-term prognosis seem more favourable. Twelve of the 23 admissions studied by Zacune et al., (1969[a]) were followed by relapse within a week of discharge, five within a month, three within two months, and three remained abstinent for at least three months and were abstinent at the time of the interview.

Perhaps the most detailed and long term follow-up study has been carried out by Clark (1962) on a group of 65 patients admitted to a provincial hospital between 1949 and 1960. The disadvantage of this study from the point of view of its generality is the atypical nature of the sample – all patients were drawn from the medical and nursing professions. The duration of follow-up varied from two to twelve years, though almost 60 per cent were followed-up for five years or more. Of those addicted to drugs under the

Table 2.6

Prognosis of narcotic addicts known to the Home Office in 1965[a b]

Known in 1965 to be dependent on narcotics	100% (n = 519)
Known in 1966 to be dependent on narcotics	77%
Known in 1967 to be dependent on narcotics	66%
Known in 1968 to be dependent on narcotics	56%
Dead in 1968	9%

[a] While confirming the chronicity of the condition it needs to be emphasised that Gobius and Hawks' data is retrospective and dependent on the adequacy of the Home Office's system of documentation, which until 1968 was not based on any compulsory notification of addicts.

[b] After Gobius and Hawks (1970).

Dangerous Drugs Acts, only 14 per cent remained drug free when discharged and only 18 per cent were able to continue their profession. The largest group was comprised of those who resorted to drugs for varying periods of time and in varying dosages since being discharged. Included in this group were a few patients who had been stabilised on regular doses of drugs and who appeared otherwise to manage their lives relatively satisfactorily providing that the drug was maintained.

Amphetamine abuse

Whatever the limitations affecting the compilation and interpretation of statistics relating to narcotic abuse, those applying to evidence of amphetamine use and misuse are manifold by comparison.

Amphetamines can be obtained on prescription from any doctor, though methylamphetamine in liquid form can only be dispensed by hospital pharmacies.

Changes in the incidence of misuse of amphetamines were first observed by Connell (1958) who described a number of patients whose use of amphetamines led to their experiencing psychotic episodes. Soon after there was evidence of an increase in the misuse of amphetamines taken in tablet form and obtained illegally (Linken, 1963; Connell, 1964, 1965[ab]. Sharpley, 1964). The principal drug involved was an amphetamine/barbiturate mixture, Drinamyl, and misuse was confined to parts of the West End of London. While it is difficult to estimate the extent of illicit use of amphetamines, since the majority of people using them neither appear before the courts nor develop symptoms necessitating medical consultation, urine screening of selected populations has confirmed an increase in the misuse of amphetamines (Scott and Willcox, 1965; Crockett and Marks, 1969).

Studies of adolescent amphetamine users show that members of this group misuse a variety of amphetamine preparations and typically substitute one for the other when supplies dictate this. While at any one time a particular drug may be favoured, evidence suggests that any attempt to control its supply will be attended by the increased use of other preparations.

Studies which have considered the chronology of drug use have consistently demonstrated that amphetamine and amphetamine/barbiturate mixtures are, with cannabis, the drugs most frequently taken first (Hawks et al., 1969; Mitcheson et al., 1970; Stimson and Ogborne, 1970[b]; Kosviner et al., 1968).

The legitimate use of these drugs is also inadequately documented, though there is some evidence that the total number of prescriptions for stimulants issued under the National Health Service has decreased in the last six years (Table 2.7).

Table 2.7
Number of prescriptions for stimulants (in millions)[a]

	Year	
	1962	1968
Number	5.4	3.9
Percentage of total prescriptions	2.7	1.5

[a] While it is not possible to ascertain the total number of amphetamine tablets represented, the figures given indicate the vast majority of prescriptions issued (they exclude those issued privately).

In the absence of any data derived from a representative base, a number of local studies have been published from which extrapolation is possible. A survey conducted in Newcastle (Kiloh and Brandon, 1962) showed that approximately 500 people in a population of 250,000 were psychologically dependent on amphetamines. The majority of these were middle-aged women who had been originally prescribed amphetamines as treatment for depression or as appetite suppressants. Extrapolating from this figure gives a rate of 200 per 100,000 of the population. A study carried out by Brandon and Smith (1962) showed that of patients receiving regular prescriptions of amphetamines or related drugs from general practitioners 21 per cent were thought by their doctors to be habituated. Wilson and Beacon (1964) in a study of 58 patients attending 11 practices (their selection is not explained) found that 58 per cent were Drinamyl-conditioned in that they said they could not do without Drinamyl. However, as only seven of the 22 patients who said they could do without Drinamyl actually ceased taking it, Wilson and Beacon's estimate of the number dependent is minimal. The fact that they do not specify how their patients were selected does, however, preclude generalisation from their results.

In contrast to the younger amphetamine user described by Connell (1964, 1965[a, b]) the amphetamine-dependent person identified in these studies usually became dependent in the course of medical treatment and did not resort to illegal supplies. They did not usually know one another or form any identifiable subculture.

That psychotic episodes could occur in persons abusing amphetamines was first demonstrated in the United Kingdom by Connell (1958) and confirmed in a group of methylamphetamine injectors by Hawks et al. (1969).

Table 2.8
Number of prescriptions for barbiturates and nonbarbiturate hypnotics (in millions)[a]

	1962		1968	
	N	% of total prescriptions	N	% of total prescriptions
Barbiturates	15.8	8.0	15.3	3.7
Nonbarbiturate hypnotics	2.6	1.3	5.8	2.2

[a] Does not include private prescriptions.

Barbiturate and nonbarbiturate hypnotic abuse

The increasing use of barbiturates and their potential for misuse has for some time been a cause for concern. Their use by narcotic addicts is a more recent phenomenon (Mitcheson et al., 1970; Alarcon, 1969[b]; Chapple, 1969).

Bewley (1968) summarised evidence from a number of sources and observed that in the past ten years there has been a marked increase in the number of overdoses with barbiturates. The suicide rate from barbiturate poisoning has more than doubled, added to which there has been a threefold increase in the number of people treated in hospitals for poisoning (Kessell, 1965; Bewley, 1966; Glatt, 1962; Brooke and Glatt, 1964).

While the absolute number of prescriptions for barbiturates and nonbarbiturate hypnotics under the National Health Service has increased over the period 1962–68, their number as a percentage of the total has decreased.

The number of prescriptions for tranquillizers has increased over the same period from 6.6 to 16 million. As this figure includes the phenothiazines it is impossible to infer an increase, if any, in the number of prescriptions for the barbiturate-like minor tranquillizers.

It needs to be noted that these figures do not include private prescriptions and so represent a minimum estimate. Where a drug like the barbiturates has abuse potential it is probable that a not inconsiderable number of private prescriptions are filled and any estimate of the total number dependent on these drugs would need to take account of this unspecified segment of the market.

Two studies of barbiturate prescribing in general practice allow some estimate of the extent of dependence on these drugs by persons receiving legitimate prescriptions. A study conducted by Adams et al. (1966) on a group practice of 10,000 patients in London showed that 407 (four per cent) were given prescriptions for barbiturates. More than half of these 407 patients had received these prescriptions for more than a year and though most of them continued to receive the drug without obvious addiction there was evidence of increasing dosage in 47 cases.

Johnson and Clift (1968) found 97 patients (1.3 per cent) who were receiving repeat prescriptions for hypnotics (74 barbiturate, 23 nonbarbiturate). While only two per cent of this group were described as severely dependent, only four patients were able to discontinue their prescriptions, suggesting that the remaining 91 were dependent on them to some extent. In both of these studies patients receiving barbiturates were more likely to be female, over 40, and married.

It is extremely difficult to estimate the extent of barbiturate dependence in the general population on the basis of the several GP surveys carried out. Bewley (1968) has suggested that it might be of the order of 150–250 per 100,000 of the population.

Informed reports from social workers, police, and hospitals, as well as drug users themselves, suggest that the use of barbiturate-type drugs has recently increased among young persons to the extent where it rivals the amphetamines. In a study of 65 heroin users Mitcheson et al. (1970) found that 62 had taken barbiturates; of these 52 had injected the drug intravenously. Forty-one admitted using methaqualone (Mandrax) illicitly. Forty had received prescriptions for barbiturates from general practitioners, 29 under the National Health Service and 18 privately. Where users were buying barbiturates illicitly it appeared that the seller was usually in receipt of a prescription for the sedatives which he later resold.

Cannabis and LSD

Estimates of the number of cannabis and LSD users in the United Kingdom derive almost entirely from the number of offences for possession of these drugs, a basis which involves the dubious assumption that convictions reflect use (Table 2.4).

Bewley (1966) has observed that until 1945 there was very little use of cannabis in the United Kingdom. Between 1945 and 1960 there was a slow increase and between 1960 and 1965 a marked increase in the use of this drug. If one assumes, as Bewley does, that for every conviction for possessing cannabis there are possibly ten or twenty people who are not convicted, the number of regular cannabis users in the United Kingdom would approximate 30 per 100,000 of the population; this figure would be doubled if occasional users were included.

A number of studies, mainly unpublished, have described the student cannabis taker, estimated in a variety of sources (Linken, 1968[a]. Binnie and Murdock, 1969) as constituting about ten per cent of the tertiary student population. Binnie and Murdock (1969) and Webb et al. (1969) both found that students who had smoked cannabis rarely used other drugs with the exception of amphetamines. The majority of users had smoked cannabis on only a few occasions and were not differentiated from nonsmokers. They did tend, however, to be more radical and permissive in their political and social attitudes and to be more often enrolled in nonscience subjects. Webb et al. (1969) found that those who had smoked cannabis had consulted a psychiatrist significantly more often and saw their general practitioners more often in the previous year. They were also more likely to report that they were regarded as trouble makers at school and had in fact committed more offences of various kinds. They also tended to be earlier and heavier users of both tobacco and alcohol and reported being drunk more often. There was no relationship between multiple drug use and continued cannabis use. Of those who had given up smoking cannabis, the majority did so because they lost interest or moved away from the source. Except in a minority of cases, there was little evidence of cannabis assuming a significant role in their lives.

There is very little objective data available on the vexing question as to whether previous cannabis use predisposes toward subsequent drug dependence. While it is frequently attested that the majority of heroin users in the United Kingdom have smoked cannabis, and for approximately half it was the first drug used, estimates as to the number of cannabis users who become heroin addicts vary considerably and in part reflect the particular group considered.

Estimates as to the number of people in the United Kingdom who have used LSD or other hallucinogens are based entirely on a few well publicised but almost certainly atypical cases and the investigations of other drug users. Stimson and Ogborne (1970[b]) found that 74 per cent of their sample of heroin users had used hallucinogens at some time, of whom half had used hallucinogens at least weekly. Only nine per cent of the total had used hallucinogens at all in the last month, however, confirming an impresson that among heroin addicts the use of LSD tends to be sporadic and self-limiting.

Unlike the situation in the United States, the use of cannabis and LSD do not appear to be closely associated in the student population. Binnie and Murdock (1969) found that only nine per cent of their tertiary students who smoked cannabis had used LSD. The comparable percentage from Webb et al. (1969) was four per cent. Nor is there a significant tendency in the United Kingdom for LSD and other hallucinogens to be used therapeutically as abreactive agents.

Bewley (1967) has reported a number of cases of short-lived psychoses in people taking LSD and has estimated from wholly informal sources (Bewley, 1968) that perhaps one to five per 100,000 of the population have experimented with LSD.

Some tentative generalisations

Any attempt to generalise about the dimensions of drug dependence in the United Kingdom is likely to be attended by numerous exceptions both as a result of the inadequate information available and the rapidly fluctuating nature of the phenomenon. Perhaps the only valid generalisation which can be offered is that the problem has assumed a bewildering variety of forms over a comparatively short period of time. Particular manifestations, for example, the epidemics of methylamphetamine and methaqualone abuse, had largely disappeared before they could be investigated and certainly before they could be understood. Individual preparations have assumed a brief prominence to be followed by others, either as a result of deliberate legislative action or, in some cases, the dictates of fashion. Drugs of quite opposite pharmacological action have been used interchangeably, and if not interchangeably then in combinations which defy pharmacological explanation.

Treatment

A constant feature of all such trends, however, has been a tendency for addicts to abuse a variety of drugs. Under these circumstances, measures – whether therapeutic or legislative – designed to cope with the abuse of a particular drug are likely to prove ineffectual in the absence of attempts to deal with the total situation. There is some recent evidence to suggest that the success with which the total amount of heroin prescribed has been reduced has been attended by an increase both in the amount of methadone prescribed by general practitioners and the amount of barbiturates misused.

The British system of treatment centres was predicated on the assumption that by supplying heroin legally to addicts, a black market would prove uneconomical. It was also assumed that by restricting the right to prescribe heroin to certain designated doctors the over-prescribing which characterised certain general practitioners would be avoided. In making this assumption it was supposed that the doctors working in treatment centres would be both more experienced and better able to assess the true needs of the addict. On the whole these two assumptions appear to have been fulfilled. Apart from some consternation following the circulation of 'Chinese heroin' (powdered heroin) which subsequently proved to be largely caffeine (personal communication: Home Office), there appears to have been little evidence of a black market in heroin developing. There is now substantial evidence of powdered heroin being sold on the black market. It is not uncommon for this heroin to be adulterated with barbiturate type drugs. Similarly, while there was initially considerable variation in the average amount of heroin prescribed by different treatment centres, in part reflecting the different character of their patient loads, the total amount of heroin prescribed by doctors working in the treatment centres has declined and variation between clinics has reduced. In the face of this decline the price of heroin on the illegal market has risen, suggesting that it is not being supplied from other sources. These developments have not been without other, less favourable consequences, as the increased use of methadone and barbiturates by heroin addicts demonstrates.

Illicit sources

The illicit market in heroin is probably supplied by over-prescription occurring in some cases (almost inevitably, if under-prescription with its attendant evils is to be avoided). The amphetamine market is almost wholly supplied by thefts from wholesale and retail chemists, though over-prescribing is also a factor. While cannabis tincture is prescribed by a limited number of doctors the illegal market in cannabis is largely supplied from illegal imports. The results of Mitcheson et al. (1970) suggest that barbiturates are mainly obtained from legal prescriptions – if not to the addict himself, at least to the primary source – though there is evidence that thefts are also increasing. These authors conclude on the basis of the evidence obtained by them that 'it is no longer sufficient for the doctor to review only those traditional middle-aged patients who come with repeated requests for sleeping tablets. Any request for sleeping tablets should be carefully considered especially when the patient is under 30, or is not personally known to the practitioner'.

Initiation

Consistent with the view that most illegally-obtained heroin is supplied by the National Health Service is the finding that potential addicts are initially supplied heroin by their associates and only rarely by someone unfamiliar to them. By establishing the approximate date at which heroin users had their initial injection of heroin and the identity of the person who had given them this injection, Alarcon (1969[a]) was able to discern both yearly incidence and source of contagion. Two major transmission trees covering 48 cases were traced. One of these trees included 32 users who could be traced back to the original initiator, the other included 16 users. Of the total 58 initiations to heroin, 46 were carried out by young men of the locality. Zacune et al. (1969[b]) in their study of largely unnotified heroin users found that personal contact with four users enabled them to interview 32 of a total of 37 users. Prior to the establishment of a treatment centre in the town studied by Zacune et al. (1969[a]) it appeared that the initial group of users existed to supply one another and generally to reinforce their identity as drug users. Studies of other populations using different drugs (e.g., Webb et al., 1969; Hawks et al., 1969) have confirmed this tendency for initiation to occur between familiar associates.

Causation

It has already been observed that drug dependence in the United Kingdom is not predominantly a manifestation of poverty or minority group membership nor does it appear to be as frequently associated with criminality as is the case in the US, though the view that criminality is never a precursor but only a consequence of drug dependence in the United Kingdom is not borne out by the facts. While the lack of relevant normative data precludes inferring causal significance it would appear from some studies that the addict population is characterised by a high incidence of familial separation and disturbance.

Hawks et al. (1969) found that 41 per cent of their methylamphetamine users had some definite or tentative evidence of neurotic distrubance in childhood. Slightly less than half had suffered parental bereavement or separation before they were 16 years old. Sixty-five per cent had not taken any examination while at school, and of those who pursued further education the majority had discontinued this prematurely. Consistent truancy from secondary school was reported by one-half of those interviewed. The degree of family pathology as assessed in terms of the frequency with which drinking problems, criminality, drug abuse and psychiatric illness in the parents and siblings was mentioned, while difficult to assess in the absence of appropriate normative data, appeared excessive. Among the addicts themselves a significant number had been heavy users of alcohol in the past. Of particular interest is the fact that those methylamphetamine users who had also used heroin were more likely to have been separated from their parents before they turned 16 than those who had not used heroin (Hawks et al., 1970). Mitcheson's et al. (1970) study of heroin addicts attending three day centres produced similar evidence of family disturbance. Fifty-two per cent of the sample had experienced separation from one or both parents for a period of at least two years before the age of sixteen. Thirty-two per cent had been separated from both parents.

Conclusions and recommendations

The studies reviewed in this paper have in the main concerned themselves with describing the characteristics of particular subjects defined as using a particular drug, admitted to a specific hospital or detained in a particular institution. While they provide a reasonably comprehensive account of the development of the British drug problem and the morbidity and mortality associated with it, they do not, by and large, consider the relationships prevailing between the variables described. That British research is largely of this demographic order is not inexplicable: the rapidity with which the problem has arisen and the need to take pre-emptive legislative action has dictated that the initial studies concern themselves with defining the extent of the problem and the characteristics of its devotees.

However understandable this preoccupation with demographic characteristics, there is an imperative need to consider not only the extent to which certain factors are disproportionately found to be associated with drug dependence, an assessment itself dependent on the existence of appropriate normative data, but also the association of factors.

Theoretical considerations aside, research into drug dependence is beset by a number of methodological problems. There exist no commonly accepted criteria of dependence and as a consequence there is immense variation in the cases studied. Conclusions are drawn from studies of identifiable cases with no assurance that they are representative of the total. In the absence of biochemical tests which allow us to assess the exact quantity and quality of drugs ingested, the determination of such information must necessarily rely on verbal report. Even were such tests available, their use would be limited to the immediate past and could tell us nothing about the addict's previous drug use. The fact that nontherapeutic use of drugs is an illegal activity increases the unreliability of self-report in any context where it is felt by the addict that the information supplied might affect his ability to get more drugs. The effect of drugs themselves on the accuracy of self-report is itself largely unknown.

Despite these qualifications, with few exceptions information as to the personal and social history of drug addicts has been based entirely on the addict's self-report. While criminal, medical and employment histories may be checked, the reliability and validity of the more personal and probably more pertinent aspects of an individual's history are largely untested. The historical nature of many of the events inquired about adds further to their inaccessibility, added to which is the fact that while no one questions the importance of social factors in the initiation and maintenance of drug dependence, we are at present comparatively inept at assessing such factors in those settings presented by the addict.

Meeting these methodological and theoretical requirements demands prospective studies which, because of the variety of conditions studied in most settings, are likely to be uneconomical undertakings unless 'at risk' groups are studied. Assuming that such groups can be identified, their division on socio-economic grounds should better permit a consideration of those more subtle psychological factors which have to date eluded assessment. It is the intervention of these factors which almost certainly accounts for the many exceptions observed when only gross social and economical variables are considered. Meeting these requirements also requires a degree of co-ordination between research and the assumption of a perspective which is denied the individual researcher. Unravelling problems like drug dependence and delinquency involving social, personal, and economic factors requires a strategy which few individual researchers can adopt. Except that such complexity is entertained the alternative seems to be a multiplicity of studies reflecting the individual idiosyncrasies of their authors and embodying a number of inevitable methodological inadequacies which prejudice their causal significance. The intractability of the causal problem is due not so much to the lack of individual research projects as to the lack of any research of sufficient dimensions to encompass the complexity of the problem.

Note

[1] The percentages given in this section need to be interpreted with caution as any drug tends to be used in combination with others and the total number shown as using particular drugs as a consequence exceeds the total known addicts. However, the same basis of comparison (i.e. the total number of known addicts) has been used in all cases.

3 Cannabis use amongst British university students*

Prevalence rates and differences between students who have tried cannabis and those who have never tried it.

ADELE KOSVINER, DAVID HAWKS AND M. G. T. WEBB

Summary

A survey is reported which involved the distribution of an anonymous questionnaire to three colleges with a total enrolment of 1,530. Responses from 1,142 subjects were obtained, giving an overall response rate of 75 per cent. The main survey had itself been preceded by an initial prevalence survey of students in seven colleges or universities with a total enrolment of 13,852, which resulted in response rates varying from 39 to 73 per cent (mean 61 per cent).

The analysis reported in this paper is confined to a comparison of students who had ever used cannabis and those who had never used it and this with variables as diverse as conventional and illicit drug use, background, political and religious orientation and activity, relationship with parents, vocational orientation and a variety of social attitudes. There were very few differences between the three colleges surveyed in the main study and no significant differences between the sexes at the one college which was co-educational.

In discussing those variables which differentiated the ever used and never used groups an attempt is made to dispense with the notion of a simple causal link between individual variables and cannabis use and instead such associations are viewed as indicative of a general style of behaviour of which cannabis is only one manifestation. Accordingly the "ever users" are described as having looser associations with traditional sources of "societal morality" and to be more rebellious in their political orientation. They tended to obtain higher neuroticism scores and to have been heavier and more precocious users of conventional drugs suggesting that they may have over time indulged in a variety of substances for reasons of their drug effect.

The distinction made between those who had ever used and those who had never used is only crude, and undoubtedly masks differences in levels and recency of use and variations in the attitudes of non-users.

---

* Shortened from a version for *British Journal of Addiction,* vol. 69, 1973, pp. 35–60.

Introduction

The prevalence of cannabis use in the UK is only spasmodically charted. Estimates in the main have derived from sources whose nature precludes generalisation to prevalence or effects of use in a more general population.

Table 3.1
Prevalence of cannabis use amongst some 'deviant' populations in the UK

Type of population	Author and year	Sample	% ever used cannabis	% used cannabis in the last month
Heroin addicts	Stimson and Ogborne, 1970	Representative sample (N = 111) of addicts being prescribed heroin at London clinics in 1969	100	61
	Anumonye and McClure, 1970	First 50 heroin users attending a treatment clinic in a North London suburb in 1968	86	
	Blumberg et al., 1973[a]	Persons attending London clinics for the first time in the period Nov. 1970–Nov. 1971 (N = 210)	98	53
Juvenile offenders	Backhouse and James, 1969	One year's intake of boys aged 14–16 years admitted to a detention centre in SE England in 1967 (N = 290)	7·5	
Patients at VD clinics	Linken, 1968[a]	252 patients under 30 years old attending a VD clinic in Middlesex	12·7	

The present study was initiated in an attempt to obtain estimates of use amongst a range of colleges and universities and thereby gain a fuller picture of use.

Estimates of the prevalence of cannabis smoking in British university populations have ranged from approximately two to 50 per cent depending on the year and type of the survey, the location of the college, and the type of student.

Bestic (1966) reports the results of a small survey of Oxford undergraduates carried out by the student magazine which estimated that two per cent had smoked cannabis. Linken in 1968[b], estimated that perhaps ten per cent of London University students had at one time smoked cannabis, with four per cent qualifying as regular users. In 1968 he estimated that the number of students using cannabis regularly did not exceed one to two per cent.

A study carried out in Leicester by Binnie and Murdoch (1969) found that eight per cent of those who returned the anonymous questionnaire (constituting only 48 per cent of the sample) had smoked cannabis. Of these two thirds had smoked less than ten times.

Most recently Young and Crutchley (1972) have reported a study carried out at a single polytechnic in the South of England in three successive years: 1968, 1969, 1970. Three courses were focused on – engineering, business studies and social science – and prevalence rates were lowest for engineering students (varying between three and 12 per cent over the three year period) and highest for social science students varying from 15 to 50 per cent. Prevalence rates (with one exception) had grown steadily over the three years, the most noticeable increase being from 15 to 40 per cent for social science students in the years 1968 to 1969.

Method

Colleges surveyed

No attempt was made to draw a stratified random sample of all colleges in the UK. Instead an attempt was made to ensure as heterogeneous a sample of colleges as our budget and the co-operation of colleges would permit. Universities and colleges in the southern half of England were somewhat arbitrarily categorised according to the age of the institution, the size of enrolment, the location, current popularity, prestige and orientation, and at least one college or university selected within each category. Letters were written to the vice-chancellors or principals of the colleges chosen and the initial selection of campuses was dictated by the willingness of the administration to allow a survey to be conducted. Although heterogeneous in the terms mentioned, the initial breakdown and choice of colleges was, therefore, to a degree arbitrary, and the eventual sample of colleges surveyed was further biased by self selection.

Design of the Study

The study was divided into two parts – an initial prevalence survey intended only to reveal the extent to which cannabis had been used by students and how often, and a more detailed questionnaire designed to enable us to look at similarities and differences amongst different kinds of users and non users, carried out in a sub-sample of colleges initially surveyed. Both questionnaires employed were anonymous and distributed in individually addressed envelopes.

Prevalence survey

The initial prevalence survey was eventually carried out in seven colleges or universities with a total enrolment of 13,852 over the period August 1968 to December 1969. The questionnaire consisted of a single sheet which, after an explanatory paragraph, simply asked the student to indicate whether he had smoked cannabis never, one to ten times or more than ten times.

The questionnaires were distributed to the total student enrolment of these colleges and response rates obtained varied from 39 to 73 per cent, with a mean of 61 per cent. The total number of returned questionnaires was 7,897 (see Table 3.2).

Main survey

The selection of those colleges or universities given the fuller questionnaire at a later date was made from these seven so as adequately to represent the range of use revealed by the initial survey. Four colleges (A, C, E and G) were so chosen, but data from college A was not included in any analysis as the response rate was too low (34 per cent). The colleges finally included in the analysis therefore were colleges C, E and G, which were surveyed between May 1969 and July 1971.

The Sample

Questionnaires were sent to the total student enrolment in colleges C and E, and to just over 33 per cent of the total enrolment in college G. Colleges C and E were all male institutions, college G was mixed. The sample in college G was drawn according to year and major discipline. The response rate for college G was slightly lower than for the other two colleges (see Table 3.3), but since for the purpose of distribution and collection the sample had been broken down into major discipline and year, some direction could be given to the bias possibly resulting from this lower rate; there was known to be a very poor response from students studying fine arts in this college (if eliminated

Table 3.2

Frequency of cannabis use (ever) – initial prevalence survey

Source	Date of survey	Number of respondents	Enrolment	Respondents of total enrolment %	Cannabis use (ever) percentages		
					Never	1 – 10 times	More than 10 times
College –							
A	August 1968	414	637	65	61	23	16
B	November 1968	1,554	2,128	73	85	11	4
C	February 1969	261	427	61	72	16	12
D	February 1969	2,236	4,140	56	90	7	3
E	April 1969	216	322	67	78	17	5
F	June 1969	2,281	3,802	60	89	7	4
G	January 1970	935	2,397	39*	76	13	11
Total		7,897	13,853				

* The means of distribution then available at this college provided no guarantee that questionnaires were received by all students. Taking those listed as non-respondents then there are almost certainly a significant number who did not receive a questionnaire.

from the sample the response rate would be 83.5 per cent, and informed opinion within the college indicated that prevalence of use would be higher amongst these students. It is therefore probable that the overall prevalence rates in college G is an underestimation (fine arts students constituting approximately 15 per cent of the desired sample).

While with an anomymous questionnaire it is impossible adequately to establish non-response bias and validity, comparing prevalence estimates from the initial and more intensive surveys (Table 3.3) gives some indication of the credibility of the findings.

Table 3.3
Comparison of findings from initial and follow-up surveys

		Response rate %	Frequency of cannabis use Percentages: Never	1–10	11+
College C	Initial survey	61	72	16	12
	Follow-up survey	82	76	15	9
College E	Initial survey	67	78	17	5
	Follow-up survey	83	72	17	10
College G	Initial survey	39	76	13	11
	Follow-up survey	72	62	18	20

Given that in college E the follow-up survey was completed ten months after the initial prevalence survey, the discrepancy in prevalence of use at this college does not seem untoward. The two surveys carried out in College C within two months gave very similar results.

While the actual number of students who had smoked cannabis is probably under represented in the figures given (interviews with some non-respondents at College C indicated that a disproportionate number were cannabis users) the relatively high response rate obtained in all three institutions limits the degree of error affecting any extrapolation. (Table 3.4).

The Questionnaire

While clearly a questionnaire approach cannot give a detailed picture of the

Table 3.4
Cannabis use (ever) in the three colleges surveyed

College	Date surveyed	Size of desired sample	Response rate %	Achieved sample	Cannabis	
					Never used	Ever used
C	May 1969	428	72†	308	75% (231)	24% (74)*
E	Feb. 1970	318	83	264	72% (190)	27% (71)*
G	June 1971	804	71‡	570	61% (348)	38% (216)*
	Overall	1,550	75	1,142	67% (769)	32% (361)

† Less than one per cent of students at any college had only used drugs other than cannabis and they are not included here.
* A further ten per cent of the population were interviewed employing a shortened form of the questionnaire; these results are not included here.
†† As mentioned in the text, the distribution of questionnaires in the college allowed the identification of areas of non-response.

subleties of every individual's attitudes and values, we hoped to go some way to avoid preconceptions by leaving many of the broader attitudinal questions and questions relating to drug use open ended, and devising coding categories *post hoc* on the basis of the responses obtained.

The adequacy of these categories was checked by having the three investigators independently code a random selection of the questionnaires.

Areas of interest

Apart from details of drug use (both illicit and conventional) and attitudes towards it, the 36 page questionnaire covered demographic and background variables: a number of attitudinal measures including such areas as political and religious orientation, anomie, the 'Puritan ethic', relationship with parents, 'permissiveness' or liberal mindedness, vocational orientation, human relationships, and so on. The questionnaire also covered a number of behavioural areas, including degree and type of social and political activity.

This interim paper focuses only on background and demographic variables, some attitudinal data, and conventional drug use, using combined data (where possible) from the three colleges mentioned.

There were no systematic differences between the sexes in College G so for the purpose of this analysis the data from this college is treated as a whole.

Overall there was a remarkable similarity of findings from the three colleges, with the result that the data have been combined in most instances in this report. Where any significant differences occur between the colleges, they are mentioned.

Limits of present analysis

Our concern in this analysis is restricted to a comparison of students who have *ever* used cannabis, with those who have *never* used it. The 'ever used' group refers to a very heterogeneous population in terms of cannabis use – ranging from people who have used it once and don't intend to again, to those who are regular users. Whilst, therefore, we might sometimes refer to 'users' and 'non-users' as a form of shorthand, it should be borne in mind throughout that we are comparing people who have at least once behaved in this way with those who have not, with any implication either behaviour may have.

Results

The test of significance used throughout is chi squared, but because this statistic is inconvenient not only when the number of observations involved is large, but also for comparisons between tables differing in size, we have included Cramer's index of association. This statistic has a range of values from zero to seven independent of the size of the table and the number of observations included (essentially chi-squared gives an indication of whether association exists and Cramer's index an indication of the degree of association). Slight differences in the total N in the tables arise from differing small numbers of students not answering the questions.

I Demographic and background factors

1 Sex

Data for this breakdown was available only from college G, the other two colleges being single sex. In this one college in 1971, 44 per cent of men had tried the drug compared to 36 per cent of women. Thus there was only a slight tendency for more men to have tried it ($X^2=3.87$, $p < 0.05$, C index=0.08).[1]

2 Age and year of college

Considering the overall sample, there was a slight tendency for first year students who had tried cannabis to be older than their contemporaries who had not, with 21 per cent (27) first-year users being 21 years or older, compared to ten per cent (28) non-users. This association did not hold in later years of college, where users and non users were almost identically distributed over age in any one year of college.

3 Socio-economic and cultural background

There were no significant differences (indeed a remakable similarity) between the distribution of users and non-users according to the socio-economic classification of father's occupation (General Register Office, Classification of Occupations, 1966). This finding applied within all three colleges equally, although there were significant differences in students' class backgrounds between the colleges themselves.

Nor were there significant differences between users and non-users in terms of their urban or rural upbringing. It is possible, however, that the source question for this data was inadequately precise (the options being 'city', 'town or suburb of city' and 'elsewhere') to elicit differences even if they existed.

The data with regard to cultural background has to be treated with caution as the numbers in 'non-British' categories were relatively small (e.g. only nine per cent (98) of the total sample being mainly brought up outside the UK). Considering the three questions ('where born', 'where mainly brought up', and 'nationality of self, mother and father') there was a tendency for more users than non-users to have been brought up outside the UK (X^2=6.46, $p < 0.02$, C index =0.08) and to have non-British nationalities (X^2= 14. 24, $p < 0.001$, C=0.11). This bias is largely accounted for by students with American nationality, or who had been mainly brought up in America. The difference is significant over all three colleges taken together, but emanates from a strong bias in this direction from colleges C and E (who had more American students) and is not upheld if college G is analysed alone. This tendency is not reflected in the overall analysis of 'where born', although a difference is apparent in colleges C and E if analysed separately from college G.

4 Family background

Broken home or disrupted family history. No significant differences were found as regards death of parents or students being separated from them for two or more years before the age of 16. Overall 12.4 per cent of students (125) had experienced the death of one or more parents, and seven per cent (87) had been separated from them before the age of 16. There was however, a difference between users' and non-users' parents having separated, but the percentages involved are small, requiring cautious interpretation. While only 6.6 per cent (71) of the total sample had parents who had separated, 11 per cent of users were so characterised compared to five per cent of non-users

($X^2=11.86$, $p<.001$, $C=0.11$).

Birth order. There was a slight tendency for non-users to be more often the only or oldest child than users, with 56 per cent (433) non-users being so characterised compared to 47 per cent (172) of users ($X^2=8.45$, $p<.02$, $C=0.09$)

5 *Educational background*

Academic achievement prior to college. Overall users tended to have passed fewer 'A' levels than non-users, with 39 per cent users compared to 29 per cent non-users having passed two or less, and 24 per cent non-users compared to 16 per cent users having passed four or more ($X^2=15.2$, $p<.001$, $C=.12$). While there was a difference between the colleges in number of passed 'A' levels, the difference between users and non-users held within each college.

Nature of secondary education. There was a slight tendency for users to be over-represented amongst students who had been to public schools (30 per cent of users compared to 24 per cent of non-users, $X^2=4.14$, $p<.05$, $C=0.06$) but otherwise there was no difference in type of school attended.

Despite more users coming from public schools (where there is a greater likelihood of boarding), users were no more likely to have boarded than non-users. They were, however, more likely to have changed school in their secondary education than non-users (27 compared to 19 per cent, $X=9.19$, $p<.01$, $C=0.09$).

6 *Personal history*

Previous nonconformity. In interpreting this data it needs to be recalled that it is based on self report and may be confounded by the tendency of those who have used cannabis being more prepared to admit to previous 'divergence' or being more honest, or both groups wanting to project a certain image.

While the validity of this data may therefore be open to question, the trends depicted in Table 3.5 held for all three colleges studied. In each of the areas enquired about people who had tried cannabis were more likely to admit non-conformity than those who had not (see Table 3.5).

Traffic offences accounted for most of the 'convictions' but more users than non-users reported offences other than traffic (see Table 3.6). The fact that only 1.4 per cent of people who had tried cannabis had any drug-related convictions provides evidence of the need to be cautious in employing drug conviction as a guide to prevalence.

Medical history. No differences between users and non users were observed

Table 3.5
Previous nonconforming behaviour

	Students admitting to listed behaviour				
	Non-users (i.e. never used) (Total N = 769)		Users (i.e. ever used) (Total N = 367)		
	N	Non-users %	N	Users %	
Truancy (more than 5 times) in primary school	23	3	32	9	$X^2=17.9$ $p<.001$, $C=0.13$
Truancy (more than 5 times) in secondary school	116	15	135	37	$X^2=68.7$ $p<.001$, $C=0.25$
Whether considered a trouble maker at school	67	9	101	28	$X^2=70.8$ $p<.001$, $C=0.25$
Whether ever gambled for money	258	34	211	55	$X^2=39.6$ $p<.001$. $C=0.19$
Whether ever consulted a psychiatrist or spent time in a mental hospital	31	4	37	10	$X^2=16.3$ $p<.001$, $C=0.12$
Whether convicted of any offences	59	8	56	15	$X^2=16.6$ $p<.001$, $C=0.12$

as regards major physical illness, and an apparent difference in colleges C and E concerning the number of times students had been to the doctor (where more users (69 per cent) than non-users (54 per cent) had made such visits) was not upheld in college G, where the percentages were almost identical.

7 *Autonomy and independence from authority*

It had been hypothesised that people who had lived away from home before coming to college, and people who had not come straight from school to

Table 3.6
Details of offences (convictions)

		Cannabis use			
		Never		Ever	
	Traffic only	48	(81%)	30	(54%)
	Political*	5		5	
	Criminal	6		16	
Other			11		26
	Drug	0	(19%)	3	(46%)
	Drug & criminal	0		2	

$X^2=10.5$ (1 d.f.)
$p < .01$, $C=0.30$

* This category comprises civil offences committed in the context of some political action, e.g., political demonstrations.

college but done something independently in between, would be more likely to have tried cannabis than those who had not. Differences in the expected direction were observed in both these cases, with 47 per cent users compared to 36 per cent non users having lived away from home before coming to college ($X^2=11.3$, $p < .001$, $C=0.10$) and 70 per cent users compared to 60 per cent non-users having done something between leaving school and coming to college, other than just a 'vacation job', ($X^2=10.1$, $p < .01$, $C=0.10$), trend findings which are consistent with the findings that first-year students who had tried cannabis tended to be older than their contemporaries who had not. Users tended also to have left secondary school slightly earlier than non-users (39.4 per cent of users compared to 31.2 per cent non-users leaving at 17 years old) ($X^2=6.3$, $p< .02$, $C=0.08$). It is difficult to interpret this data without further cross comparison. It could be that age is the relevant factor, but given that the university environment appears to exert a levelling effect (with the association between use and age within year, diminishing in later years) it seems more likely that the way in which the time was spent is rather more important – with those students who exhibit some 'break' from conventional reliance on parents and school being more likely to try cannabis.

It was also hypothesised that the more independent a student was in his living arrangements at college the more likely he would be to have tried cannabis. That is to say, those students with their own flat would be more likely to have tried cannabis. In addition it was thought that those living in less conventional ways, i.e., cohabiting or living with people of of both sexes, would be more likely to have smoked. The data supported both these hypotheses, with 18 per cent (64) users compared to 7 per cent (52) non-users living in 'less conventional' settings ($X^2=34.9$, $p < .001$, $C=0.18$). Considering college G alone, 47 per cent of users (103) compared to 26 per cent non-users (91) were living in their own flat ($X^2=25.5$, $p < .001$, $C=0.21$). The question was asked in slightly different forms for colleges C and E but the trend, although less marked, was in the same direction, ($X^2=4.5$, $p < .05$, $C=0.09$).

8 *Vocational orientation*

It was hypothesised that people who had tried cannabis would be more likely to be interested in the arts and social sciences than in other disciplines. In this connection it was noted whether A level subjects had been mainly arts or sciences, and in addition the main field of study chosen at college was recorded. Employing these two indicators the differences were in the expected direction, with 65 per cent (216) of users compared to 50 per cent (360) non-users having done mainly arts 'A' levels ($X^2=23.4$, $p < .001$, $C=0.15$) and users being over represented amongst arts and social science subjects at college.

II Some attitudinal, behavioural and personality measures

1 *Religion*

It was hypothesised that strong religious beliefs would deter people from trying cannabis. Students were, therefore, asked in which religion, if any, they were brought up; their religion now, and their attendance at religious services in the last year.

The association of religious affiliation and cannabis use was evident in all three areas, most especially in whether the student claimed a current religious affiliation and the frequency of attendance at religious services, and to a lesser extent on whether students had been brought up with a religion. Type of religion did not differentiate users and non-users, in terms of either past or present affiliation.

Considering only those who had been brought up with religious beliefs (995 or 88 per cent of the total sample), a large proportion (42 per cent) had since abandoned these beliefs. This trend was more marked in those who had tried

Table 3.7
Religious affiliation

	Cannabis use: Never (Total N = 769) N	Non-users %	Ever (Total N = 367) N	Users %	
Students brought up in a religion	684	90	311	85	X^2=5.17 p< .05, C=0.07
Students having a religion now	418	55	124	34	X^2=45.3 p<.001, C=0.20
Students attending religious services once a month or more in the last year	210	28	24	7	X^2=65.2 p< .001, C=0.24

cannabis, with 60 per cent of users (187) compared to 39 per cent of non-users (266) having abandoned this affiliation.

2 *Political attitudes and activities*

Attitudes. Students were asked how they would vote should there be an election 'tomorrow'. Whilst there was little difference between users and non-users as regards the 'conventional' parties (Conservative, Liberal and Labour), there was a tendency for more users to adopt what could be called a 'non-establishment' position. If one combined students who said they would not vote at all – either because they were not interested or thought it futile –and those who said they would vote communist or other socialist (not Labour Party), 26.3 per cent of those who had tried cannabis fell into this category compared to 8.3 per cent of those who had not.

Political activity. Fifty per cent of users compared to 36 per cent of non-users had engaged in some kind of political activity in the last month, in the form of going to political meetings or demonstrations. There was a slight but significant trend for more users to belong to political clubs or organisations in college than non-users (p< .05, C=0.08). The same trend was not observed in membership of such organisations outside of college.

5 *Social and personal relationships*

Degree and type of social activity. Asking students to check a list of recreational activities indicated that users were more likely to engage in such activities than non-users, and were more likely to take part in a 'gregarious' rather than solitary fashion – that is with friends rather than alone.

Users were slightly *less* likely than non-users to belong to social recreational organisations both in college (28 per cent of users compared to 19 per cent) and outside college (59 compared to 41 per cent). There was no difference between the groups in the degree to which they reported regularly engaging in other activities.

Friendship patterns. No differences in the answers given by users and non-users were observed to such questions as 'of your six closest friends how many did you know before college?', whether they considered they belonged to a close group of friends, and whether they knew people at college before going there. Concerning relationships with the opposite sex (defined as 'been out with at least three times'), non-users were slightly more likely either not to have had such a relationship in the last year (17 per cent non-users compared to six per cent users), or to have had only one or two such relationships (56 compared to 48 per cent users). Users were more likely than non-users to have had three or more such relationships (46 compared to 27 per cent non-users). There were no differences, however, in length of the longest relationship. Thus whilst users were more likely to have had such relationships, and had more of them, they were not any more or less continuous or permanent than those of non-users.

4 *Satisfaction with course of study*

In order to gain an impression of whether there is an association between use and satisfaction with present course of study, we asked a number of related questions: whether students felt their course of study was worth while, whether they wanted to change their course, whether they had changed their main course and whether they anticipated leaving college before they attained their degree. In all these areas users were more likely to express dissatisfaction than non-users (see Table 3.8).

It cannot of course be inferred from such association that the use of cannabis was instrumental in causing this dissatisfaction.

5 *Other attitudinal indicators*

In addition to the data described so far, preliminary analysis of a number of other attitude scales suggests that users are likely to be more 'alienated' than

Table 3.8
Students' satisfaction with course of study

	Those wanting to change course		Those saying course of study not worthwhile		Those anticipating leaving college before completing degree		Those who had already changed course	
	N	%	N	%	N	%	N	%
Ever used (Total N=367)	59	16	111	31	62	17	62	17
Never used (Total N=769)	79	10	122	16	56	7	74	9
	X^2=8.0, p < .01, C=0.08		X^2=34.2, p < .001 C=0.17		X^2=25.0 p < .001 C=*0.15*		X^2=12.6 p < .001 C=0.11	

non-users (as measured by Sroles' five item scale of anomie), to have less affinity with their parents (for example, only 26 per cent of users said they shared their parents' view of life compared to 41 per cent non-users), to be less in agreement with what might be called the 'Puritan ethic', and more liberal or permissive in their attitudes to societal, social and sexual issues.

6 *Personality measures*

Students who had tried cannabis tended to obtain higher scores on both extraversion and neuroticism as measured by the short form of the Eysenck Personality Inventory.

A shortened version of Crumbaugh's 'purpose in life' test based on Frankl's notions of 'noögenic neurosis' and 'existential vacuum' was included with the intention of measuring the degree of meaning in life a subject experiences. This scale was shortened after being analysed for internal consistency on other groups of tertiary students, and repetitive items, or those likely to be

Table 3.9
Extraversion and neuroticism scores from EPI*

	Extraversion		Neuroticism	
	Mean	SD	Mean	SD
Never used	3·44	1·51	2·65	1·55
Ever used	3·83	1·45	3·25	1·58
Comparative norms from sample of normal population (Eysenck and Eysenck, 1964)	3·76	1·68	2·30	1·52

* Differences between users and non-users are significant on both indices ($p < \cdot 001$ 't' test) most noticeably on neuroticism.

heavily biased by religious attitudes, removed. The initial analysis of this test suggested users score lower (i.e., report 'less purpose') than non-users.

III Conventional drug use and attitudes toward illicit drug use

1 Use of Tobacco

Students who had used cannabis were much more likely to have smoked tobacco than non-users (77 per cent compared to 33 per cent). Considering only those students who had ever smoked tobacco (N=537), cannabis users were also more likely to have been heavier smokers at the time they smoked most, with 31 per cent of those who had used cannabis compared to 21 per cent who had not, having smoked more than 20 cigarettes a day.

There was also a slight (but not significant) tendency for users to have started smoking tobacco at an earlier age, with 60 per cent users compared to 48 per cent non-users having started before they were 18 (C=0.13). A sizable proportion of students who had smoked tobacco reported they had now stopped (28 per cent), and amongst these there were more non-cannabis users than cannabis users (34 and 23 per cent, respectively). Despite their being heavier smokers cannabis users were not significantly more concerned about their use of tobacco than non-users, though there was a slight trend in this direction (66 per cent users expressing some concern compared to 56 per cent non-users (C=0.10)).

Table 3.10
Most cigarettes ever smoked (daily)

Cannabis Use:	Under 5	6–10	11–20	21–30	31–40	40+
Never	98 (37%)	47 (18%)	64 (24%)	41 (16%)	10 (4%)	4 (1%)
Ever	55 (19%)	52 (18%)	93 (32%)	54 (19%)	19 (7%)	15 (5%)

$X^2=27{\cdot}6$, $p < {\cdot}001$, $C=0{\cdot}22$

2 *Use of Alcohol*

A similar pattern emerges for alcohol use – more users than non-users reported that they had been drunk (subjectively defined) and been drunk more often, with only eight per cent of users compared with 31 per cent of non-users saying they had never been drunk, and 36 per cent compared to 13 per cent saying they had been drunk more than ten times ($X^2=123.4$, $p < .001$, (3 d.f.), $C=0.33$). There was also a slight tendency for users to drink more than non-users on any one occasion ($p < .05$, $C=0.10$) but no significant difference between the groups in frequency of drinking in the last two months.

3 *Attitudes to cannabis and other drug use*

Not surprisingly cannabis users were more in favour of cannabis generally than non-smokers, and also tended to have more friends who used it (41 per cent of users estimated that more than 40 per cent of their friends smoked, compared to three per cent of non-users).

Asked whether they thought people who used cannabis differed from those who did not, the two groups split more or less evenly (54 per cent of users thinking they did, compared to 47 per cent of non-users). More non-users said they didn't know. Of those students who thought they did differ, the most favoured response amongst users was that users had more social and personal freedom. Non-users tended to think users had a more negative or passive outlook on life, as well as differing in other ways.

Asked whether they thought cannabis did more harm than good, or vice versa, as one would expect more users thought it did more good (24 compared to three per cent non-users) while more non-users thought it did more harm (43 compared to six per cent users), but also more users said they could not answer as it depended on the person (70 compared to 53 per cent non-users).

A similar pattern emerges when the answers to the questions 'what are some of the good things that can be said about cannabis?' and 'what are some of the bad things?' are analysed. Non-users tended to say 'nothing good can be said' more often than users (19 per cent non-users compared to two per cent users), but users did not in the same way tend to say 'nothing bad can be said' any more than non-users (four per cent compared to two per cent non-users). Eighty per cent said the good things were increasing pleasure and aesthetic appreciation. Pleasure also rated high amongst non-users (38 per cent while 20 per cent non-users said they didn't know).

Turning to the 'bad things' more non-users were concerned about what they saw as the possibility of progression to harder drugs (either through contact with source of supply or the need to seek 'bigger kicks') than users (41 per cent compared to 23 per cent users). The most frequent answer for users (31 per cent) was negative psychological effects such as apathy and slight paranoia. Only seven per cent of users and four per cent non-users chose negative physical effects as the main 'bad effect'. Relatively few users and non-users (13 and two per cent) attributed the bad effects primarily to the illegal status of cannabis.

Although more users (79 per cent) than non-users (44 per cent) thought cannabis should be legalised, a substantial proportion of all students (56 per cent) thought that it should. Amongst students answering 'yes' were those (both users and non-users) who thought that if it were legalised, fewer people would smoke it for the 'wrong' reasons, (e.g., because it involved subterfuge or because it was élitist).

Cannabis users and non-users differed very little in their attitudes to injecting drugs. While more users had seen people fix a drug (26 per cent compared to nine per cent non-users), few had any friends who fixed (ten per cent compared to four per cent) and the vast majority of both groups (98 per cent non-users, 94 per cent users) said they would not themselves fix, given the opportunity. Less than one per per cent of users had in fact ever fixed a drug.

Discussion

As has been emphasised throughout, the present paper has been concerned with people who have ever tried cannabis. It may be that differences between users and non-users emanate primarily from certain types of users. The percentage differences between the two groups are in many instances quite small, and it seems likely from initial analyses based on a further breakdown of the user group, that the more frequent or heavier users are more often or more strongly characterised by the differentiating attributes than the less frequent users who are more similar to non-users.

In discussing the possible temporal relationship between the variables included in this study it seems profitable to abandon the notion of simple causal links between certain psychosocial variables and cannabis use, and instead to view any such associations as indicative of a general style of behaviour or orientation, with cannabis use (or the preparedness to try cannabis) being only one possible feature of this general style.

The postulation of a general style is consistent with recent studies in the field of young people's drug use. Weiner (1970), in his study of drug use amongst school children, employed the word 'precocity' to describe the association of use with smoking tobacco, drinking alcohol, associating with older children, having more experience with the opposite sex and the like. Orford (1974), in his study of student drinking habits, described an 'adventurous pleasure-seeking' dimension, and Young and Crutchley (1972), finding associations between cannabis use, hedonism, certain political, religious and social attitudes, invoked the concept of the 'bohemian' student. If the broader social background of the students in the present study are considered no clear picture emerges in terms of class or cultural origins. That users were over represented amongst students with American nationality or those brought up in the USA, and yet not amongst those merely born there, suggests that cultural environment (in the form of parents or peers) may be of some importance, although no differences are apparent when other environmental indices such as urban/rural dwelling or social class are considered.

On the other hand a pattern does emerge from the personal history data which can suggest that users display *looser associations with traditional sources of 'societal morality'*. Although further cross comparison is required it may be noted that users tended to have more disrupted family backgrounds (in the form of parents separating for other than 'natural causes'), to be less likely to be the first born child, to have more diverse schooling (changed school more often), to have lived away from home before coming to college, to have done something in between school and college and to have less affinity with their parents.

The family and school are traditionally the two main socialising institutions in society. The less central, stable and unquestioned such institutions are to the individual, and the more alternative orientations he has experienced, the more likely he is to question conventional societal norms, including the prohibition of cannabis. If it is assumed that parental separation *may* lead a child to question family norms, that first born children *tend* to get more 'socialising', that changing schools makes it *less* likely that any one such institution will play so central a role in an individual's life, that living away from home and not coming directly from school to college increases the likelihood of being exposed to alternative viewpoints, it may be hypothesised that people who try cannabis have experienced less close or unique alignment with sources of conventional socialisation than those who have not. The fact that contemporary religious affiliation is associated with not trying cannabis and that more users have displayed nonconforming behaviour in the past is consistent with such a view. At least some of the findings suggest that students who had smoked cannabis may perceive less pay-off from conformity. Although university students in general are a relatively 'successful' group in terms of having achieved a desired societal goal, it was the case that those who had tried cannabis had passed relatively fewer 'A' levels than non-users, were relatively less satisfied with their courses and displayed relatively more 'anomie' and less 'purpose'. Without wishing to imply any causal relationship between the above variables and use it might be suggested that those achieving relatively less success (in terms of 'A' levels) or perceiving relatively less possibility of pay-off from conformity (more pessimistic about their course of study and the future) would be more likely to question conventional goals and instead think in terms of other options (cf. Jessor et al., 1968; Cloward and Ohlin, 1960).

If we turn now to consider more current attitudes and behaviours it was the case that as a general thing users tended to be more politically active, and slightly more of the opinion that there was something they personally could do in correcting what they considered to be 'basically wrong' with western society. They tended also to be more left wing and to be inclined either not to vote at all for parliamentary parties or to choose 'minority' left wing parties. Taken together these tendencies suggest an orientation closer to 'rebellion' than 'retreatism' (Merton, 1957).

Another area where consistent differences are apparent is in the use of illicit drugs, where users appear to have been heavier and more precocious users of tobacco and alcohol. This finding together with the fact that the user tended to get higher neuroticism scores on the Eysenck Personality Inventory suggests that users may have historically indulged in a variety of substances for reasons of their drug effect. There is, however, very little difference between the two groups in terms of their attitudes to 'fixing' harder drugs.

A point which cannot be too strongly emphasised is that in the previous discussion differences between the two groups have been the focus of attention. Many students in the generic user group do not display the 'characteristic' differentiating attributes, and many non-users do. Further multifactorial analyses are required to differentiate types of users and non users, and until such analyses have been completed the ideas expressed in this section are of necessity generalisations. It must also be remembered that we are not in any sense talking about the effects of cannabis use but rather about a general style of life of which cannabis use may be a part.

Note

[1] There was a difference between the colleges in so far as more users had tried cannabis before coming to university in college G than in the other colleges (26 compared to 8 per cent of users in colleges C and E). While this could be a function of the time difference between the surveys or the institutions attracting different sorts of students it does not invalidate the combination of the data for the purpose of looking at use and relative age.

4 Abuse of methylamphetamine*

DAVID HAWKS, MARTIN MITCHESON,
ALAN OGBORNE AND GRIFFITH EDWARDS

Summary

Seventy-four regular users of methylamphetamine injections were interviewed in four settings by use of a relatively structured standardised questionary. All but two had injected methylamphetamine within the previous 48 hours and had on average been using methylamphetamine continuously for 19 months.

Significant features found in those interviewed were British nationality, single status, under 25 years of age, and a history of parental separation, absence or bereavement. Educational standards were poor and a history of consistent truancy from secondary school was frequently reported.

Comparison of their best and present occupations showed that downward drift had occurred. Forty-one per cent of the sample had some definite or tentative evidence of neurotic disturbance in childhood. Twenty-three per cent, had been sentenced to detention centre, approved school or Borstal training, and 20 per cent had been sentenced to prison. Sixty five per cent had been charged with offences of one sort and 24 per cent had been convicted of both drug and non-drug offences.

A significant number had been heavy drinkers in the past, while most had been, and in many cases still were, multiple drug users who had first started to use drugs between the ages of 16 and 20 years. They tended to have obtained methylamphetamine initially from people they knew or from sellers. While the majority were currently getting methylamphetamine from doctors, the fact that 40 per cent gave non-medical agents as their major source of drugs suggests that a significant number were supplementing their supplies from illicit sources. More than one-half were rated as being continually involved in the 'drug scene'.

Most of those interviewed accepted frequent psychotic episodes as a side-effect of their use of methylamphetamine. Malnutrition, weight loss, and sleep disturbance were frequent.

---

* Condensed from a paper in the *British Medical Journal,* vol. 2, 1969, pp. 715–21.

Introduction

In the summer of 1968 an epidemic of methylamphetamine injecting occurred in London. Young people with amphetamine psychosis were encountered by medical and social work agencies (*Lancet,* 1968; Glatt. 1968; James, 1968) and phrases such as 'meth head' and 'speed freak' became part of the underground vocabulary. Some doctors working in private practice or hospitals prescribed methylamphetamine as a substitute for cocaine. By the spring of 1968, however, two doctors were prescribing quantities of the drug to an extent which contributed directly to the growth of the illicit market. In October the manufacturers, by arrangement with the Ministry of Health and the British Medical Association, withdrew methylamphetamine from retail pharmacists, and this particular epidemic was curtailed.

The aim of this paper is to report the characteristics of some of the young people who were involved in this epidemic and to describe the effect which the drug had on them.

The study

The study lasted from the beginning of June to the end of July 1968. Those interviewed were a relatively heterogeneous if not representative sample of methylamphetamine users drawn from four different settings, all in London.

Setting	No. of subjects interviewed
Single-handed general practice which included a large number of patients using amphetamines	33
Group practice treating a number of addicts by clinical and community means	12
Outpatient clinic of a psychiatric hospital	15
Community centre run by a central London church	14

Results

Description of sample

Demographic. The sample was predominantly of British nationality (97 per cent).[1] The ratio of males to females was about 4:1. Seventy-four per cent were single, seven per cent were currently married, nine per cent admitted to cohabiting, and another nine per cent were either separated or divorced. The average age of those interviewed was 21.5 years, with a standard deviation of

3.5 years and a range of 17–36 years. Eighty-two per cent were under 25 years of age.

Of the total sample slightly less than half (34) had suffered parental bereavement or separation before they were 16 years old. Comparison of the fathers' socio-economic grouping with that of economically active and retired males aged 15 and over in the Greater London area (General Register Office, 1967) showed that the fathers diverged very little from this norm.

Family Pathology. In 18 per cent of cases the subject's father or father surrogate had a drinking problem which was defined in terms of social, physical, or mental impairment of a non-transitory kind. Seven per cent of fathers had criminal convictions and in three per cent there was evidence of drug abuse other than alcoholism. Five per cent had either been admitted to a psychiatric hospital or consulted a psychiatrist. In nine per cent insufficient information was obtained. The incidence of social pathology amongst the mothers or mother surrogates was much lower. No attempt was made to differentiate between the siblings of the same subject, so that if *any* sibling had a drinking problem this was noted. As a consequence the actual degree of disturbance present in siblings of a comparable age is unknown, since many of the subjects had siblings considerably younger than themselves. Even so, seven per cent of the subjects had siblings who displayed a drinking problem and 16 per cent had siblings who abused other drugs. Nineteen per cent had siblings with criminal convictions and 12 per cent had siblings who had a history of psychiatric disorder. No relevant information relating to siblings was obtained in five per cent of cases.

Current situation

Diet. Only 23 per cent had had what could be regarded as three adequate meals in the previous 24 hours. Seventy-six per cent of the sample had observed a significant weight loss since starting to use methylamphetamine.

Employment and income. Forty per cent claimed to be currently employed (about half in regular jobs) while 57 per cent were not working at all. Two women described themselves as housewives.

Residence. Thirty-eight per cent were either living with their parents or wife and 43 per cent had some other fixed abode.

'Involvement'. Assessing the extent to which those interviewed were involved in the drug scene, we found that 61 per cent were 'continually involved' in that they spent most of their time either obtaining or 'fixing' drugs and were constantly in the company of other drug users. Thirty-one per cent appeared to be only 'occasionally involved', and seven per cent were isolated from the scene, since their only contact with other drug users occurred when they

collected their prescriptions.

Sleep. Only 22 per cent had slept for more than two hours in each and every one of the previous seven 24-hour periods, while four had not slept for this length of time in any of the previous seven 24-hour periods.

Personal history

Schooling. The average age at leaving school was 15.38 years, with a range of 13–18 years. Eight per cent left school before reaching 15, 61 per cent left in the year they turned 15, while 30 per cent continued their formal education beyond the permissible leaving age. Sixty-five per cent had not taken any examinations while at school. The majority (81 per cent) had not pursued any further education on leaving school, and of the ten per cent who did part time courses 80 per cent had discontinued these. A similar trend was apparent among those who began full-time further education: of the nine per cent who started 78 per cent had discontinued this at the time of the interview. Consistent truancy, defined as frequent absence for one or more half-days per week, was relatively rare in primary school, being found in only one per cent; three per cent admitted to occasional absences. By contrast consistent truancy was relatively common in secondary school, being reported in 43 per cent of cases, while a further eight per cent were occasionally truant. In both instances the figures given are minimum estimates, as in 30 per cent of cases, information was not obtained for primary schooling and in 22 per cent for secondary schooling. Truancy in secondary school mainly occurred in the year in which the subjects left school and often immediately preceded their leaving.

Employment. Thirty-four per cent of the sample had entered some form of apprenticeship but two-thirds of these had discontinued this training and only 11 per cent had completed their course. Most of those interviewed had at best been employed in semi-skilled occupations. Compared with their fathers they were employed in occupations having a lower socio-economic classification. A comparison of their best and present occupations showed that there had been a downward drift.

Medical and psychiatric history. Forty-one per cent of the sample had some tentative or definite evidence of neurotic disturbance in childhood. Definite psychological disturbance was inferred from actual psychiatric referral, while frequent and intense nightmares, school refusal, and eating and sleeping disturbances were accepted as tentative evidence of disturbance. Eleven per cent of the sample had been referred to a psychiatrist during adolescence for treatment which was not associated with their drug-taking.

Criminality. Twenty-three per cent of the subjects had been sentenced to detention centre, approved school, or Borstal training, and 20 per cent had been sentenced to prison (excluding remand). In all, 32 per cent of the total sample had been sentenced to one or other institution and 11 per cent had been sentenced to both. A larger percentage of the sample admitted to delinquent or criminal behaviour, though in many instances this did not result in prosecution. Sixty-nine per cent admitted to stealing, 19 per cent to breaking and entering, 22 per cent to vandalism, and 42 per cent to the illegal use of a motor-car. Twenty-two per cent had been charged with violence, usually resisting arrest and using abusive language. Forty-five per cent of the sample had been charged with a drug offence, and almost all had been frequently searched by the police. An identical percentage (45) had been charged with other (non-drug) offences. Sixty-five per cent of the sample had been charged with offences of one sort or another and 24 per cent had been convicted of both drug and non-drug offences.

Sexual Behaviour. Twenty-four per cent of the males and 56 per cent of the females questioned stated that they first had sexual intercourse when aged 15 or less. In only three per cent of cases, all male, was sexual intercourse denied. In a further 11 per cent of cases, again all male, the relevant information was not obtained. Five per cent of males admitted to prostitution, compared with 31 per cent of females. Half of the females admitted to homosexual activites, compared with 19 per cent of the males. In eight per cent of cases, all males, insufficient information was obtained on this question.

Drug history

Use of alcohol. Whereas 89 per cent of the subjects had drunk alcohol on fewer than three days in the previous week and 58 per cent had not had a drink at all in that period, 24 per cent of the sample reported evidence of problem drinking in the past. In most cases problem drinking predated the use of other drugs. Only three per cent of the sample reported having a drink on each of the previous seven days.

Table 4.1 gives the mean age at which drugs were first used together with the frequency with which they were reported as having been taken. While the age of first use varied from 12 to 35 (depending on the drug in question) usually drugs were first taken between the ages of 16 and 20. That the subjects included in the sample had been, and in many cases still were, multiple drug users is illustrated by the fact that over half reported having taken heroin, methadone, hallucinogens, sedatives and tranquillizers, cannabis, amphetamine/barbiturate tablets, or amphetamine tablets in addition to methylamphetamine. The fact that all of these drugs were taken in the main between the ages of 16 and 20 suggests that they were used concurrently.

Table 4.2 shows that as well as their regular use of methylamphetamine about half of the sample had at one time been regular users of cannabis, amphetamine/barbiturate tablets, heroin or amphetamine tablets. About 20 per cent were at one time regular users of hallucinogens, sedatives and tranquillizers, methadone or cocaine. As regards their *current* use as well as their present use of methylamphetamine, about 30 per cent of the sample were also regular users of amphetamine/barbiturate tablets, methadone, cannabis or heroin. Sixteen per cent continued to use sedatives and tranquillizers at regular intervals and 11 per cent used amphetamine tablets regularly. A comparison of maximum intensity of use and current intensity of use shows that in all cases, with the exception of methylamphetamine and methadone, maximum use exceeded present use.

There was considerable variation in the quantity taken either maximumly or currently (table 4.3), and in the case of both methylamphetamine and heroin the average maximum dose exceeded the average current dose. This decrease in dose is particularly significant in the case of heroin, where it parallels a decrease in the number of persons currently using heroin. The decrease in the average dose of methylamphetamine taken reflects a diminution in the quantity reported taken, as all of those included in the sample were currently using methylamphetamine.

Methylamphetamine: supply and pattern of use

Table 4.4 shows that initial suppliers tended to be either people the addict knew or sellers. By contrast the majority of those interviewed said that their current major source of supply was a doctor. This significant increase in the number of persons receiving methylamphetamine from medical practitioners is partly a reflection of the fact that three of the settings in which patients were seen were medical establishments. What is significant, however, is the fact that so many bought methylamphetamine initially from people they did not know, or at most had only a passing acquaintance with. The finding that 40 per cent gave non-medical sources as their current major source of supply despite the fact that the majority were also getting methylamphetamine from doctors suggests that a significant number were supplementing their supplies from illicit sources. This is also confirmed by the fact that 23 per cent gave a 'seller' as their current major source of supply.

In all, those included in the sample had used methylamphetamine for an average of 19 months, though the length of use varied from two months to ten years. Only three per cent of cases had used methylamphetamine for three months or less, suggesting that in this sample at least there had been no

Table 4.1

Mean age at which drugs were first taken and the frequency of their report

	Mean age at first use	Standard deviation	Range	N (Frequency of report)	Not taken	Not known
				%		
Amphetamine tablets	16.88	2.40	12–23	54 (73)	16	4
Amphetamine/barbiturate mixtures	16.96	2.42	13–25	65 (88)	7	2
Cannabis	17.16	2.14	12–23	67 (91)	5	2
Sedatives and tranquillizers	18.64	2.51	14–25	39 (53)	31	
Other (mainly ephedrine)	18.66	4.22	14–25	6 (8)	66	2
Cocaine	18.67	2.42	14–24	34 (46)	33	7
Glue and solvents	18.76	3.65	14–28	13 (18)	58	3
Other opiates (mainly opium)	18.96	2.18	15–25	28 (38)	39	7
Hallucinogens	19.24	2.35	16–26	37 (50)	33	4
Heroin	19.82	3.45	14–34	64 (86)	10	0
Methylamphetamine injections	19.82	3.20	15–35	74 (100)	0	0
Ritalin (methylphenidate) or preludin phenmetrazine injections	19.88	2.39	15–24	17 (23)	54	3
Methadone	20.95	3.53	16–34	44 (59)	28	2

tendency for methylamphetamine to have been first taken following the restriction of heroin and cocaine in April 1968, though the indirect influence of restrictions placed on individual doctors cannot be discounted.

In contrast to the finding of Kramer et al. (1967) only a minority (eight per cent) of those interviewed in the present study reported a cyclic pattern of use.

Table 4.2

Maximum and current intensity of drug use (percentages in the body of the table)

	Methyl-amphet-amine-injec-tions	Canna-bis	Amphet-amine/barbit-urate mixtures	Heroin	Amphet-amine tab-lets	Meth-adone	Seda-tives and tran-quilli-zers	Hallu-cino-gens	Co-caine	Other op-iates	Rita-lin or prelu-din injec-tions	Glue and solvents
Maximum intensity of use												
Known to have taken but nothing more recorded	3	4	5	0	12	4	5	7	8	5	5	4
Isolated use	0	8	1	8	4	15	3	8	14	22	12	11
Intermittent use	1	26	20	28	12	19	19	23	12	18	8	3
Regular use	95	45	61	50	42	23	24	15	19	1	1	3
Not taken	0	7	9	14	22	38	46	45	46	53	73	78
Not known	1	0	3	0	8	1	3	3	1	1	0	1
Current intensity of use:												
Not using now	3*	35	40	36	49	20	23	28	38	35	20	19
Occasional use	1	32	11	28	11	14	12	19	5	7	4	0
Regular use	96	24	34	22	11	25	16	3	4	1	0	0
Not taken ever	0	7	12	14	23	38	42	45	47	53	73	80
Not known	0	1	4	0	7	3	7	5	5	4	3	1

* The 3% shown as not currently using methylamphetamine represent two subjects who had not injected methylamphetamine within the previous 48 hours (the period accepted as defining current use of methylamphetamine) but who were otherwise regular users of the drug.

Table 4.3

Maximum and current dose of methylamphetamine and heroin

	Daily dose of methylamphetamine (ampoules)[a]		Daily dose of heroin (grains)	
	Maximum	Current	Maximum	Current
Mean	8.65	5.00	2.92	1.27
Standard deviation	8.46	2.34	3.43	1.77
Range	2–20	1–12	1–16	1–5
N	67	72	50	30[b]
Not known	7	2	14	7
Not taken ever	0	0	10	10
Not taken now		0		27

a One ampoule of methylamphetamine contains 30 mg. and 1 grain of heroin is equivalent to about 60 mg.

b Included among the 30 subjects whose current dose of heroin was known are 17 whose current daily dose was less than 1 gr. (60 mg.). Some of those using very low doses were, however, regular users.

Table 4.4

Initial and current major source of supply of methylamphetamine

	Initial supplier	Current major source of supply
	%	%
Doctor	8	57
Person known to subject	47	16
Other giver	9	1
Seller	32	23
Not known	4	3

By far the greatest number (70 per cent) appeared to use methylamphetamine continuously, abstinences of one or two days occurring when they were unable to get supplies. Thirty-one per cent reported that they had undergone one or more 'voluntary' (non-hospital) withdrawals.

Heroin: supply and pattern of use

Those who had used heroin began taking it daily on an average of 17 weeks after first injecting it, though individuals varied considerably (range 0 to 84 weeks). In 11 per cent of cases the rate of progression could not be established. Table 4.5 gives the initial and current major source of supply.

Table 4.5
Initial and current major source of supply of heroin

	Initial supplier	Current major source of supply
	%	%
Doctor	3	8
Person known to subject	53	15
Other giver	5	1
Seller	23	26
Not applicable	14	45
Not known	3	5

Nineteen per cent claimed to have used heroin continuously. That the majority of the subjects who reported using heroin had been physically dependent on it is suggested by the fact that 57 per cent reported suffering withdrawal symptoms.

Side-effects of methylamphetamine

All subjects were asked whether they had experienced 'the horrors' when taking methylamphetamine. In almost all cases the subjects then described the various adverse effects experienced. On those isolated occasions in which subjects asked what was meant they were instructed to describe any effect of their taking methylamphetamine. The question was phrased in this way in order to avoid stereotyped answers – nevertheless, when coding the responses the answers given were cast in conventional psychiatric categories.

Table 4.6 shows that, with the exception of olfactory hallucinations, these

Table 4.6

Delusional and hallucinatory side-effects of methylamphetamine abuse

	%		%
Delusions of persecution	77	Tactile hallucinations	38
Ideas of reference	55	'Bugs'*	24
Visual hallucinations	54	Olfactory hallucinations	9
Auditory hallucinations	59		

* Bugs were not distinguished from tactile hallucinations in 31% of cases.

phenomena were frequently reported – so frequently as to be accepted and adapted to by the methylamphetamine user. Despite their familiarity most of the subjects had no insight into the unreality of the delusional and hallucinatory phenomena at the time of their occurrence, though 58 per cent stated that they appreciated their delusional nature now. Fourteen per cent still appeared to lack insight. In five per cent of cases insight appeared to be variable, present on some occasions but absent on others, and in eight per cent of cases the degree of insight could not be established. Only 15 per cent of those questioned claimed to have insight at the time of their occurrence.

Delusions of persecution and ideas of reference most often referred to police activity, and in some cases probably had their basis in frequent police searches. That these assumed true psychotic proportions, however, is illustrated by their vividness and irrationality. Visual hallucinations almost invariably reflected concern with the police and tended to be more common at night and when the subject was alone. The most common form of auditory hallucination was for the subject to hear his name called, usually with ominous implications. Formication was the most frequent tactile hallucination and itching was also common.

It did appear that these phenomena were to some extent dose-related, though a more common correlate was the degree of sleep deprivation of the subject. That this should be the case is hardly surprising when it is considered that sleeplessness itself is accompanied by an increase in hallucinogenic phenomena.

Other effects were equally prominent. Hyperactivity was reported in 49 per cent of cases and anxiety amounting to panic in 36 per cent of subjects. Aggression was felt by 45 per cent of those questioned but was rarely acted out. The majority of those who reported feeling aggressive said they felt irritable and short tempered. Aggression, agitation, and anxiety were most frequently associated with 'coming down' and were at least partly contributed to by the need to obtain further supplies of the drug.

Being 'hung up' was often reported (78 per cent). While subjects varied considerably in their description of this phenomenon, and in some cases used it merely to refer to dependence, it was most frequently used with reference to a pattern of obsessional rumination and compulsive behaviour. Subjects reported obsessionally tearing up pieces of paper or tickets, meticulously searching drawers and pockets, and re-reading without comprehension.

Thought disorder was also reported in half the cases and was described as 'like having too many thoughts in your head at once . . . great rapidity of thought . . . enabling one to anticipate what others are going to say.' In some cases methylamphetamine was described as 'sharpening' thought.

Discussion

The design and execution of the study is open to several criticisms. The final strategy represents a compromise between the niceties of research method and the limitations imposed by realities of the situation. While considerable care was exercised in the design and standardisation of the questionary and its subsequent coding, its use was affected by several factors over which we had no control. Patients were frequently in a very agitated state, often coming to the interview after injecting methylamphetamine or else threatening to terminate the interview to accomplish this. The garrulousness caused by methylamphetamine made the interviews exercises in discursiveness and imposed extreme difficulties in ensuring that comparable answers were obtained to standard questions. The fact that in some instances the information was not obtained attests to these difficulties. Seeing patients in various and in some cases unconventional settings also imposed limitations which were justified only by the desire to survey a heterogeneous sample.

The difficulties in conducting the interview must raise questions as to the validity of the information obtained – as does the fact that we were never able to obtain independent evidence about the accuracy of the information given. The estimates of anti-social and criminal behaviour obtained are therefore likely to be underestimates rather than overestimates. Despite these reservations we were impressed by the willingness with which subjects talked about their criminal involvement once assured of the confidentiality of their answers – a willingness no doubt facilitated by their use of methylamphetamine.

Who are the Methylamphetamine Users?

It is obvious that methylamphetamine users do not conform to any one stereotype. In the sample were middle class girls brought up, and in some cases continuing to live, in conventional middle class homes, and East End boys who had been involved in a variety of criminal activities since early adolescence. What was common to these various subjects could often be directly attributed to the drugs they were taking.

To what extent does personality disturbance in childhood precede drug use in adolescence? While the data obtained in this study are no substitute for those obtained from school records and interviews with parents, they do suggest that a significant proportion of those interviewed displayed personality problems before becoming drug users. The fact that 45 per cent of the sample were consistent truants from secondary school and that 41 per cent showed neurotic disturbances in childhood is at least indicative of the importance of pre-drug adjustment, though the absence of normative data prevents one from attaching more significance to these findings.

The finding also that half the girls interviewed admitted to homosexual activities suggests some failure of psychosexual development. That 46 per cent of the sample had suffered either parental bereavement or separation before they had turned 16 and the apparently excessive degree of social pathology in the parents and siblings of those interviewed is likely to have contributed to their maladjustment.

Of equal importance to the role of personality disturbance in drug abuse is the individual's involvement in a pre-existing deviant subculture. Reconstructing a person's subcultural affiliations, however, is no less difficult than delineating his premorbid personality. Nevertheless, we consider that a significant proportion of methylamphetamine users were members of a delinquent subculture and that their membership of this subculture, in so far as it reinforced anti-social activities, contributed to their later adoption of drugs.

The fact that so many of the sample were initially (and currently) supplied heroin or methylamphetamine by people they knew reinforces the view that there exists within the drug subculture a 'grey market', in which drugs are the currency of previous and present friendship. That a significant percentage bought their drugs initially from sellers whom they did not know and in many cases continued to rely on these sources emphasises, however, that drugs are also deployed for commercial purposes within this society. Sociological field research is sorely needed for better understanding of these processes.

Drug of choice

The evidence suggests that to talk of methylamphetamine takers as if they were a singular type of person exhibiting a circumscribed deviance is fallacious. To focus on methylamphetamine as the problem is quite arbitrary and puts untoward emphasis on the particular drug taken at one point in time, frequently in the context of a long history of drug taking. It would be arbitrary even to give most of those interviewed a specific identity as methylamphetamine users, since many of them were currently using other drugs as well.

Methylamphetamine use must be seen in the context of other drug use which was extensive in the past and is extensive in the present. We were very impressed with the ease with which a methylamphetamine user would use heroin when this was available and the comparable ease with which methylamphetamine was substituted for heroin. The willingness of those interviewed to alternate between two drugs with such totally contrasting pharmacological action suggests that any theory which seeks to relate specific drug choice to personality or to a particular type of reaction against society is simple-minded.

The frequency of childhood neurotic disturbance and previous problem drinking reported by those interviewed suggests that not only should present methylamphetamine use be seen in the setting of other drug use but that it must itself be seen as only one type of symptom manifestation. How many of those seen would otherwise have exhibited prodromal symptoms of alcohol addiction is an interesting question which this study raises but does not answer.

Consequences of methylamphetamine use

The phenomenology of amphetamine psychosis as related to us by these subjects confirms the classical account given by Connell (1958). The frequent occurrence of these episodes suggests that those seen in hospital today represent a small proportion of the total occurring in the community.

That anyone taking high doses of methylamphetamine by injection for long can lead a normal life is very doubtful, though some of those interviewed made adjustments which allowed them to approximate this state. Some, for example, took barbiturates at night to ensure they slept, and others took tranquillizers during the day to prevent too great excitement; yet others ensured they ate an adequate diet and thus counteracted the weight loss and malnutrition associated with methylamphetamine use.

The frequency of sleep disturbance, weight loss, malnutrition, and physical complications, together with the frequency of psychotic disturbance, all point, however, to the extreme difficulty the methylamphetamine user would experience in maintaining a job and normal social and personal relations. Indirectly, their use of methylamphetamine often led those interviewed into illegal activities directed at obtaining money for further supplies and thus into involvement with an anti-social subculture. It certainly could not be argued from the evidence obtained that the adverse effects of methylamphetamine are attributable to society's response to the methylamphetamine user – the damage suffered by the user, whatever society's reaction, is largely determined by the drug he has taken.

Implications for policy

To suggest that the findings of a rapidly mounted study carried out in circumstances deserving of critical scrutiny have implications for policy is to display a rash temerity.

The principal implication of this study is the need for further investigation. Nevertheless, the results do suggest certain relationships warranting further comment. The role of pre-morbid personality deserves further study, as does the means of introducing and maintaining the drug habit. The need to view the use of any one drug in a historical context suggests that longitudinal studies will be more profitable than those concerned with behaviour at any one point in time.

Policies of prevention or treatment are unlikely to prove efficacious if they focus on one particular drug or drugs. It would, for example, be misleading to talk of the 'treatment of methylamphetamine abuse' rather than to consider the help required by disturbed young persons who might in addition be taking methylamphetamine. This is not to suggest, however, that their use of methylamphetamine can be considered irrelevant.

That methylamphetamine was so readily available during the period over which the study was conducted is itself a disturbing feature. Eight per cent of those questioned reported obtaining their initial supply from doctors. The view of some doctors that methylamphetamine was a less dangerous drug than cocaine undoubtedly contributed to their willingness to supply this drug as a substitute for cocaine. Again the evidence of this study suggests that there is little validity in this assumption. Methylamphetamine is not a substance which can be considered suitable for medical 'maintenance' prescribing.

While the drug problem is not going to be solved by restrictive measures directed against any one drug there is an obvious need within the total programme for action to be taken against the danger presented by massive overprescribing of a dangerous substance. Action directed against one drug is likely to be unsuccessful in the long run, however, except that the question of overprescribing *per se* is dealt with, as the recent increase in the use of amphetamine sulphate illustrates.

Note

[1] In all cases where percentages are quoted they have been calculated with reference to the total number of 74. They therefore represent minimum estimates. Where the relevant information was not obtained in all cases this is indicated.

5 Sedative abuse by heroin addicts*

MARTIN MITCHESON, JAMES DAVIDSON,
DAVID HAWKS, LAURA HITCHENS
and SARAH MALONE

Summary

The pattern of drug abuse is constantly changing. A development is the extensive abuse of barbiturates by heroin addicts. Sixty-five heroin addicts were interviewed in the summer of 1969 and 62 had taken barbiturates. Eighty per cent admitted to injecting barbiturates at some time. During the month before the interview a legitimate prescription was the immediate source in approximately half the cases. Where an illegitimate source was given, the ultimate source was often medical. It is suggested that any request for sleeping tablets should be carefully considered and that pharmacists and wholesalers should review their security arrangements.

Introduction

Heroin dependency is usually only a part of multiple drug abuse. The commonest drugs associated with heroin abuse in the UK have been cocaine, cannabis and amphetamines. Of 33 heroin addicts seen by Bewley in 1963 and 1964, only five had taken barbiturates and three of these were Canadians (Bewley, 1965). However, in 1967 66 per cent of heroin users remanded in a London prison took barbiturates (James, 1969), and in a study of methylamphetamine injectors in the summer of 1968 sedative abuse was recorded in 53 per cent of cases (Hawks et al., 1969). Barbiturate abuse amongst heroin addicts in North America has become increasingly common during the past ten years (Hamburger, 1964; Cumberlidge, 1968; Chambers, 1969).

The authors investigated barbiturate abuse among 65 heroin addicts interviewed in the summer of 1969.

---

* Condensed from a paper in the *Lancet,* vol. 1, 1970, pp. 606–7.

Materials and methods

Sixty-five people were interviewed during May, June and July 1969 at three day centres open to heroin addicts – one in South London (38), one in Central London (11), and one in a provincial town (16).

In sex and age composition this group was not significantly different from a random sample of patients attending London drug treatment clinics who were interviewed over approximately the same period (Ogborne and Stimson, 1969). Fifty-four of the sample were male and 11 were female; they were, on average over a year younger than the clinic patients and there were fewer older addicts. The mean age was 23.1, with a range of 17–37 (SD 1.4). Both groups were equally likely to have a regular address. It had been expected that persons visiting the day centres would be less likely to be employed and this was confirmed.

Alcohol, cannabis, heroin and methadone injections had been taken by all patients at least once; amphetamine or amphetamine/barbiturate tablets and

Table 5.1
Frequency of drugs used

Drug	Ever used No.	Ever used %	% ever used daily	% ever used weekly	% used in last month	% used daily in last month
Alcohol	65	100	52	34	35	3
Amphetamine and amphetamine/barbiturate tablets	64	99	57	29	32	19
Cannabis	65	100	77	8	49	12
Cocaine*	50	77	59	8	25	9
Hallucinogens	48	74	8	27	9	0
Heroin	65	100	100	0	91	66
Methylamphetamine injections	64	99	95	3	2	0
Methadone injections	65	100	NK†	NK†	83	65
Barbiturates*	62	95	75	12	72	37

* Information lacking in one case. Columns 3 and 4 are mutally exclusive.
† NK = not known.
All percentages in the body of the table are calculated in the terms of the total sample, N = 65.

methylamphetamine injections by all but one. The only drug to have been used daily by everybody interviewed was heroin (this being the criterion for inclusion in the sample).

Heroin was also the commonest drug to have been used during the last month and to have been taken daily over the last month. Cannabis and methylamphetamine, which in the past had been taken daily by most patients, had in the last month been taken less than barbiturates.

Sedative use and abuse

Each heroin addict was asked why he first took barbiturates, the first source of the drug, and the route of administration. Three main reasons were given for using sedatives: to sleep because the subject was sleeping badly; to sleep to evade symptoms of opiate withdrawal; or for hedonistic reasons (the subjects being asked whether they had taken the drug for 'kicks'). The second reason – to evade withdrawal symptoms – includes both motivated attempts to reduce the intake of opiates, and involuntary withdrawal symptoms incurred where the subject had used his prescription too quickly and sought a period of oblivion until his next prescription was due to be collected. Where an addict had taken the drug for more than one reason the least proper reason is listed, e.g., a patient listed as using drugs for hedonistic reasons is likely also to have taken them for sleeping at some other time.

The initial source and reasons for using barbiturates are given in Table 5.2.

Table 5.2

Initial source of barbiturate and reason for trial

	Source				
Reason	Hospital inpatient	Hospital outpatient or general practitioner	Family	Illicit	Total
Sleep	7	13	3	4	27
Sleep to avoid withdrawal	1	5*	0	6	12
Hedonistic	0	2	3	18	23
Total	8	20	6	28	62†

* Includes one subject who took drugs for sedation when using excessive stimulants.

† Information was insufficient for one subject to be included in this table; and information was lacking in one case (see Table 5.1).

Barbiturates were more likely to be initially abused when obtained from non-medical sources ($X^2=11.51$; 1 DF; $P < 0.001$).

At some time, 42 said they had taken barbiturates for kicks, and 52 (80 per cent of those interviewed) had injected barbiturates, all but one intravenously. It seems that either the figure of 42 is an underestimate of hedonistic use, or else that the heroin addict is so accustomed to injecting opiates that ten individuals regarded the injection of the contents of a barbiturate capsule as a normal method of inducing sleep. The mean maximum regular consumption in the course of 24 hours was stated as 4.7 capsules of barbiturate (range 1–20, SD 4.3). The exact quantity of barbiturates cannot be estimated, since a capsule may contain between 60 and 300 mg. As a consequence of their use or abuse of sedatives, 21 patients had taken an overdose of barbiturates; 14 of these had been admitted to hospital as a result.

Of those who had obtained and used barbiturates in the month before interview, the number giving a doctor as their principal source was approximately equal to that giving a non-medical source. In addition, 12 whose principal source of barbiturates was medical, also obtained supplies from non-medical sources; four obtaining barbiturates principally from non-medical sources also received a prescription. Thirty-four had injected barbiturates during the previous month.

Table 5.3

Principal source of barbiturates in previous month

Source	No.	%
Hospital	8	17
General practitioner:		
NHS prescription	13	28
Private prescription	3	6
Friend or acquaintance	21	45
Professional seller	2	4
TOTAL	47	100

Discussion

Fashions in drug abuse change remarkably quickly. The epidemic of methylamphetamine injection seems to have been terminated promptly when the drug was withdrawn from the retail market in October 1968; and, although the subjects in the present study claimed to have obtained the occasional ampoule, the incidence of amphetamine abuse dropped dramatically. The consumption of methaqualone with diphenhydramine by heroin addicts, which was common in the previous winter, seemed to be declining when the interviews were carried out.

Although it may be possible to work on a stabilised dose of an opiate, this is very much more difficult in a state of intoxication induced by sedatives (Dole, 1965). Drug users usually claim that their abuse of sedatives is a result of the absence of methylamphetamine and the reduced quantities of heroin and cocaine available. It is not suggested that the drug situation would be improved by making opiates and amphetamines more freely available, but rather that increasing control over any one group of drugs is likely to result in some increase in the abuse of other substances.

The practical implication of the research findings that 80 per cent of these heroin addicts had injected barbiturates is that an increasing demand for sedatives can be expected in the illicit market. This illicit market is traditionally supplied directly or indirectly from medical prescriptions or thefts from wholesale and retail chemists. The figures quoted above minimise the extent to which medical prescriptions supply the illicit market; since, where an illicit source was given as the immediate source of the drug, the ultimate source was almost always a prescription or theft from a pharmacy.

It is suggested that all persons concerned in the handling, prescribing, and dispensing of sedatives should consider their security precautions. It is no longer sufficient for the doctor to review only middle aged dependent patients who come with repeated requests for sleeping tablets. Any request for sleeping tablets should be carefully considered, especially when the patient is under 30, or is not personally known to the practitioner. Further, the possibility of younger members of the family abusing unused sleeping tablets is by no means negligible.

6 Heroin users in a provincial town and their follow-up over a three year period*

DAVID HAWKS

Summary

In December 1967 initial contact was made with four heroin users in a provincial town, and through their network of friends 37 confirmed heroin users were traced. Personal and social characteristics and patterns of drug use are described. A research office was set up which maintained contact and functioned as an informal day-centre. Further data were collected after intervals of one, two and three years. Few of those at liberty gave up using drugs, but approximately half the subjects worked full time for the greater part of the follow-up period. Real availability of an alternative choice to the continuing life of addiction may be more important in determining favourable outcome than formal treatment. A prescribing treatment policy may however fragment the cohesion of a drug subculture where the previous unifying influence has been the search for drugs.

Introduction

The study of heroin users in a large city is beset by many difficulties. Communication between the different agencies dealing with users is uncertain and the movement of the users themselves such that their follow-up is hazarded. The advantages of studying use in a provincial town are, therefore, considerable. The particular advantages of studying use in the town described here were that almost from the outset a policy of co-ordination and containment was adopted which both gave some assurance that the vast majority of users were known to the research team and allowed information to be collected on them from a variety of sources. While in time the cohort increasingly dispersed, it is nevertheless the case that for the three years during which they were followed-up a degree of personal contact was

* This composite paper has been specially written for inclusion in this book. The authors of the original papers were Adele Kosviner, Martin Mitcheson, Alan Ogborne, Jim Zacune, Kenneth Myers, Gerry Stimson, Sarah Malone, Laura Hitchins, Griffith Edwards and David Hawks.

maintained with the majority, which is unusual except in a treatment context.

In describing this study and, in doing so, condensing three separate papers considerable space will be given to outlining the original survey where the basic methodology is set out and the areas of enquiry depicted. In that the follow-up papers employed the same methodology and made comparisons on the same variables, less space will be devoted to them.

The original survey [1]

The survey reported here is an intensive investigation of the extent and nature of heroin use in one town. The essential advantage of this approach is that it offers more than a history of individuals – it provides an opportunity to build up a picture of an addict's subculture and of the social forces determining and maintaining addiction. The town is compact and long established, with a population of under 100,000. It has an unusually high proportion of middle class people; light manufacturing industry and services, including a university and a technical college, are the predominant employers.

Method

Scope

The aim was to interview all the heroin users who lived in or around the town. People at the university were not included unless they had been resident locally before going to university. A heroin user was defined as anyone using the drug at the time of the study or within the previous three months in any dosage.

Contacting the subjects

Contact was first established with four heroin users attending a weekly discussion group held by a local psychiatrist. Through them others were contacted, sometimes by spontaneous introduction to friends, sometimes by more persistent enquiry. The only exceptions to this approach were that two users were contacted through their general practitioners and that those in institutions were contacted through those institutions.

Two furnished rooms were rented in the centre of the town where the researchers lived and conducted most of the interviews. These rooms came to be treated by many of the users as an informal meeting place for coffee and companionship.

Coverage

There is no way of confirming that all the heroin users in the town were contacted but names obtained through the co-operation of the users corresponded very closely with those from official sources and from the town's doctors, all of whom were contacted. A structured interview was given as soon as possible after each user was contacted. The initial fieldwork was done in December 1967 and January 1968.

Validity

Information gained from the initial interview was checked with information from official sources; in only a few cases were there discrepancies and these were generally minor. That the subjects were heroin users was confirmed in 22 cases by direct observation of self-injection and in the other cases by hospital notes, general practitioners or friends.

Findings

The extent of heroin use

The names of 47 suspected users were assembled with the help of a psychiatrist and other official sources: 31 of these suspects were confirmed as heroin users, ten were not and six had left the town. All authorities had underestimated the extent of the problem and six users were unknown to any of them. Thirty-one of the 37 confirmed heroin users were interviewed and basic information on the other six was obtained from official sources and from their friends.

Characteristics of the users

Demographic details. Thirty-one were male and six were female. Their ages ranged from 16 to 33, the mean age being 20 years 7 months (18 for females, 21 for males). Thirty-one (84 per cent) were aged 21 or less and only two were over 25. Only one was married; he had no children and was not living with his wife.

Because of the age of the users, it would be unrealistic to assess social class on the basis of their own occupation. Classification of social class was based on parents' occupations, using the Registrar General's definitions (General Register Office, Classification of Occupations, 1966[a]).

The 33 subjects on whom information was available were distributed fairly evenly between classes I, II, and III; none was in classes IV or V. There was a

Table 6.1
Socio-economic groups of users' parents and of occupied and retired males in the town population

	Distribution of users' parents		Distribution of town population (1961)
Groups	No.	%	%
1, 2, 3, 4, 13	20	54	19
5–17 except 13	13	35	81
Not known	4	11	–
Total	37	100	100

striking tendency for the parents to be in professional, rather than commercial, occupations. Using the Registrar General's detailed socio-economic groups the sample can be compared with the population of the town (General Register Office, Census, 1966[b], see Table 6.1). Groups 1–4 and 13 are, broadly, employers, managers, professional people and farmers. Even assuming that the four 'not knowns' fell in groups 5–17, the difference between the numbers of users in the two socio-economic groupings (see Table 6.1) and the expected numbers, based on the distribution of the town population, is statistically significant ($X^2=29.5$; $P < 0.0005$).

Family structure and residence. Twenty-six of the users' parents were married and living together. The parents of the remaining 9 were either divorced, separated or both not alive. Comparable data on the incidence of 'broken homes' in the town population is not available. The majority of subjects (23) were living at home with their parents.

Education. The majority of the subjects went to the kinds of schools where they would have had relatively good chances of getting academic qualifications and of going on to higher education (21 had attended grammar, direct-grant or independent schools).

Despite these opportunities, the mean age of leaving school was just over 16 years, with only nine subjects remaining at school after this age. Nineteen had, however, gone on to some form of full time further education at technical college, art school or university, though 13 failed to complete these courses. In all, 19 people had failed to complete a course either at school or in further part time or full time education.

Occupation. Fourteen were in full time employment, nine were unemployed, seven were students (either at university or the local technical college) and seven were in hospital or other institution. Of the last group, six had been unemployed and one employed immediately before admission. The jobs held were generally unskilled or semi-skilled, such as kitchen worker, clerk or laundry hand.

Drug use, medical and psychiatric history, delinquency.

Seventeen of those not in institutions were daily users of heroin, and 13 were irregular users. Of those in institutions three were using heroin daily and three irregularly on admission (one not known).

First use of drugs. The average age at which drugs were first used illicitly was 15 for girls and 16 for boys. All the 30 subjects whose history of drug use was obtained had tried both cannabis and amphetamines before taking heroin. Quite a high proportion (12) had injected themselves with another drug before trying heroin. Most frequently this drug was methylamphetamine, but other substances injected included pethidine, vodka, pentobarbitone and a solution of cannabis.

First use of heroin. The average age at which heroin was first tried was 16 for girls and 18 for boys. Nearly half the users took their first heroin between one and two years after they had first tried a drug; only four had taken it after a shorter interval. Twenty-three subjects injected heroin the first time they used it.

Source and dosage of heroin. Five subjects were receiving heroin on prescription when the study began and 17 by its end, reflecting a change in the prescribing policy of local doctors. Supplies for those not on prescription were generally obtained by different users going each week to 'score' (buy) from registered addicts in London. There was no evidence of anyone 'pushing' heroin; the arrangement appeared to be a co-operative rota system rather than a commerical enterprise. The amounts being used by daily users outside institutions range from gr.$\frac{1}{2}$ (30 mg.) to gr.4 (240 mg.), the mean dosage being gr.$1\frac{1}{2}$ (90 mg.). The drug most often used with heroin was methylamphetamine.

Medical and psychiatric history. While no clinical examination was carried out, information was obtained on previous hospital treatment and known complications of drug taking. Before drug use four subjects had been in touch with psychiatric services, three had had brief attendances at child guidance clinics and one had attended a psychiatric outpatients' department. After the onset of drug use 18 (nearly half the total) had been admitted to hospital. Eleven had been inpatients in a psychiatric hospital, five had been admitted to general hospitals for physical complications, either jaundice or pneumonia, and two had records of admission to both general and psychiatric hospitals. Fourteen of the total had either had a diagnosed episode of hepatitis or themselves reported an attack of jaundice. A further five gave a history of sepsis or abscesses resulting from non-sterile injections but not all had received medical attention for this.

Delinquency. Twenty of the sample were known to have had convictions. The crimes not involving drugs were generally petty. Of the ten people who had been convicted of non-drug offences, three had committed them before using any drugs at all and seven between first trying drugs and first trying heroin. There was only one person who was convicted of a non-drug offence after heroin use began and this person had already been convicted of such a crime before the onset of heroin use. Of the 13 people who had been convicted of drug offences only two were convicted before they started using heroin. Half the convictions were for 'soft' drugs only.

One year later [2]

The original cohort of 37, together with those resident in the town or taking up residence in the town who, subsequent to the initial survey, became regular or irregular users of heroin, were interviewed over the period September to December 1968. Twenty-seven of the original 37 users visited the research office during the course of the year as did 11 of the 14 'new' users. Thirty-five of the original sample were either reinterviewed directly or basic information was obtained on them from a variety of sources. All of the new users were given a structured questionnaire similar to that given the original cohort a year earlier.

The continuing presence of the research workers in the town allowed the completeness of the original survey to be checked. One of those initially included, on whom only indirect information was available, was subsequently shown not to be a heroin user while four, who were only irregular users at the time of the original survey, were included as new cases.

Table 6.2 compares the heroin users in the 1967 and 1968 samples.

Careful monitoring of the original cohort and the new cases allowed consideration of the impact of the new treatment policies adopted after April 1968. The principal change was from a illicit dependence to a dependence on the containment unit as the main source of drugs. Whereas in April only five users were 'registered', there were 15 in December who received their prescriptions from the local clinic; the number had been even higher (21) in the course of the year. As a consequence, while the total amount of heroin in circulation increased there was less dependence on the illicit market and less evidence of illicit heroin.

The impact of such changes on the original group was to fragment it, revealing that the original close association was based essentially on the need

Table 6.2 Heroin users in 1967 and 1968 samples

	First survey	Status at end of Dec. 1968: Original 1967 sample	Status at end of Dec. 1968: Additional cases first contacted in 1968
Total	37	36	14
Sex:			
male	31	30	12
female	6	6	2
Average age:			
male	21	22	21
female	18	19	18.5
Marital status:			
married	1	2	–
single	36	34	14
Residential status:			
resident in town	37	32	11
left town	–	4	3
resident 3 years before interview	37	36	7
resident less than 3 years before interview	–	–	7
Employment:			
employed full time	14	16	2
unemployed	9	14	10
students	7	4	2
institutionalised	7	2	–
Social class:			
I	10	10	2
II	11	11	1
III	12	13	3
IV	–	2	5
V	–	–	1
unknown	4	–	2
Drug use status:			
daily use of heroin	17	16	8
regular use of heroin	13	12	6
institutionalised	7	2	–
not using heroin presently	–	6	–
Daily users' dosage:			
range	30–240 mg. ($\frac{1}{2}$–4 grains)	10–300 mg. ($\frac{1}{6}$–5 grains)	
mean dosage	90 mg. ($1\frac{1}{2}$ grains)	87 mg. ($1\frac{1}{2}$ grains)	
Hospital treatment related to drugs:			
subjects admitted	18	11 (23 admissions)	3
Delinquency:			
subject with non-drug offences (theft)	10	2	5
subjects with drug offences	13	4	8

to obtain illicit supplies. The new users had, from the outset, little contact with the original cohort, except fortuitously through the containment unit. Those not primarily resident in the town constituted a separate sub-group. The new users were also notable in that they had a history of more serious delinquency. For their part, the original cohort showed little change over the twelve months during which they were followed up.

Two years later [3]

In the closing months of 1969 the original 36 users, together with 27 subsequent users of whom 13 were first included in 1969, were followed up using a variety of means. Table 6.3 compares the sources of information employed over the three years.

Table 6.3
Sources of information

	1967	1968	1969
	%	%	%
Official records only	1 (3)	4 (8)	6 (10)
Information from other users	2 (5)	5 (10)	4 (6)
Informal personal contact	1 (3)	5 (10)	5 (8)
Interview at end of year	33 (89)	36 (72)	48 (76)
Total included	37	50	63

If personal interview was refused or proved impossible, the schedule was completed, as far as possible, from informal conversation and information received during the year. The diminution of personal contact indicated in Table 6.3 reflects the gradual dispersal of the cohort. Even so, 43 individuals visited the research office during the year, 28 of them more than ten times.

Compared to the previous year, fewer were fully employed and more correspondingly were unemployed or in part time work. One half of the sample were either unemployed, spasmodically employed or in an institution.

The addition of new cases from non-professional or managerial backgrounds resulted in a sample more typical of the local population. Even so, those from the professional or managerial classes were significantly over-represented in the sample.

Comparing the frequency with which heroin was taken at the time of interview for each of the three years shows a very much smaller proportion of the sample were using heroin on a regular basis at the end of 1969 than had been the case in the two previous years. Even so, only ten of those at liberty had not used heroin at some time during 1969.

Table 6.4
Heroin and opiate use

	At time of interview			During year
	1967	1968	1969	1969
	%	%	%	%
Heroin				
Daily	17 (46)	24 (48)	6 (10)	20 (32)
Irregular	13 (35)	18 (36)	14 (22)	29 (46)
None	–	6 (12)	28 (45)	10 (16)
Institution or dead	7 (19)	2 (4)	9 (14)	2 (3)
Uncertain			5 (8)	2 (3)
Any opiate				
Daily			25 (40)	40 (64)
Irregular			6 (10)	14 (22)
None			19 (30)	5 (8)
Institution or dead			9 (14)	2 (3)
Uncertain			4 (6)	2 (3)

Compared with 1968 there had been a reduction in the use of heroin, cocaine and methedrine (the latter was withdrawn from retail pharmacies in October 1968) and an increase in the use of methadone, barbiturates and oral amphetamines, the latter reflecting the ban on methedrine. The same trends were observed nationally.

While the vast majority (33/40) of those who were daily users of opiates were on prescription, seven users consumed opiates daily for at least a month and 13 on a more infrequent basis without receiving a prescription.

Thirteen per cent (14) of the cohort were convicted for a non-drug offence during the year, while 22 per cent (24) were convicted of drug offences, proportions very similar to 1968. Only 25 per cent spent some time in custody during 1969. Somewhat surprisingly, there was no difference in the rate of

Table 6.5
Comparison of frequency of drug taking during 1968 and 1969 (original 36 cases)

Drug	Year	None		Irregular use		Daily use		Total	Difference
		N	%	N	%	N	%		
Heroin	68	8	25	4	12	20	63	32	$P<0.05$
	69	6	20	13	40	13	40		x^2 6.5
Methadone	68	10	32	5	16	16	52	31	N.S.
	69	4	13	7	23	20	64		x^2 5.5
Other opiates	68	25	78	3	9	4	13	32	N.S.
	69	25	78	7	22	0	0		x^2 3.9
Barbiturates	68	23	72	4	12	5	16	32	$P<0.01$
	69	8	25	11	34	13	41		x^2 13.6
Oral amphetamines	68	25	83	3	10	2	7	30	$P<0.01$
	69	12	40	13	43	5	17		x^2 10.8
Cocaine	68	14	48	12	41	3	11	29	$P<0.05$
	69	24	83	4	14	1	3		x^2 6.4

conviction for those receiving prescriptions and those not (27/32 per cent). Twenty-five per cent were admitted to hospital for drug treatment, reflecting the local policy of refusing to prescribe opiates to users following their discharge, though all but two left within three months.

Abstinence, or irregular use of opiates, did not appear to be related to a conviction for a drug or non-drug offence, previous hospital admissions, age of first drug use or age of present heroin use, though the smallness of the numbers precluded statistical test. On the other hand, there was an apparent association with not having received a prescription (it is to be noted that most of those who were abstinent or irregular users had only ever been irregular users). Not using any drug except alcohol or cannabis was most compatible with working, while the illicit use of drugs was least compatible with working.

Three years later [4]

The continued dispersal of the cohort made it increasingly difficult to ensure a comprehensive follow-up. As a consequence, the third year follow-up was confined to those who constituted the original cohort. The virtue of such concentration is that it permits the comparison of this group over a period of three years undiluted by the addition of those identified in later years.

Follow-up questionnaires were completed on 34 of the original cohort of 36 in December 1970. The remaining two had died. Thirty-three per cent had not been in the town in which the original survey had been carried out at all in

Table 6.6
Comparison of frequency of drug taking during 1968, 1969 and 1970 (original 36 cases)

Drug	Year	None		Irregular use		Daily use		Total
		N	%	N	%	N	%	N
Heroin	68	8	25	4	12	20	63	32
	69	6	20	13	40	13	40	
	70	15	42	10	28	4	11	29
Methadone	68	10	32	5	16	16	52	31
	69	4	13	7	23	20	64	
	70	5	14	11	31	14	38	30
Barbiturates	68	23	72	4	12	5	16	32
	69	8	25	11	34	13	41	
	70	12	33	15	42	2	6	29
Amphetamines	68	25	83	3	10	2	7	30
	69	12	40	13	43	5	17	
	70	8	22	18	50	3	8	29
Cocaine	68	14	48	12	41	3	11	29
	69	24	83	4	14	1	3	
	70	21	58	8	22	0	0	29

1970, while 36 per cent had spent all of 1970 in the town.

Apart from there being a greater number married in 1970, a trend which in any case only reflects the increasing age of the cohort, there had been little change in the marital or employment status of the group. Slightly less than one-half were known to be employed full time.

Comparing the frequency of drug use during each of the three years 1968, 1969 and 1970 reveals that the frequency of use of most drugs diminished. Whereas in 1968 63 per cent of the sample were daily users of heroin, in 1970 the proportion was 11 per cent. The use of barbiturates having increased during 1969 diminished in 1970, though 42 per cent still continued to use barbiturates irregularly. Amphetamines continued to be used sporadically.

As might be expected, receiving a prescription was closely associated with the frequency of use of any opiate. Thirteen of those using opiates daily received a prescription, compared to one who did not. Irregular use of opiates was by no means incompatible with not receiving a prescription, however, and of the 11 claiming to use opiates irregularly ten did not receive a prescription.

While a daily use of opiates did not appear to be closely associated with employment status in the month prior to interview (with five daily users in full time employment, compared with six who did not use opiates at all) obtaining a prescription for the greater part of the year did appear to be closely associated with being unemployed for most of the year.

Hospitalisation was as frequent in 1970 as in previous years, the majority immediately relapsing to drugs on discharge, while convictions were lower with only 14 per cent convicted for any offence during the year.

Discussion

Extrapolation from so small a base is a hazardous business, particularly as there is evidence to suggest that the group was atypical in some of its attributes. Even so, many of the trends observed found parallel on the national scene and at least some of the conclusions reached appear to have implications for broader policy.

1 The heterogeneity of users

Even within this relatively small and homogeneous sample there was no characteristic common to all users. Who are the addicts must, therefore, be answered in terms of a comprehensive typology, rather than in terms of a single set of descriptive variables.

2 The polymorphous nature of misuse

While the intention had been to study a group of heroin users, it immediately became apparent that heroin use could only be a convenient shorthand for polyuse. A majority of those included in the cohort used a variety of drugs, often substituting one for another as availability dictated. Moreover, it was clear that any restriction in the supply of one drug, whether the result of official policy or merely fortuitously, resulted in a greater recourse to others. Any treatment policy which addresses only one group of drugs is, in such circumstances, unlikely to prove effective; it is also likely to discourage those who may not yet be using opiates from seeking help.

3 The chronic course of heroin use

While there was a trend for the frequency of use to diminish, it was nevertheless apparent that few of those at liberty gave up using drugs altogether. Most replaced regular use with more sporadic use. Similarly, while many were admitted to hospital for treatment, most discharged themselves after only relatively brief periods and almost immediately reverted to using drugs.

4 The 'normality' of continuing drug use

Despite the evidence of continuing social and physical damage observed in some users, approximately one-half of the sample managed to work full time for the greater part of the follow-up period. Many lived at home or else had a stable abode and avoided further criminal involvement.

5 The imperative necessity of finding real alternatives

While the numbers studied do not permit a rigorous test of factors related to abstinence, long term abstinence did not appear to be related to receiving treatment at one of the special treatment centres. On the other hand, it did appear in the few cases in which it occurred to be related to the availability of accessible and attractive alternatives to a drug centred way of life. Except that those responsible for the rehabilitation of users address themselves to this issue, it seems likely that the majority of those treated will relapse.

6 The desirability of adopting a co-ordinated policy

The particular town in which this study was carried out adopted a co-ordinated policy of containment at the outset. While it subsequently changed details of its procedures, it did so after consultation between all the parties involved. An important benefit of such a co-ordinated approach was that some of the misunderstandings which otherwise abound when a number of agencies are involved in the treatment of the same cases were avoided and the addicts themselves presented with a more consistent policy. Another advantage, fostered in part by the comparative smallness of the town was that information relating to the addicts was available from a large number of sources, with the result that a complete monitoring was more nearly approximated.

Notes

[1] Condensed from a paper originally published in the *Lancet,* vol. 1, 1968, pp. 1189–92.

[2] Condensed from a paper originally published in the *International Journal of the Addictions,* vol. 4, 1969, pp. 557–70.

[3] Condensed from a paper originally published in the *British Journal of Addictions,* vol. 66, 1971, pp. 129–40.

[4] This aspect of the study has not been published previously.

7 Appraisal

It must not be assumed that a research unit is able without prejudice to assess its own work – that is properly the function of others with less investment in the answer. What will be attempted here is a partial review of the shortcomings of the approaches illustrated by this group of papers, and a listing of some of the directions which might be pursued in future research. Neither review nor listing would pretend to be complete.

The professional epidemiologist might well object that to describe the work reported in the papers which are being discussed as in any strict sense a contribution to epidemiology, is presumptuous. He would point out that the most basic conditions for epidemiological research are that what is to constitute the case should be strictly defined, that the study population should then be delineated and demarcated, that the representativeness of sampling should be ensured or any likely bias identified, that cases should then be adequately counted. Probably none of the reported studies would meet these criteria. In such a situation the purist response would be to dismiss the value of the great majority of so far available studies of drug using populations from any part of the world. A more charitable judgement would be one which took full cognizance of the manifest shortcomings but which acknowledged that much of the existing work has its evolutionary place in the development of studies in an area beset by peculiarly difficult practical problems.

As is perhaps inevitable in so new an area of research many of the projects described in this section are descriptive. They have described the characteristics of a variety of drug users without attempting to test any explicit hypotheses and without in some cases fully exploiting their own data. At a time when even so basic information as the ethnic and social class composition of the addict population is unknown such descriptive research is justifiable and even necessary. However it will be apparent that the number and variety of drug abusers is such that this demographic exercise can be inordinately prolonged. At some stage an attempt to categorise must be made and few of the studies reviewed have to-date made this attempt, to some extent as a result of the small numbers involved in their samples. While the smallness of the numbers is partly a reflection of the field itself, the failure to cross-tabulate attributes of the same samples is less explicable unless it is allowed that the urgency which has attended research in the drug field precludes the use of more sophisticated forms of analysis. Whatever the historical justification for the present situation there is an imperative need to consider not only the extent to which certain factors are disproportionally found to be associated with drug dependence (an assessment which is itself dependent on the existence of normative data), but also the association of those factors with each other. Lacking a set of categories which can be universally applied to all addicts or even addicts using particular drugs, it is at least arguable that any universality which exists is to be found in the relationship between variables rather than in the predominance of the variables themselves. Thus while the average age at which drugs were first used may vary considerably depending on the population studied, it might nevertheless be shown in any of a variety of samples that the younger the age of first use, the poorer the prognosis and the greater the diversity of drugs tried.

Except that normative data is available or specifically collected, inferences about the disproportionate representation of certain factors in the background or present characteristics of addicts must remain hazardous. While at times the extremity of some of the distributions almost certainly justifies the assumption of their significance, in other instances they almost certainly do not diverge significantly from the norm for the appropriate age group. In part the deficiency owes its origin to the paucity of such normative data. Truancy rates for Inner London are extremely difficult to obtain, and data relating to the percentage of children who are separated from their parents for a period of one year or more before the age of 15 is non-existent for the general population. What is perhaps less defensible is the failure to collect relevant normative data, though even here there are extenuating circumstances. The collection of data with the intention of comparing it with that collected on drug using samples is bound to produce a certain amount of anxiety. What is lacking in any of the published research in this field is a comparison of a drug using sample with a cohort drawn from the same schools or neighbourhoods. Until such comparisons are made, whether directly or indirectly, the etiological importance of a number of factors and even their disproportionate representation in samples of drug users, must remain a matter for surmise.

Of equal cause for comment is the failure to date to address some of the methodological problems rampant in this field. Reliance on the recollection of a single respondent provides only dubious assurance of accuracy. Reliance on the recall of a respondent who may be motivated to mislead his questioner, who may not be orientated at the time or on the occasion in question, and who may have the greatest difficulty even when well intentioned in providing the details requested, can only provide modest comfort. Where such recollections can be substantiated by another observer or checked against other documents, or where the effects of the drugs themselves are known and can therefore be acknowledged, or where the anonymity of the respondent can be guaranteed and accepted as guaranteed by the respondent himself, the enquiry is lent some greater respectability. At present it must be acknowledged however that few of these assurances operate. In the main the studies reported have relied on the report of a single observer and where documentation exists it has pertained only to a limited number of the areas of interest, or has derived from the same dubious source. The degree and nature of intoxication has not always been assessed and if assessed subjectively not substantiated by urine analysis; even if relatively objective evidence of intoxication were available its effect on recall and other cognitive functions is largely unknown. Lacking these safeguards most studies rest their claim to validity on the assurance of anonymity given the respondent and their impression of co-operativeness, together with some internal and external checks on the consistency with which some details are reported.

Nor is the reliability of the interviewer better assured. With the exception of the pilot stage in some of the research reported, respondents were not interviewed by more than one interviewer either on the same or successive occasions, nor were different methods always employed to obtain the same information as would be recommended to eliminate artifacts due to the method of data collection employed. That such safeguards are not often implemented in other social science research can provide little comfort when the peculiar difficulties of ensuring validity in this area are considered.

The difficulties associated with retrospective enquiries both with regard to the adequacy of the data and the problem of inferring causality, are such that it is tempting to pursue only prospective studies. Apart from the difficulties involved in maintaining the continuity of such studies and ensuring the follow-up of adequate numbers, there are problems peculiar to the field of drug dependence which beset this approach. The fact that drug dependence of any persistence, and particularly opiate addiction is a relatively rare condition even in the most vulnerable age groups, means that any attempt to study prospectively the actual development of dependence must either contend with very large samples or else over-sample those regarded as 'at risk'. For those at risk to be identified presumes the availability of certain information, or else the existence of strong theoretical models regarding the causation of dependence. Notwithstanding the relative lack of such theory there is a need for studies which structure their enquiry in order to test certain hypotheses either by reference to normative data which is already available, or by making internal comparisons between carefully selected sub-samples. If such a strategy had no other virtue it would greatly reduce the number of individual variables considered and instead focus attention on a limited number of synthetic variables.

Two other strategies recommend themselves though they may both be thought appropriate to a later stage in the evolution of research in the drug field. The first might be termed the 'controlling out of socio-economic variables'. It is well attested that most forms of deviance have strong socio-economic correlates, though whether these are causative or merely reflect societal definitions of deviance is problematic. What is clear however is that a fairly predictable proportion of the total variance is accounted for by socio-economic variables. This being the case there is much to recommend controlling such variables out, and concentrating instead on the elucidation of those other variables which even in populations having similar socio-economic characteristics result in differing manifestations of drug dependence. These other variables, which normally account for much less of the variance, might under such circumstances attain greater prominence. For example, the incidence of drug dependence might be studied in an area of high prevalance where exposure is fairly uniformly ensured by the operation of the same social variables. The detailed study and comparison of those who become dependent at different stages of the innovation process, or who remain immune, can be expected to reveal the operation of those more subtle variables whose influence is usually disguised by the effect of grosser (and more easily measured) socio-economic variables. Such a research strategy is but a general prescription for including in the research purview the 'negative case' or person who despite the odds does not become dependent. Research which concentrates exclusively on those who are known to be dependent, will fail to acknolwedge the operation of a process of immunity which in addition to being instructive in itself may tell us much about the etiology of addiction.

Prognostications as to what are likely to prove in future to be the most productive lines of research are bound to be contentious – worthwhileness being highly subjective and prediction an uncertain art. Much research attests to the fact that those who have misused one drug tend also to have misused others, whether licitly or illicitly, and one obvious development would be to pursue studies which considered the individual's abuse of a variety of substances and which does not confine itself to any one – the general characteristics of the individual and the general social processes which result in drug seeking. It would also seem important to put some part of the research investment toward the study of society's multi-faceted reaction to drug use and the drug user, believing this to be relevant both to the etiology of dependence and what happens for better or worse to the drug user. Epidemiological research is often hopefully seen as providing the underpinning of preventive strategies but with drugs perhaps the greatest ambivalence is reserved for research which has prevention as its objective. While in an area where the condition is both difficult to treat and subject to frequent relapse, prevention has a certain logical imperative, the gap between what is logically required and what is possible is huge, and this not only because of a certain lack of 'leverage' but also because of the paucity of predictive models.

In summary, the fairest appraisal of the state of the art might be that the art form of drug epidemiology (at least as illustrated by this present batch of papers), is still at a fairly primitive stage of development. There is certainly no room for complacency, but even with an awareness of all the difficulties ringing in the ears there is some sense of a way ahead.

Part II Treatment populations and treatment organisation

8 The British Approach to the Treatment of Heroin Addiction*

GRIFFITH EDWARDS

Summary

The legal context of the British approach to the treatment of heroin addiction is summarised and the assumptions implicit in such an approach listed. Included in the latter are hypotheses relating to the prevention of new cases and the nature of the treatment offered. The actual situation is described and limitations in the hypotheses identified – new patients may not need heroin but may nevertheless demand to be registered; doctors may not show the right discernment in ascertaining the correct dosage; not everyone will prove invulnerable to the black market; the prescription of heroin and the building of abstinence motivation may prove mutually exclusive activities; there will be a temptation to compulsorily admit those patients who cannot be stabilised and the stabilised addict may himself prove to be a figment of the legislator's imagination.

Means are proposed whereby some of these difficulties may be overcome – means which include the vigorous and adequate implementation of the system; the support of those doctors working the system; the provision of attractive and accessible career alternatives to addicts; the further legislative control of prescribing and investment in prevention of a basic kind.

Introduction

Every month between 50 and 100 young people have walked into drug treatment centres asking – or demanding – that they be taken on as registered addicts. The ill-looking and under-nourished adolescent sitting in a corner of the outpatient hall witnesses the fact that one more drug-taker has grown tired

---

* Condensed from a paper which appeared in the *Lancet*, vol. 1, 1969, pp. 768–72.

of reliance on the black market and is now wanting his free and legal supply of NHS heroin.

The law

The legal context within which the doctor takes on the treatment of this patient is admirably clear. Deriving from the Dangerous Drugs Acts of 1965 and 1967, the Dangerous Drugs (Notification of Addicts) Regulations 1968, which came into operation on 22 February 1968, and the Supply to Addicts Regulations, which came into force on 16 April 1968, in essence laid down between them the following rules:

1 Heroin and cocaine 'unless given for the relief of pain due to organic disease or injury' may be prescribed only by doctors specially licensed by the Home Secretary. National Health Service consultants who treat heroin addiction in hospitals or in units nominated by a regional hospital board or board of governors will be considered for a licence, as will junior staff of sufficient seniority and in some circumstances private doctors. It is not proposed to issue licences to general practitioners.

2 The Government is empowered at any time by the introduction of further regulations, to limit prescribing of other dangerous drugs in similar manner. This of course does not include the amphetamines or barbiturates.

3 A licence is valid for prescribing only at a named hospital which, in London at least, largely means the new special centres sited in teaching hospitals.

4 Any doctor seeing a patient whom he has reason to suppose is addicted must within seven days furnish in writing certain particulars to the Home Office – this is a statutory requirement and is not dependent on the patient consenting to such notification.

The regulations mean that the addict in this country is still as ever to be treated as a sick person and that it is the medical profession which is required by society to accept responsibility for the addict's care – there is no abrupt departure from the fundamental ethic of the 'British system', but the way in which the system is now in practice to be worked is certainly a break with the past. Until 1968 any doctor who so wished could supply any narcotic in any amount (provided he kept proper records) to anyone he chose, could charge fees for such prescribing, and was under no official obligation to notify. Intemperate prescribing by a handful of doctors under this old dispensation was thought by the second Brain Committee to have been responsible for the great increase in heroin addiction which has occurred during recent years – addicts were getting much more generous prescriptions than they needed, selling the surplus, and thus spreading the 'infection'.

The aim of the 1968 provisions was to retain a humane ethic but at the same time eliminate possibility of the system being purposefully or carelessly abused. The situation existing immediately before the introduction of the new regulations and the expected impact of the regulations has been discussed by Connell (1969).

Hypotheses which underlie the system

The central hypotheses on which the system now rests seem generally to be perceived as being six in number.

A Three hypotheses on prevention of occurrence of new cases

1 The clinic doctor will not start a new patient on heroin unless he is absolutely sure that the patient is addicted and truly needs the drug.
2 The doctor in the new centre will prescribe conservatively and this will much lessen the risk of his patient having surplus heroin to sell.
3 By the controlled medical prescribing of heroin the likelihood of a well-organised criminal black market is diminished – why buy expensive illegal heroin when legal heroin is free? The Mafia, it is believed, will see any attempt by them to move on to the British scene as likely to be undercut and unprofitable.

B Three hypothese relating to treatment are then offered

1 Addicts are taken on by the clinics not for the continuing handout of drugs but for treatment: the patient may not initially be motivated to accept withdrawal but, through contact with clinic staff, motivation will gradually be built, dosage gradually decreased, and the offer of admission for withdrawal finally accepted.
2 Since successful treatment ultimately depends on the patient's own motivation, there is no place for the use of compulsory admission procedures.
3 There are believed to be some patients who cannot – or cannot for the time being – function without the drug, but who on a regular maintenance dose can live a normal and useful life as 'stabilised addicts': such patients will be maintained on heroin rather than have their drug withdrawn.

The situation

The law then is written with clarity, the hypotheses underlying the latter-day British system are identifiable, the new centres are in action, and the Department of Health and Social Security gives every evidence of energetic concern. The situation appears to be very much more under control than a year ago. To suggest therefore that all is not well might seem faint-hearted or even churlish.

All is not well – this is of course not to say that everything is wrong. My contention is that the law is in some ways inadequate, and that the hypotheses which underlie the British approach are in some instances unsound. My aim therefore in this article is to identify a number of specific difficulties arising in the working of a system which, though based on a humane ethic, nonetheless in practice generates a number of perplexing and, indeed at times, destructive situations.

The difficulties of the six hypotheses

1 The new patient who does not need heroin but demands to be registered

In addict language the phrase 'to turn someone on' means to initiate that person into addiction. The fear of every doctor working in a treatment centre is that he will do just that – a lad will come to the clinic saying that he needs heroin but who has never or only occasionally used the drug, and if we incautiously give him the prescription for which he asks it is we who are accidentally guilty of playing the pusher's traditional role.

The only safe procedure is to insist that any new patient who is seeking to be registered should first agree to a brief hospital admission so that he can be observed for manifestation of withdrawal symptoms – in most cases this is probably the only near totally reliable safeguard against turning on the chipper. There can, however, be little doubt that, as the treatment centres are today operating, this safeguard is by no means always observed. It would be improper to blame the clinics concerned, and the excuse may fairly be made that pressure of work and limitation of facilities puts such extreme counsels of caution sometimes beyond the limit of practical possibilities.

The new patient who is demanding to be registered therefore poses not one problem but rather a number of potential difficulties:

(a) An overstretched clinic may accidentally turn a non-addict into an addict.

(b) If refused heroin, a non-addict may simply go on to another and perhaps more dangerous drug.

(b) The patient whose needs are not gratified may bully, exploit, manipulate, and indeed terrorise his family.

(d) Failure of communication between clinics may result in the adolescent who has been refused at one centre being given heroin at another.

2 Conservative prescribing

The second hypothesis which underlies current policy is that clinic doctors have the requisite skill to be able to provide addicts with just the right amount of heroin – not so little that they suffer chronically from sub-acute withdrawal symptoms, and not so much that they have surplus of the narcotic to sell.

On what criteria is this nice assessment of the correct dosage made? No available biochemical tests tell us what dose a patient is on: heroin is fairly rapidly cleared from the blood, and a blood-level would (if available) be more indicative of the time of the last dose than of the daily dosage. The only way to determine the patient's physiological need with certainty is therefore once more to insist on hospital admission for assessment by titration of drug against withdrawal symptoms, and once more the realities of case-load mean that such a procedure is by no means always instigated. In the absence of inpatient assessment different consultants adopt various strategies – some for instance make it a rule that no patient is given more than half the requested dose, and that no patient will ever subsequently have the initial dose increased. But what is physiologically enough may not in the addict's view be enough psychologically – he is looking for sufficient heroin not just to 'keep him straight' but to 'give him a buzz'.

With this difficulty in determining the not too little, not too much, but just right, quantity of the drug, it is not surprising that the black market is still stocked by NHS heroin. Prescribing by the new clinics is certainly more accurate than it was before they came into being, and the black market price of heroin has in consequence gone up from about £1 to about £3 per 60 mg. The hypothesis that over-prescribing by the clinics can be eliminated – as opposed to diminished – is at present, however, an over-bold hope. The unanswered question is the extent of that diminution.

3 The hope of undercutting the black market.

The aim of the British system is to deprive a criminally organised black market of its potential customers. There can be no doubt that in Britain the majority of addicted heroin users are, for most of the time, going to be poor prospects for the black marketeer, but the system in fact cuts down but in no way eliminates the potential population of black market customers, of which the following groups can be identified:

(i) People who are using a little heroin but who do not want to get registered, or who have been refused registration.

(ii) Registered addicts who find their NHS supply insufficient.

(iii) Hospital-treated addicts who on discharge relapse and who may then exist for a period on black market supplies before re-registering.

So much for the market – its size cannot at present be accurately assessed, but it is certainly not negligible. What sources feed it?

(a) *NHS over-prescription.* Since over-prescribing occurs, despite every effort by the clinics to be conservative, there can be no doubt that virtually all the heroin which can today be bought illegally is of NHS origin.[1]

(b) *Illegally imported heroin.* There are common reports by addicts of supplies of 'Chinese heroin' having arrived in London, but the rumours are not substantiated. However, one of the inevitable illogicalities of a system which aims both at tight prescribing and at pre-empting the Mafia is that successfully conservative prescribing sends the black market price of heroin rocketing, and must make London seem to organised crime an increasingly attractive scene of operation. Although the professional or international criminal has not yet gone into the heroin business in Britain, there is no reason to suppose that we shall for ever remain free from his activities.

(c) *Substitute drugs and prescribing doctors.* At present the regulations which have been introduced apply only to heroin and cocaine. Such a situation inevitably invites a misguided or unscrupulous doctor to go into business as a prescriber, keeping one jump ahead of successively introduced regulations. There is at present increasing evidence that morphine and ampoules of methadone are being distributed by such sources, and the 1968 epidemic of intravenous methylamphetamine use stemmed largely from prescribing at £2 per script by private doctors.

We must conclude therefore that the British system may eliminate that part of the black market trade which would otherwise be profiting from supplying most established addicts, but that it nevertheless leaves an illicit market which though small may be very dangerous – only a small black market may be necessary continually to breed new cases of addiction. And the irresponsible doctor rather than the professional criminal may be the greater danger.

4 The building of motivation

The hypothesis that the clinics will with one hand give the addict heroin while with the other hand build his motivation to come off the drug is attractive, but is it plausible? The following factors might perhaps be expected to provide motivation for withdrawal, but the evidence to date is that the hope is not often fulfilled.

(a) The clinic staff could go all out to offer reality help to the addict, aiding him with accommodation and financial problems, and generally showing kindness and evident concern, so that a transference is built up, communication is established and maintained, and the patient gradually won round to accepting the staff's view that he should come off drugs. However, the result of such a humane policy may sadly be the reverse of that intended: the drug taker is protected from all adverse social consequences of his addiction, and all motivation for withdrawal is sapped.

(b) The alternative policy would be to limit the clinic's activity to prescribing heroin, to hold out the offer of withdrawal, and to refuse to do anything to protect the addict from the social consequences of his behaviour, hoping that his suffering will drive him to accept help. Such an approach to the care of a sick person would to many doctors seem distasteful, and its consequence might be to destroy any hope of a good and therapeutically useful relationship being maintained.

5 Compulsion

Should the clinic doctor be allowed powers in certain circumstances to sign an order for compulsory admission?

A patient who was being prescribed heroin by a clinic came along each week looking more ill and with his skin horribly excoriated: he was obtaining black market supplies of methylamphetamine and was injecting barbiturates intravenously. He resolutely refused hospital admission. In such a case it might sometimes be possible so to interpret the Mental Health Act, 1959, as to secure three-day or 28-day admission on Order, but usually no really effective measure of control is available.

6 The stabilised addict

The concept of stabilisation is again one which presents difficulties.

(a) Is a concept, which derives from a time when the majority of addicts were older and probably less emotionally disturbed than those we now see, one which has any applicability to other than a tiny minority of today's adolescent drug takers? No hard evidence is at present to hand, but the impression of many of the clinic doctors would probably be that the majority of young heroin takers to not settle to a job, or otherwise manage their lives responsibily, do not keep to the prescribed dose, and tend to acquire drugs other than those prescribed. And the patient who is taking heroin is, unless he is very careful, at risk from the complications of unsterile injections and of overdose: maintenance means for him continued exposure to very serious risk.

(b) In the USA there has now been considerable experience with the substitution of maintenance methadone ('Physeptone'), for injected heroin – a far safer regimen. In Britain, however, there are no powers to compel the patient to accept a choice which he will almost certainly consider a very poor second-best to the pleasures of an intravenous narcotic.

(c) The problem of determining what is to be considered the maintenance dose has already been touched on – whether it is enough to prevent withdrawal symptoms or whether enough to satisfy desire for pleasurable experience. Whether what is for any particular addict to be considered a maintenance dose today is still to him a satisfactory dose in three months' time seems very improbable, and if we do not satisfy him there is again the likelihood of his recourse to the black market. Should maintenance policy envisage gradual increase of dosage to, say, 600 mg. per day, so that the habituation process is, as it were, super-saturated? But perhaps a patient on 600 mg. has a comfortable ability to vary his daily intake within certain limits without distress, and he may therefore when short of money sell 60 mg. or so per day to someone else.

Overcoming the difficulties

The purpose of this paper is to propose not that the British system is unworkable but something much to the contrary. A system which sees the addict as someone in need of help is totally to be preferred to one which treats him only as a criminal, and there need therefore be no embarrassment in admitting that the medically determined approach brings with it many difficulties. Some of these difficulties have been outlined – how are they to be met?

1 Vigorous implementation

The British system might fail – and this would be tragic – not because of any fundamental flaw in its conception but simply because of lack of really resolute determination to implement it. One may suspect that the American experiment with 'ambulatory treatment' (American Medical Association, 1963) failed in part for just this reason. The need therefore is to ensure that the special centres are properly financed and properly staffed, so that they are indeed treatment units, rather than maintenance or containment centres or places for mere drug hand-out. The following specific points can be made:–

(a) There should be adequate facilities to enable the rule to be implemented that no new patient will be registered without prior admission for stabilisation.
(b) No patient should ever have his dose of heroin increased without prior admission for observation.
(c) Staffing should be adequate to ensure that every patient – other, perhaps, than middle aged and truly stabilised addicts – is seen at least once a week and is given adequate clinic time.
(d) The day to day running of clinics should not be left to juniors or

inexperienced staff.

(e) Clerical and other staffing should be adequate to permit proper documentation.

(f) There should be continuity between clinic and inpatient care and the phase of rehabilitation.

2 Continuing definition of the doctor's role and of doctor–patient relationship

The problem of the feelings about himself of the doctor who works in these clinics is something which deserves sensitive consideration. He is practising a form of treatment which carries considerable strains: he may find himself constantly questioning the ethical premises of his own actions; self-questioning is at times likely to be complemented by the questioning and criticism of his colleagues; his patients are likely to submit him to every variety of emotional manipulation. If he is to continue to function successfully as a therapist he is going to need support, and opportunity for discussion, and on his continuing willingness and ability to work the system will of course ultimately depend the system's success. Unsupported, he may find himself either becoming increasingly punitive and engaging in endless ill-natured wrangling and reproach, or alternatively going to the opposite extreme and becoming over-permissive and perhaps over-identifying with his patients.

3 The building of motivation

The British system, in so far as it is concerned with getting patients off drugs as opposed to maintenance, must seem to many critics to be batting on a poor wicket – to motivate patients to surrender their heroin-taking habit when they get their heroin free and are not subject to prosecution must seem to many American experts to be flying in the face of reality. The fact is, however, that we know already that some addicts will in these seemingly unhopeful circumstances give up drugs – the problem is to multiply their numbers. We have to know more about how to motivate people, and it seems likely that the answer is to be found neither in the direction of making things tougher, nor in the investment of more social worker hours in removal of transient reality difficulties, but in presenting to the addict a (to him) clearly perceivable, attractive, and seemingly workable alternative career to that of being an addict.

Can compulsion provide motivation? There seems to be some likelihood that during the next few years there will be pressure in Britain for introduction of legislation which will in certain circumstances permit compulsory treatment, and it seems possible too that many doctors would welcome some increased powers within a framework of mental health legislation. However, the design of such legislation would present difficulties, for, if every patient is to feel himself at the mercy of the clinic's sudden and quixotic decision to commit him to a closed institution, the whole basis of trust is likely to be destroyed. But to ask for slightly greater legal powers to aid treatment is a very different matter from countenancing an escalation of punitive legal measures, which might well be the dangerous reaction of society if the present system is not made to work.

4 The legislative control of prescribing

Another hazard to the system is that of having its intention frustrated by the unscrupulous doctor who prescribes substitute drugs and keeps one jump ahead of acts and regulations. It seems inevitable that legislation must eventually be introduced which will directly aim at frightening off such doctors or putting them out of business, rather than the legislation chasing drug after drug. Would it not be possible to enact legislation which would make it an offence for any doctor other than a licensed doctor to prescribe psychoactive substances to any person whom he has reason to believe to be addicted or to be in danger of addiction, other than for the relief of pain or for the legitimate treatment of a withdrawal emergency?

5 Research

Research should not be regarded as an optional extra. The British system should indeed be seen in itself as an action experiment, and the results of that experiment should be constantly monitored, with a willingness, on the basis of research results, intelligently to change course. Much fundamental research is also needed on such matters as habituation phenomena, the relationship between heroin dose and ability to function socially or interpersonally, and attitude–change techniques which can successfully confront the patient with the dangers of his habit and increase his motivation. The hospital ward and the therapeutic community need to be studied as social systems which can win affiliations and bring about attitude change: the aim should constantly be to focus studies on the attitudes, values, needs, relationships, and expectations of the addict, and in so doing results may be expected which directly bear on methods by which the treatment system may be strengthened.

Prevention and the wider background

The British system is supposed to be not only a method of treating the individual but also a method of preventing the spread of addiction. It is unlikely, however, that narrowly focused attention on the drug is by itself going to solve the drug problem, important though the control of the 'infectious agent' must certainly be considered. Health education in terms of warning the teenage population about the dangers of drugs is of uncertain worth. Prevention is certainly assisted by certain obvious measures – conservative prescribing, preventing irresponsible doctors from exploiting the situation, continuing police action against drug importation and increased action against drug thefts from such places as warehouses, and the greatest care by manufacturers in the marketing of potentially abusable substances. But besides these direct responses to the declared problem we must obviously think too of prevention at the root level – measures to aid the troubled child and troubled family before drug taking is an added symptom, and measures to aid the troubled community. Such sentiments as these have of course a familiarly pious and Utopian ring, but it is probably only in a country which is willing to invest very generously in the whole wide, costly, and endlessly demanding business of aiding the distressed individual, and preventing the emergence of communities that are poor or cheated, that the so-called British system of treating the drug addict can be expected to work. Whether Britain at a time of many transitions is a country which can make the system work remains to be seen.

Note

[1] In 1976 this is no longer the case. Illegally imported heroin is available.

9 Patterns of behaviour of heroin addicts*

G. V. STIMSON

Summary

Four groups of addicts with different patterns of behaviour were found in a representative sample of addicts who were attending London drug dependency clinics and who had heroin prescribed for them. The patterns of behaviour of two groups, the Stables and the Junkies, seemed fairly consistent over time, while the Loners and Two Worlders had both shown some recent change. The variety of behaviour suggests that there should be a multi-modality approach to treatment and policy. Particular approaches (maintenance, therapeutic community, piecemeal change) are likely to suit particular types of addicts.

Introduction

Most reports on heroin addicts in the United Kingdom have by implication or omission tended to treat them as homogenous with respect to social functioning. Only two reports have been found which looked at differences within samples (Frankau and Stanwell, 1961; Gardner and Connell, 1970). While little comparison of addicts has been conducted within one investigation, a review of the literature does suggest that there may be different types of addicts or different patterns of behaviour among addicts.

The present report is of an investigation into social functioning of heroin addicts with the aim of looking for diversity within the population. In 1968, policy changes in this country, in effect restricted the prescription of heroin to the then new drug dependency clinics (Edwards, 1969). For the first time it was feasible to take samples of addicts under treatment.

Method

Sample

A representative sample of addicts attending London drug dependency clinics

* Shortened from a paper which appeared in the *International Journal of the Addictions,* vol. 7, 1973, pp. 671–91.

was selected. The sample was approximately one in three of all those receiving heroin at the time of the study (March–November 1969). One hundred and eleven of the 128 selected were interviewed (response rate 86.7 per cent). Fuller details of the selection and basic characteristics of the sample together with evidence of reliability and validity have been described elsewhere (Stimson and Ogborne, 1970[b]).

Data collection

Respondents were interviewed using a structured schedule. The current situation was chosen as the main focus and operationally was generally defined as the three-month period prior to the interview.

Areas covered in the interview were: (1) current life characteristics (in the last three months) – employment, criminal activity, source of income, contact with other addicts, pattern of drug use, conditions of drug use, injection techniques, physical complications and overdose, hospitalisation, residential stability, sleep pattern, eating habits, social contacts, and social visibility; (2) addiction history characteristics (from beginning of addiction to present) – employment, convictions, physical complications and overdose, hospitalisation, drug experience, and age at start of drug use; (3) background characteristics (prior to onset of addiction) – employment, convictions, relationship with parents, and education; (4) treatment experience – abstinence, clinic attendance, and prescription.

Analysis

Four key areas were chosen as relevant to describing the behaviour of addicts: (1) current pattern of employment, (2) current source of income, (3) current involvement in criminal activities. and (4) current involvement or contact with other addicts.

Findings

Results – I the four scales to measure the key areas of behaviour

Four scales representing the four key areas of behaviour were developed using principal components analysis or Guttman techniques. Scales were validated using criterion variables.

Employment rating. This was based on current employment status and the amount of time worked in the last three months. The score range was 0–2, with a high score indicating a high level of employment. This scale divided the sample into three approximately equal groups.

Irregular income. One point for each source reported as a source of income in the last month: 'stealing things', 'selling things', 'money from friends', 'shoplifting', 'own earnings', (score reversed), 'pawning things', 'selling drugs'. The score range was 0–7, with a high score indicating more sources of income and income of an illicit or unconventional nature (mean 1.75, standard deviation 1.79).

Criminal activity. One point for each of the following items reported on a check list in the previous three months: 'obtained things by false pretences', 'received stolen goods', 'stolen from a shop', 'sold drugs', 'been in illegal possession of drugs'. The score range was 0–5, with a high score indicating that more criminal activities were reported. The scale has the cumulative properties of a Guttman scale; a low score indicates that only drug activities were reported ('selling drugs' and/or 'been in illegal possession of drugs') and a high score indicates that some criminal activity of an acquisitive sort was reported in addition to the two drug activities (mean 1.80 SD 1.35).

Involvement with addicts. Weighted scoring: 'number of addicts known', 41 or more score 1; 'number out of three closest friends using heroin', none score 0, one or two score 2, three score 4; 'number out of three closest friends ever using heroin' (scoring as for previous item); 'number out of three closest friends addicted to heroin' (scoring as in previous item); 'visited Piccadilly in last week', 'yes' score 2; 'no' score 0. The score range was 0–15, with a high score indicating high contact with other addicts (mean 6.9, SD 3.4).

Results – II the cluster analysis

Respondents were compared for similarity of profile on the four scales using cluster analysis. The method of cluster analysis used was Class I (Everitt, in press, 1974). Class 1 proceeds by taking the two individuals who are farthest apart in the test space (as defined here by the four scales) and then to each of these adds the next nearest individual. As each individual is added, a new mean for that group is calculated and the next individual placed in the group is the one closest to that mean. When all individuals have been assigned to a group, their distance from the final mean of their group and the mean of the other groups is calculated. This is done because each group mean shifts by the addition of new members and thus an individual originally placed in one group may end up nearer the mean of another by the end of the allocation procedure. Such individuals are reassigned to the group that they are now nearest to, and means are again calculated until distance between members in groups is smallest and distance between groups greatest.

The first analysis divides the data into two groups and then the procedure is repeated for three groups, four groups and so on. A statistical device, the 'density of points' is incorporated as an aid to determining the optimum number of groups. This is based on the number of points (individuals) who are within one standard deviation of the group mean for each group. The greater the density the more discrete the groups. The analysis was performed on the male sample on whom there was complete data (n=76). The input was the scores of the sample on the four scales: employment rating, irregular income, criminal activity and involvement with addicts. The optimum solution (based on density of points, group size, and the meaningfulness of the group scores) was four groups of size 25, 13, 22 and 16. The means and standard deviations for the groups on the four scales and the overall means and standard deviations for the sample are shown in Table 9.1.

Group I (25 respondents, 32.9 per cent of sample) had the highest employment rating. This group had the lowest score on irregular income, showing that most received income from their own earnings only; and the lowest score on criminal activities, with nine reporting no criminal activities, 14 reporting activities which would be offences under the drug laws only, and only two reporting some other crime in addition ('stolen from a shop' and 'received stolen goods'). They had the lowest scores on involvement with addicts and an examination of the interview schedules showed that they tended to have only one of three friends using heroin. Members of this group thus tended to be employed, were supported by their own earnings, admitted to few criminal activities except those concerning drugs, and had little contact with other addicts. The group approaches to some extent the ideal of the 'stable addict' and will be called *Stables*. It must be noted that this 'stability' is relative to the rest of the sample.

Group II (13 respondents, 17.1 per cent of the sample) were opposite to the first group on all four key variables. They had low employment ratings and the highest scores on irregular income, indicating that their incomes derived from illicit and unconventional sources (i.e. 'stealing things', 'selling things', 'money from friends', 'shoplifting', 'pawning things', 'selling drugs'). They had high scores on criminal activities (all admitted to criminal activities, eight to both drug and acquisitive activities, five to drug activities only), and had the highest involvement with addicts scores, indicating that most of their friends were addicts. This group is like the 'junkie' or 'hustler' described in the literature (Bestic, 1966: Laurie, 1967: Sutter, 1966: Preble and Casey, 1969) and will be called *Junkies*.

Group III (22 respondents, 28.9 per cent of sample) were similar to the Junkies in that they had low employment ratings yet they did not have such high irregular income scores. An examination of the schedules showed that this group tended to be supported from Social Security benefits, an item that was not included in the irregular income scale for methodological reasons.

Table 9.1
Group scores on key variables

Scale	Group scores*									
	Group I Mean	(Stables) SD	Group II Mean	(Junkies) SD	Group III Mean	(Loners) SD	Group IV Mean	(Two Worlders) SD	Total Mean	Sample SD
Employment rating	1.80	0.40	0.15	0.36	0.27	0.45	1.50	0.61	1.00	0.87
Irregular income	0.32	0.73	4.31	1.53	2.05	1.14	1.63	1.36	1.78	1.78
Criminal activities	0.72	0.72	3.23	1.25	1.14	0.75	3.32	0.98	1.82	1.47
Involvement with addicts	4.19	3.75	12.94	2.43	5.80	4.82	8.20	5.10	7.00	5.21
N	25		13		22		16		76	

* A high score (compared to overall mean for variable) is consistent with the labelling of the variable, e.g., a high score on criminal activity indicates a high degree of criminal activity.

They also had relatively low criminal activities scores. (Three reported no crime, 14 reported drug activities only, five reported in addition some crime of an acquisitive sort.) They had low involvement with addicts scores but not as low as the Stable group. Thus this group had one of the characteristics of the Junkie group – low employment ratings. They were lower than the Junkies on irregular income, criminal activities, and involvement with addicts but not as low as the Stables. This group appears to be neither part of the drug subculture (because they tend not to be involved with other addicts) nor part of the conventional world (because of their low level of employment) and will be called *Loners*.

Group IV (16 respondents, 21 per cent of sample) were next highest to the Stables on employment rating. They had low irregular income scores, indicating that they tended to be supported by their employment only. However, they were similar to the Junkies in their criminal activities scores (all except one reporting both drug activities and activities of an acquisitive nature) and they had the second highest involvement with addicts scores. As the addicts in this group were similar in some respects to the Stables (on employment rating and irregular income) but in other respects to the Junkies (on involvement with addicts and criminal activities), they will be called *Two Worlders* after the similar group described by Meyer et al. (1965).

Results –III Characteristics of the four groups on other variables

Statistical comparison between the four groups of addicts was generally by chi-square or by reference to Latscha's (1953) or Finney's (1948) contingency tables. All differences below are significant at beyond the 0.05 level (the majority beyond 0.01) unless stated in terms of *tendency*, where the difference is in a direction expected from results on other similar variables but not significant. Results are summarised in Table 9.2.

Pattern of drug use. The Stables (Group I) were being prescribed the most heroin (more than 60 mg. per day), were the most satisfied with the amount being prescribed, were least likely to run out of the heroin that was being prescribed for them, were least likely to use extra heroin (including 'Chinese' heroin), and least likely to use other drugs which were not being prescribed for them. The Junkies (Group II) and the Two Worlders (Group IV) were almost opposite to the Stables. They received little heroin on prescription (60 mg. per day or less), were not satisfied with the amount being prescribed, ran out of the amount they were being prescribed, used extra heroin (including 'Chinese' heroin), and used extra non-opiate drugs which were not being prescribed for them. The Loners (Group III) were like the Stables in some respects. They were being prescribed a large amount of heroin (more than 60 mg. per day)

Table 9.2
Summary characteristics of the four groups [a c]

	Stables	Junkies	Loners	Two Worlders
Current characteristics				
Employment	+	–	–	+
Crime	–	+	–	+
Involvement with addicts	–	+	–	+
Income from:				
own earnings	+	–	–	+
Social Security benefits	–	–	+	–
stealing and hustling	–	+	–	–
Amount of heroin prescribed	+	–	+	–
Extra use of non-prescribed heroin	–	+	O	–
Extra use of other non-prescribed drugs	–	+	+	+
Public drug use	–	+	–	–
Social drug use	–	+	–	+
Physical complications and overdose	–	+	O	–
Clean injection techniques (?)[b]	O	–	+	+
Recent hospitalisation	–	+	+	–
Stable residentially	+	–	–	+
Regular eating	+	–	–	+
Regular sleeping	+	–	–	+
In contact with family	+	–	+	+
Girlfriends mostly drug users	–	+	O	+
Visible as an addict	–	+	+	–
Currently on probation	–	–	–	+
Addiction history characteristics (from beginning of addiction to present)				
Employment	+	–	–	–
Crime	–	+	+	+
Physical complications and overdose	–	+	+	–
Hospitalisation for complications	–	+	+	–
Extent of drug experience	–	+	+	+
Drug use began late	+	–	–	–
Background characteristics (prior to addiction)				
Employment(?)	+	–	O	–
Crime(?)	–	+	–	–
Separation from parents	–	+	+	–
Got on well with parents	+	–	–	+
Treatment experience				
No recent change in amount being prescribed(?)	+	–	–	–

a + = yes or high on the characteristic
– = no or low on the characteristic
O = intermediate or midway on the characteristic
b (?) indicates that the finding is tentative
c Characteristics on which groups are not particularly distinguished are excluded.

but unlike the Stables they reported that they were not satisfied with the amount being prescribed. Like the Stables they were less likely to use extra heroin or to use 'Chinese' heroin, but like the Junkies and the Two Worlders they did run out of heroin and used other non-prescribed drugs. There was no difference between groups in the proportions being prescribed methadone in addition to heroin (82 per cent of total sample).

Consistency of patterns of behaviour over time. The addiction histories, i.e. from onset of addiction to the present, of the four groups were examined to see whether the four patterns of behaviour reflected different stages in the natural history of addiction. The addiction history characteristics of the Stables and the Junkies were similar to their present characteristics. In the past as in the present, they differed in the same direction on the extent of their employment, crime, physical complications and overdose, hospitalisation for physical complications, and extent of drug experience. They thus seem to represent fairly consistent patterns of behaviour over time. The Two Worlders and the Loners have both shown some recent change. The Two Worlders had a lower level of employment in the past than in the present. The Loners appear to have been more like the Junkies in the past, having a high rate of past convictions and a high incidence of past physical complications. Both crime and complications were lower for them in the present. There was a tentative finding that they had recently improved their injection techniques.

Treatment experience. It was possible that the different patterns of behaviour reflected different treatment experiences of the four groups. Several crude indicators of treatment were examined. There was no difference between the groups in the type of clinics, the length of time attending the clinic, the frequency of attendance at the clinic, or the frequency of picking up heroin at the chemists. There was a difference in the frequency of abstinence. It was found that the Junkies had been abstinent more frequently than members of the other groups. This reflected their greater degree of imprisonment, for their abstinence had been in prison rather than in hospital. There was a tendency for the Stables to have had less change in the amount of heroin being prescribed for them in the last month.

Background characteristics. Before the onset of addiction, similar differences between the Junkies and the Stables were found. Prior to addiction the Stables tended to have had a higher level of employment than the Junkies, to have been convicted less, to report less separation from their parents, and to report that they got on well with their parents. The Junkies tended to report the opposite. The Loners and the Two Worlders were intermediate between the other two groups prior to addiction. Tentatively, some of the differences between the groups can therefore be traced to before the onset of addiction. There was no difference between the groups on the type of school attended, age left school, school adjustment (truancy, etc.), dropping out of school, age first smoked cigarettes, age first drunk alcohol, place of birth, or social class.

Patterns of behaviour of the females. The females were not included in the cluster analysis due to difficulties encountered in assigning employment ratings to the ten of them who were classified as housewives. The female group (N=27) was too small for a separate cluster analysis. Their scores were compared to scores of male groups and they were placed in the groups to which their scores were most similar. This proved a relatively easy task. The females were then compared on seven variables which had distinguished the male groups ('use of non-prescribed drugs', 'total number of convictions', 'residential stability', 'physical complications', 'sleep pattern', 'eating habits', and 'junkieness rating'. It was predicted that the group differences on these variables would be in the same direction as for the male groups and this was confirmed.

Discussion

Pattern of behaviour and drug dosage

A striking difference between the groups concerned the amount of heroin that was being prescribed for them by the clinics. The Stables and the Loners received the most (more than 60 mg. per day) and the Junkies and the Two Worlders received the least (60 mg. per day or less). Certain formulations of addict behaviour suggest that a legal supply of drugs enables normal social functioning and that when the drug is illegally obtained and expensive, there is a consequent enforced criminality to ensure a supply, which in turn causes disrupted social functioning (Schur, 1966; Lindesmith, 1966). All members of this sample obtain heroin on prescription and so the presence or absence of legal supplies cannot be tested against functioning. However, the fact that the groups are being prescribed differing amounts might indicate that they will have different propensities or needs to buy extra supplies on the black market.

The true amount of heroin (if there is one) needed to enable normal social functioning cannot be determined here as this would have to take into account the tolerance level of the individual, about which nothing is known in this investigation. For the present, in examining the relationship of dose to behaviour, the bold assumption is made that tolerance of 'the right dose' is similar for each group. Are the Stables able to function in a normal manner because they are being prescribed large amounts of heroin and the Junkies unable to function normally because they do not receive enough heroin? Just comparing these two groups would support this and would suggest that prescribing more to the Junkies would mean that they would have to buy less on the black market, and thus spend less time mixing with other drug users to ensure supplies, spend less time in criminal activities to raise finances for supplies, and have more time available to work. Characteristics of the other two groups cast doubt on this hypothesis. The Loners receive as much heroin as the Stables, yet, while they do not use much extra heroin, they do use other non-prescribed drugs (unlike the Stables) and they are not employed. Then again, the Two Worlders are similar in drug use pattern to the Junkies, for they receive little heroin and buy extra heroin and other drugs, and yet they are employed, unlike the Junkies.

It has been suggested that the more interruptions an addict has in his addiction, through imprisonment and so on, the more opportunities the clinic has to cut down the amount prescribed to him. It was the case that the Junkies had been in prison more often than any of the other groups and that the Stables had been in prison the least. It would also be thought that the more the addict is able to exhibit to the clinic that he can function well while on heroin, the less likely the clinic will be to reduce the amount of heroin being prescribed to him. It is indicative here that there was a tendency for the Stables to have had no recent change in the amount of heroin they were being prescribed. The dose prescribed and its relationship to behaviour would thus seem to be more a result of the interaction of the addict and the clinic rather than a pharmacological effect of the drug. The nature of the relationship between functioning and dose, whether the dose is reduced and functioning affected or whether the dose is reduced as a response to poor functioning, needs further investigation.

Drug use and physical complications

The pattern of drug use and the circumstances of drug use of the Stables may explain their low incidence of overdose and infection. Their more controlled use of drugs suggests that they are unlikely to use drugs in unusual quantities or combinations which would be likely to increase the risk of overdose. It is not known if they inject drugs prescribed for them that are not designed to be injected, but the fact that they are unlikely to use extra non-prescribed drugs would be expected to lower the risk of this. (Mitcheson et al., 1970, have shown a high incidence of sedative injections among some heroin addicts.) Consequently there would be less risk of abscesses which may be caused by use of drugs in this way (only two Stables reported abscesses in the last three months). Their solitary use of drugs means that one source of infection, the sharing of syringes, will be a rare event, and in fact none reported that they had had hepatitis (which among addicts is usually syringe transmitted) in the previous three months.

Three aspects of the style of drug use of the Junkies increase their risk of complications. Firstly, their more extensive use of non-prescribed drugs no doubt increases their chances of injecting drugs which are not designed to be injected; secondly, their social use of drugs increases their chances of sharing injection equipment; and thirdly, they report the least care in the way they prepare and administer their injections. It is not surprising that they report the highest incidence of complications.

The drug use of the Loners is a solitary activity and they take care with the preparation of their injections. It would be expected that they would have a low incidence of physical complications, yet while the incidence is not as high as among the Junkies it is still higher than among the Stables and the Two Worlders. The three cases of abscesses and two cases of overdose reported by the Loners may be connected with their use of drugs which are not being prescribed for them. However, three of the Loners had recently had hepatitis, yet only one Loner reported sharing a syringe in the last week. Possibly more of the Loners do share syringes and the time limit imposed by the question was too short. A more plausible reason is that the Loners have recently changed their injection techniques and now take more care as a result of recently experiencing hepatitis. Some support for this was found in a statement by one Loner that he had shared syringes in the past but had stopped doing so because he had had hepatitis. Further support for this suggestion of a recent change is that in the past (before the last three months), the Loners had as high an incidence of physical complications as the Junkies.

The drug use of the Two Worlders is a social activity, like that of the Junkies. Their drug use is not, however, as public as that of the Junkies, for the Two Worlders inject themselves more often when they are at home than when they are in public places. It may be – but there is no evidence for this – that although the Two Worlder has nearly as much contact with other addicts as the Junkie, the style of contact is different. It is thought that he interacts with addicts and uses drugs socially but does not lead the full time life of a 'street junkie' and so tends to use his drugs more often at home than when in public places. It is implied that the Two Worlder is a Junkie some of the time but not all of the time. If this is correct it would follow that the Two Worlder has only some of the characteristics of the Junkie. Thus, although like the Junkie he uses extra drugs and although he uses drugs socially (both of which it has been argued above increase the risk of overdose and physical complications), the Two Worlder is in fact very careful in the way he prepares his injections and the incidence of complications is low.

The population investigated was a very specific one: those addicts attending treatment clinics in London who were being prescribed heroin. The sample was representative of the 372 addicts being prescribed heroin out of the 827 addicts attending the 13 selected clinics in London in March – April 1969. Those being prescribed heroin are under half the total clinic population, most of the rest receiving methadone. When the clinics first opened in 1968, heroin was probably prescribed to most patients. In the first few months of operation the amount of heroin being prescribed was reduced (Connell, 1971), the numbers being prescribed heroin fell, and many were transferred to methadone. Little is known about the doctor/addict relationship and how the amount prescribed is arrived at except that it may resemble a bargaining situation. If this is so, those addicts who have continued to be prescribed heroin may be more competent in bargaining with their doctors than others.

The sample had some addicts who were already on the way to being prescribed methadone only or no drugs at all. A large proportion (27 per cent) reported that the amount of heroin that they were being prescribed had been reduced in the last month. Most (82 per cent) were being prescribed methadone in addition to heroin, which suggests that they were being gradually transferred to a methadone-only regime. In fact at follow-up through records one year later, 23 per cent had been transferred to methadone only and 12 per cent were no longer being prescribed heroin or methadone. The sample thus seems to have been comprised of those who were being maintained on heroin and those whose prescriptions were being changed and reduced.

The single most important finding of this investigation is that the population of heroin addicts being prescribed heroin is quite varied with respect to behaviour. The fact of this variety suggests that different treatment modalities will be needed for different addicts.

One of the ideas behind the prescription of drugs to addicts in the United Kingdom was that the addict would be able to lead a 'fairly normal life' while getting his drug of addiction, but not otherwise (Ministry of Health, 1926). This concept was formulated when addicts were different in many respects from those of today, but within the sample investigated one group, the Stables, manages relatively well while addicted. Information which would be a crucial test of the Stable hypothesis is not available, that is, whether these particular addicts are functioning *better* on heroin than they would be off. Despite this lack of evidence as no rival method of treatment has been shown to be successful with addicts, and because the Stables are functioning satisfactorily while being prescribed heroin, it seems that a cautious approach would be to continue to prescribe for them.

The investigation has shown that not all addicts lead a 'fairly normal life' when heroin is prescribed for them. The three other groups of addicts fare less well, either using extra drugs in addition to those prescribed and/or having socially disorganised behaviour. For the Junkies and Loners the pattern of behaviour increases the risk of physical complications. It may be that despite this they are better off prescribed than not. There is no evidence for this, just as there is no evidence whether the Stables would function better or worse if they were no longer being prescribed heroin.

The Junkies and the Two Worlders are highly involved in the drug subculture and while the Two Worlders have maintained some links with the conventional world (they are playing both 'scenes'), the Junkies' participation and involvement in the drug way of life appears in fact to be their whole way of life. Burroughs' (1966) dictum – 'Junk is not a kick. It is a way of life' – applies to this group more than the others. One treatment approach might be to offer an alternative subculture made as attractive and cohesive as the drug subculture but which has a drug-free orientation. One thinks here of therapeutic communities such as Synanon and Daytop in the United States, and in this country Phoenix in London and Alpha in Portsmouth. Such communities transform the stigma attached to being an addict and turn the stigma to its best advantage. 'Addiction' becomes a qualification for a new life and a new occupation as an 'addiction specialist' who can take on the role of therapist. At the same time, the addict is provided with intense social support. For the person, like the Junkie, who has a 24-hour day involvement with the drug scene, a therapeutic community which can provide a 24-hour day environment is likely to have considerable impact.

It has been intimated that the Two Worlders may be suitable for the therapeutic community approach from the point of view of their involvement in the subculture. However, they are relatively conventional in some areas of their lives. Although they appear always to have been intermediate between the Junkies and the Stables, it was noticed that they had had some recent change to more employment. Meyer et al., (1965) suggest that the goal of treatment should be the modification of behaviour in areas such as work and crime, rather than total abstinence. As the Two Worlders already have some links outside the drug scene, this piecemeal approach may work for them.

The most difficult group is the Loners. They are withdrawn from both the conventional and the drug world. They may be the most psychologically disturbed group, for it has been suggested that the deviant who leads a solitary existence is most troubled because he has little social support for this deviance (Lemert, 1964; Rubington, 1968). In face of the social reaction to addiction, the Junkies have the support of the subculture while the Stables do not need this support because they hide their addiction by their low social visibility as addicts. It could also be that the Loners are the most 'addicted' group, for their drug intake appears to be the highest. Because of their solitary existence, one doubts if they would fit into a tightly knit therapeutic community; on the other hand they do not seem to be able to function well when prescribed heroin. It could be that this group would be most suited to individual therapy but this is expensive and rarely available for addicts. This group will perhaps remain permanently addicted, or if drug free, might be expected still to have social problems and to continue from one crisis to another with the aid of those offering treatment and help.

Concluding note and caveat.

While this investigation sheds some light on the characteristics of heroin addicts under the British policy of prescribing it does not provide conclusive evidence either way on the question of the viability of prescribing heroin. This warning is necessary for two reasons: (a) this is a cross-sectional study with no control comparisons and little information on the status of the population over time, and (b) little is known here of the type of treatment given, for example, it is not known whether the addicts who exhibit socially disorganised behaviour would be more or less disorganised if they were to be prescribed more heroin.

10 British opiate users: I People approaching London drug treatment centres*

HERBERT H. BLUMBERG, S. DARYL COHEN,
B. ELIZABETH DRONFIELD, ELIZABETH A. MORDECAI,
J. COLIN ROBERTS AND DAVID HAWKS

Summary

Interviews were secured with over 90 per cent of a sample of 230 people all of whom had *fixed* drugs, had approached any outpatient drug treatment centre in Greater London during the one-year period commencing mid-November 1970, and had no significant previous clinic contact. Results include descriptions of family and demographic background, current life styles, illegal activities, initial and current drug use, periods of abstention, and physical complications.

Males constituted 80 per cent of the sample. Most of the respondents were between 18 and 25 years of age. About half of the respondents held full time employment at the time of interview. About 25 per cent of the sample had been convicted of at least one non-drug offence in the previous year, but the majority of these respondents also had at least one conviction prior to their first fix. Most respondents had at least tried a wide variety of drugs, including the injection of sedatives and of 'Chinese' heroin. From the time of first fix of heroin or methadone, there was a median interval of about one year before respondents 'first fixed daily for seven days', and a further interval of about two years before approaching a drug clinic – but this is subject to considerable variability. On average about half of respondents' acquaintances who had fixed had also come to clinics. The main reason given as to why the remainder did not do so was simply that they did not use enough opiates to warrant it.

Sample

As part of a long term study of opiate users, people approaching the drug treatment centres ('clinics') in Greater London during 1971 were interviewed

---

* Condensed from a paper which appeared in the *International Journal of the Addictions,* vol. 9, 1974, pp. 1–23.

approximately at the time of their first clinic appointments.

To be included in our sample three requirements had to be met: (a) he/she had to have *fixed* (i.e., injected intravenously in a non-medical context) any drug at some time in the past (virtually all respondents had fixed opiates); (b) he/she had to be seen by a doctor at the clinic;[1] and (c) he/she must not have received an opiate script or scripts, on an outpatient basis, covering more than seven consecutive days before mid-November 1970 from any of the clinics in the UK since their founding in 1968.

Of the 230 people whom we wanted to interview, 210 were actually interviewed, giving a response rate of over 90 per cent.[2]

Method

The interviews were highly structured and lasted approximately 45–90 minutes. The areas covered were (a) family and demographic background; (b) current life style attitudes, general social activities, illegal acts, friends, accomodation, use of social agencies, and ratings made by the interviewer concerning appearance and demeanor; and (c) drugs – early use, current use, periods of abstention, and physical complications resulting from use. Many of the questions were derived from the survey carried out by Stimson and Ogborne (1970[b]). Additional information was derived from clinic notes and from forms filled out by the doctors at the clinics. This additional information also provided checks on the validity of some of the answers given by respondents.

In general, *identical* data analyses have been carried out *separately* for the 112 *'odd-numbered'* and 98 *'even-numbered'* respondents.[3] The 'odd' group has been used to test hypotheses, to form descriptions, and discover which items were related to particular key variables. The 'even' group was used to attempt to replicate the findings. Most of the findings reported in this paper have been thus replicated, but for a few of the analyses it was decided in advance to include all respondents together, in order to have a sample of adequate size for those particular analyses. Except where they are described as 'trends' or 'tendencies', all of the findings reported in this paper were statistically significant, at least at the 5 per cent level, on *both* groups (or in the single combined group, for those few analyses that were carried out only once). The factorial structure of the variables is in fact such that very few of the significant differences in the 'odd' group were not replicated in the 'even' group.

Procedural variables

A few variables provide checks on sample homogenity across time and clinics. Sequential respondent number (higher numbers being allocated as the year proceeded) had no consistent significant relationship with any other variables. This suggests that clinic treatment policy and the chracteristics of people approaching clinics did not change systematically over the course of the year.

Personal background

Some of the background characteristics of the sample are summarized in Table 10.1.

Table 10.1
Background characteristics of the sample

Item	Description
Sex	167 male, 43 female.
Age	26% late teens, 72% 20–29 years of age, 2% 30 years or more.
Birthplace	Over 90% UK (majority in or near London).
Education	Approximately similar to British norms.
Employment	39% full time, 4% part time, 50% unemployed, 7% housewife, student, misc.
Personality	Low on aggression and authoritarianism, 'normal' on anxiety and extraversion.

Family and demographic variables

Sex, age and place of birth. There were 16 per cent male respondents and 43 females. Approximately 26 per cent of the respondents were in their late teenage years, 72 per cent were in their 20s, and two per cent were 30 years of age or older. Median present age was 21.7 years. Age was not significantly related to any other important variables except that younger respondents were more extraverted (General Survey, adapted from Couch, 1960). Although age was positively correlated with age of first fix, this was to be expected simply because older respondents had had more of a chance to have their first fixes at a later age.

More than 90 per cent of the respondents were born in the UK and grew up there: however, clinics do not generally provide even initial appointments for anyone not eligible to be under the National Health Service. Of all respondents, 46 per cent were born in Greater London, 20 per cent in another major city, 29 per cent were born in a town or suburb (including suburbs of Greater London), and five per cent in rural areas. Thus the majority of those approaching London drug clinics have grown up in or near London.

Upbringing. Incidence or parental death appears to be no higher in the present population than in samples of psychiatric patients or normal controls (cf. Birtchnell, 1969, 1970). The parents of 20 per cent of the sample were (alive and) living apart from each other.

About 33 per cent of the respondents had been separated from one or both parents for more than a year before the age of 15 (22 per cent had been away from both parents, nine per cent from just their fathers, and two per cent from just their mothers (cf. Bowlby, 1970). Just under 74 per cent of all the respondents were brought up by their natural parents, 17 per cent by one parent or other family member, four per cent by adopted parents, and five institutionally.

On average, respondents had between two and three siblings. Out of the approximately 180 respondents who had at least one sibling, 20 reported that one or more sibs had fixed, 70 said that one or more sibs had smoked cannabis, and 55 had at least one sib who had been convicted of something.

Education and employment

Respondents were asked about the highest examination they had completed; 59 per cent had not completed any, 22 per cent had at least one 'O' Level or Certificate of Secondary Education, four per cent a vocational exam, ten per cent at least one 'A' level, three per cent had entered a degree or diploma programme, and the remaining two per cent had at least a first degree or teaching diploma. The sample does not appear to differ markedly in this respect from the national averages for Great Britain (Central Statistical Office, 1971). As might be expected in any population the more educated respondents were less likely to have court convictions and were rated by the interviewer as being especially co-operative.

At the time of interview, about 39 per cent of all respondents were working full time, four per cent part time, 50 per cent were unemployed, and seven per cent housewives, students and miscellaneous. The rate unemployed would be lower if the present sample were completely comparable to those used in most previous studies – i.e., which excluded people who approach clinics without being 'taken on' (this latter group have a relatively high rate of unemployment). The several indices of employment were in general significantly intercorrelated: present work status (interview), present work status (clinic notes), amount of employment (number of weeks worked in the past year), and the doctor's rating of how much he expected the respondent to be employed 'in the near future.'

Respondents were asked where their money had come from in the four weeks preceding the interview. Out of 205 respondents (each of whom was specifically asked about every alternative), 66 per cent indicated at least some money from own (or spouse's) earnings, 49 per cent borrowing from (or sharing with) friends, 38 per cent money from relatives, 37 per cent selling things (except drugs), 34 per cent social security, 32 per cent selling drugs and 22 per cent stealing.

Out of 206 respondents, 76 answered 'yes' to whether they had ever lost a job because of their drugs use. When asked for a possible explanation, respondents less often cited (a) the mere fact of being discovered as a person who used drugs than (b) other reasons, such as poor performance (with or without discovery of drug use). However, it is at least possible that even if they had not been using drugs, the respondents might have had a similar overall jobless rate.

Personality and attitude

Respondents appeared to score low on aggression and authoritarianism (cf. Kohn and Mercer, 1971) and to have normal scores on anxiety and extraversion (four scales adapted from the General Survey; Couch, 1960)[4] Extraversion and neuroticism scores were in a normal range as measured on a short version of the Eysenck Personality Inventory (EPI); this is in keeping with previous findings cited by Mott (1972) and may in part be due to drug use.

Current life style (apart from drugs)

Social agencies, friends and residence

Of the 100 respondents who were asked about the amount of contact they had ever had with various social agencies, 81 had had some contact with the Department of Health and Social Security, 70 with the probation service (includes probation reports), 63 with a solicitor or legal advice people, 27 with various forms of local authority social work assistance, 23 with Release (an advisory service), 18 with various day centres (Chelsea Centre, St. Martin-in-the-Fields, etc.), 16 with BIT (information service), and eight with a drug hostel (a surprisingly low number, perhaps).

As a rough index of their involvement with other people using opiates, respondents were asked, 'About how many people do you know now to say hello to who have probably fixed at least once?' (Stimson and Ogborne, 1970b). Those who knew more people also had higher scores on the following: anxiety (EPI), aggression (General Survey), number of arrests in the twelve months prior to interview, sum of admitted illegal activities (in the three months prior to interview), doctor's rating of continued employment in the near future as being *unlikely* (but there was no actual relationship with other employment indices), and having less wish to come off fixing completely.

Few respondents had had more than three addresses in the course of the preceding 12 months. A number of questions were asked about the place which was occupied *longest* during the preceding year: 48 per cent of the respondents lived with their families (with or without cohabitee and/or others), 28 per cent with spouse/cohatibee (with or without non-relatives), 16 per cent with non-relatives only, and ten per cent alone. The average number of other people living with the respondent was 2.5; and for one third of the sample other people in the place were fixing besides themselves.

At the time of interview, 20 per cent of the respondents were married and living with their spouses, 19 per cent lived with their steady boy/girl friends, 25 per cent had steady boy/girl friends with whom they were not living, leaving 34 per cent who said they had no such liaisons.

Illegal activities

Four selected indices of illegal activities were all found to be rather closely intercorrelated: number of convictions prior to the previous 12 months, number of different admitted illegal activities in the past three months (whether charged or not), convictions (as recorded in the clinic notes), and doctor's estimate of whether the respondent 'is likely to go to prison' in the near future. Examination of various data indicates that very few of the respondents had ever carried out any violent crimes – indeed very few of the crimes committed would be likely to be regarded as serious.

The following are all *percentages of the 208 people* who were asked questions about court convictions. There were 80 per cent who had had at least one conviction; 46 per cent had had a conviction in the 12 months prior to interview; and 69 per cent had had one prior to that. There were 52 per cent who had been convicted of at least one *drug* offence; 28 per cent in the year prior to interview; and 37 per cent before that. There were 59 per cent who had been convicted of at least one *non-drug* offence; 25 per cent during the year prior to interview; 52 per cent prior to that.

Of 103 people who were asked how many convictions they had had *prior* to their first fix, 47 per cent had had at least one. Only 13 per cent of the 103 people had been convicted of a non-drug offence during the year prior to interview without having had any convictions prior to their first fix.

The number of charges and convictions may be as large as it is for a number of reasons, including the fact that the sample may well constitute a group who are watched especially closely by the police. In the present samples of opiate users, although the median number of arrests in the 12 months prior to interview was 0.6, the median reported number of 'times searched' was 4.0.

As noted earlier, those with more education had fewer convictions prior to the year before interview, and women had fewer convictions than men during the year prior to interview.

A description of the admitted illegal activities (all of which related to the three months prior to interview, whether the respondent was charged or not) is as follows: 95 per cent of the respondents had been (not surprisingly) in illegal possession of drugs, 50 per cent had sold drugs, 41 per cent had received goods knowing them to have been stolen, 33 per cent had stolen things from a shop, and 22 per cent had obtained something by false pretences. These items were asked as a checklist to which the interviewee was asked to respond 'yes' or 'no'.

Those who had engaged in more illegal activities reported a higher frequency of 'being on the street after midnight'. The doctor rated them as more likely to be unemployed in the near future even though, perhaps surprisingly, their employment records did not differ substantially from those of respondents with fewer admitted illegal activities.

Self-reported illegal activities were also positively related to various drug items: having more friends who fix, being more likely to ask the doctor for drugs, having more hospitalisations related to drug use (in the past, including the year prior to interview), being more likely to admit to swapping or lending prescribed drugs, using a larger number of different drugs, disliking to fix sleepers.

Drug use and related issues

Early use

The decision to start using a drug or to start fixing must be subject to social, personality and motivational, and (although often overlooked) cognitive considerations. Once the drug is tried these considerations would still be relevant to continued use, but added to them would be further mechanisms of conditioning and possible physiological addiction.

Before starting to fix, respondents in the present study knew (fairly well) a median of about nine people who had fixed. Only about two per cent of the respondents had not known *any* such people. It is *not* the case that respondents have commonly been turned on to fixing by 'pushers' whom they hardly knew.

As regards motivation, a number of needs and drives would appear to be particularly relevant to initial drug use – among them, curiosity drive for new experiences, the need for anxiety reduction and, particularly where use is related to one's social context, affiliative needs. Not only might initial drug use follow from these specific needs and drives, but also one might suggest that opiates provide *generalised* need reduction and that withdrawal symptoms represent in part a return of the needs which have been eased.

Social factors are especially relevant in determining whether one *encounters* opiates. Once opiates are present, social factors are still relevant but only insofar as they interact with one's needs, one's personality and other individual factors. The *number* of occasions that an opiate and syringe are both on hand before a person actually first fixes the opiate would seem to provide at least one reasonably useful index of these individual factors – that is, an index of personal readiness to try opiates. What is of relevance here are the large individual differences on this index among our respondents.

For 60 per cent of the respondents, an opiate and syringe had been on hand fewer than ten times before they fixed the opiate (in the majority of these cases this fix took place on the very first occasion); for 13 per cent the materials had been on hand between ten and about 100 times; and for 27 per cent of the sample, use did not occur until the material had been on hand for at least about 100 times (or else continually for periods summing to at least 100 days).

The number of times an opiate and syringe were on hand (before fixing) was found to be related to only three other variables – all three of the correlations being positive and small but statistically significant (in both the odd and even sub-samples): low aggression, low anxiety, and number of older siblings.

Cognitive factors and conscious decision clearly have some part in determining whether or not a person would try opiates. A small sample (30 respondents) were asked whether their first opiate fix was planned in advance: 18 described it as 'unplanned' (but that is not to say it was unexpected), eight more said it was unplanned but they were 'seeking an occasion', and for four it was planned in advance. Thus a clear minority had *anticipated* their first opiate fix. Moreover, as regards their willingness to try it when the occasion of their first opiate fix did arise, all but three of the 30 respondents described themselves as 'willing' and the remaining three were uncertain (but not unwilling). This is in accord with the findings of Chein

(1964) and cf. Rathod (1972) regarding 'initiation on a convivial basis'.

Recent use

For each of a variety of drugs and classes of drugs respondents were asked about: frequency of use, liking, need, ease of obtainability, source, and intent for future use. The main results are given in Table 10.2 There were also questions about friends' drug use.

Table 10.2

Characteristics of drug use

Substance	Frequency	Liking	Need	Obtainability	Intent
Cannabis	2.3	3.5	1.3	4.4	3.0
Amphetamines[a]	1.2	2.4	1.2	4.1	2.4
Heroin [b]	2.7	4.7	2.8	4.1	2.5
Methadone [c]	3.8	4.0	2.9	4.6	2.2
Other opiates	1.9	3.6	2.0	3.0	2.2
Cocaine	1.3	4.2	1.5	1.7	2.6
Tobacco	5.0	4.3	3.3	–	2.7
Methedrine	1.0	3.8	1.3	1.3	2.6
Alcohol	2.6	2.9	1.3	–	3.0
Sleepers [d]	1.4	2.0	1.4	4.6	2.0
Sniffing	1.0	2.1	1.0	–	1.8
Psychedelics	1.1	2.9	1.2	3.9	2.6
Coffee/tea	4.9	4.6	2.7	–	–

Note: respondents who had never tried a particular drug are excluded from all means for that drug. Entries are mean figures for those respondents who were given an opiate script by the clinic. In several cases, the means for those not given an opiate script differ from the figures in this table, but the overall pattern of the present table would not be very much changed by taking these differences into account. The numerical scales are not strictly linear but can reasonably be used for rough comparisons within columns (the standard error of the mean is between 0.2 and 0.4 for most of the entries).

Frequency was measured on a scale ranging from 1 (not taken in the past four weeks) to 5 (taken daily).

Liking was measured on a scale ranging from 1 (dislike) to 5 (like a lot).

Need was measured on a scale ranging from 1 (no need) to 4 (strong need).

Obtainability was measured on a scale ranging from 1 (very difficult to obtain) to 5 (very easy to obtain).

Intent was measured on a scale ranging from 1 (trying to get off completely) to 5 (trying to increase).

[a] The means refer to oral amphetamines. Figures for injected amphetamines are similar.

[b] The means refer to English heroin but the figures for Chinese heroin are similar.

[c] Means refer to methadone ampoules.

[d] Means refer to injected sleepers and tranquillizers, oral use being more frequent and disliked less.

Frequency of use

Most of the respondents had at the very least *tried* most of the drugs and drug classes that were asked about – over 90 per cent had tried cannabis, oral amphetamines, English heroin, methadone ampoules, other opiates, and oral sleepers and tranquillizers. About 89 per cent had at least tried powdered ('Chinese') heroin and 83 per cent had fixed sleepers – high prevalences indicating a sizable black market in Chinese heroin, and a matter of concern given the rate of physical complications among people fixing adulterated substances and sleepers.

About 87 per cent of the respondents had tried psychedelics, 76 per cent fixing amphetamines, 75 per cent methedrine ampoules, and 56 per cent cocaine.

Apart from tobacco and coffee or tea, the drugs most frequently used by respondents were in fact heroin and methadone, followed by alcohol and cannabis (for both of which the average use was just under weekly in the month prior to coming to clinic). Hardly any respondents had been using methadone linctus or tablets.

On average, respondents indicated that they were using about the same amount of heroin and methadone as one year prior to being interviewed, though there was some tendency for use to be greater at the time of interview. Median estimated daily use of heroin was about 50 mg., with 25 per cent of the sample claiming to use over 100 mg. Mostly, this was Chinese heroin, which (being in powder form) is open to adulteration. Consequently, estimates of weight are subject to inaccuracy. Median estimated daily use of methadone ampoules was about ten mg., with nearly half of the respondents (included below the median) not using any, and 25 per cent reporting use of more than about 40 mg.

Liking, need, obtainability and intent

As the fixing of sleepers and tranquillizers is significantly correlated with the incidence of abcesses (in the present data), and these in turn would contribute to an increased rate of septicaemia (although our sample was not large enough to confirm this), it is reassuring to note that respondents do not express much liking or need for fixing them (in contrast with their higher liking and need for heroin and methadone). The figures in the last column of Table 10.2 suggest that respondents are trying to cut down on their use of opiates as well as of sleepers and tranquillizers. It is of interest to note that two drugs which have been very infrequently prescribed in the past year or two, namely cocaine and methedrine ampoules, were both rated as relatively difficult to obtain. This is evidence that concomitant increase in illicit supply does not inevitably occur, but one must be careful about extrapolating from such observations to other drugs or to some point in the future.

Friends' drug use

Respondents were also asked various questions about their three 'closest friends' (whom they identified by initials or other anonymous symbols). For 56 per cent of the respondents all three of these friends had taken drugs orally at least (excluding cannabis and alcohol and drugs taken as prescribed), and for 80 per cent two, at least, of the three friends had done so. For 60 per cent of the respondents all three closest friends had tried cannabis, and for 81 per cent at least two of the three had done so. For 80 per cent at least one of the three friends had fixed.

Abstention

Respondents were asked how many periods of abstention from fixing and oral methadone (lasting at least a fortnight) they had had since they first started fixing regularly (that is, daily for seven days or more). About 37 per cent of the respondents had had no such abstentions, 30 per cent had had one or two, 17 per cent three or four, ten per cent five or six, and six per cent had had seven or more abstentions. Only 16 per cent of the respondents had had one or more abstentions commencing in hospital, and for most of these there was only one. About 24 per cent had had one or more abstentions in prison, and for most of these this was on only one occasion. Of those respondents who had had at least one abstention, the longest abstention for the majority of them lasted no more than about ten weeks, but for 23 per cent it had lasted at least about a year.

There were 77 respondents (33 per cent of the sample) who reported at least one period of abstention from opiates in the *twelve months prior to being interviewed.* These respondents were asked a number of questions about their most recent abstentions. Of those who explained the circumstances, in 44 cases the most recent abstention resulted from their own decision, and in only a further six cases was it due to 'no means of obtaining supplies'. In six cases the abstention was initiated by being in hospital, and in seven by being in prison (but these figures might be overly high because a recent hospitalisation or court referral in some cases led to a respondent coming to clinic and, therefore, to being interviewed as part of the sample).

About two-thirds of the abstentions were effected by stopping quickly, and one-third by stopping gradually. Respondents were asked: 'If you wanted to stop fixing completely, which of the following could be effective for you *in the long run?'* While the answers may in part reflect liking for the particular method suggested, it is still noteworthy that procedures in which the respondent would stop on his/her own decision or in which the doctor would slowly reduce overall script size were the most likely to be endorsed; those involving various forms of compulsory treatment were least endorsed.

Contact with clinic

A series of questions was asked separately of the respondent and the doctor about the initial consultations up until the time the doctor conveyed to the respondent a final decision about his/her preparedness, or otherwise, to prescribe opitates or other drugs. The data from these series are internally and mutually consistent but, with some notable exceptions, are not related to major external variables. In the information given by the doctors, the main cluster[5] or significantly intercorrelated items consisted of the following: certainty that the patient should be taken on by the clinic, lack of open dispute about the amount or kind of drugs to be prescribed, a rating that the patient appeared to be truthful, and description of the overall relationship with the patient as being a good one. This last item was, in turn, related to (a) a positive response to a question about liking the patient, (b) a feeling that the patient was unlikely to break off treatment against advice in the near future, and (c) a respondent's being more likely to be given a regular opiate script than to be among those who (asked for drugs but) were not given any regular opiate script.

There is substantial agreement between the respondent and the doctor as to whether the respondent asked for drugs before the script decision. And there is also substantial agreement as to whether there was a good relationship between the doctor and respondent. The respondent's rating of a good relationship is, in turn, part of a significantly intercorrelated cluster which also contains the following items: respondent feels that the doctor liked him/her, that the doctor acted openly, that the doctor believed what he/she (the respondent) said, and that he/she (the respondent) acted in a friendly manner.

In addition to being asked how many of their acquaintances had had occasion to fix drugs, respondents were also asked how many of these had come to a clinic and why the others had not. The median of the figures given for a number of acquaintances known (who had fixed) was compared with the median of the figures given for the number who had come to a clinic. The ratio of these two medians was approximately 2:1 – i.e., half of the people who had fixed had come to a clinic.[6] Nevertheless, there are some respondents who have had most of their acquaintances come to a clinic, while some respondents claim to know upwards of 100 people who have fixed opiates, few of whom had come to a clinic. The main reasons respondents gave to an open question as to why they themselves had come were either that their drug use had become too expensive in the absence of a legal supply or that they wanted to cut down or stop using. The main reason given as to why some of their acquaintances had *not* come to a clinic was that they did not use frequently enough to merit wanting treatment, but another reason commonly cited seemed to amount to not wanting involvement with the clinic and/or official bodies (cf. O'Malley et al., 1972).

Conclusions

Reticence in approaching the drug treatment centres

The data indicate that at least 50 per cent of those who approached a clinic had first injected an opiate three years (or more) previously. At least half of the sample had injected opiates 'daily for at least seven days', two years before they approached a clinic, and 37 per cent (of those who had ever fixed daily for a week) used opiates without any abstentions over a fortnight. Enquiries made of respondents regarding their associates who had fixed suggested that perhaps one-half of the latter were not registered with clinics.

These items of information together suggest that at any one time a considerable number of people are using opiates, possibly on at least a fairly frequent basis, without being known to the drug treatment centres. Statistics compiled on the basis of the numbers attending these centres are likely, therefore, to considerably underestimate the numbers using opiates in the population. Added to the number who are at any one time not known to the clinics are those who, having approached clinics, are not prescribed opiates, and whose contact therefore is likely to be extremely tenuous. A preliminary follow-up (of early respondents) about eight months after the initial interview indicated that of 20 who had been given at least an initial opiate script, 12 were still coming to clinic regularly, whereas of 14 who were *not* given such a script, only one was still coming to clinic ($\chi^2 = 7.62$, $P < .01$). To the extent that a number of those not given prescriptions might not, in fact, be using opiates (a negative urine was associated with the decision not to offer a prescription), the number actually using opiates but not in touch with clinics will be diminished. However, it is notable that the majority of those refused scripts and having a negative urine at least claimed to have been using opiates in the immediate past.

The reasons given for not approaching clinics were various but included the statement that opiate need or use was insufficient to warrant this, reluctance to be notified to official bodies, and the feeling that little advantage could be achieved since the majority registered with clinics were not prescribed heroin anyway.

Implications for treatment policy

One must consider the possibility – although it is in no way proven by the present data – that reluctance on the part of opiate users to approach the clinics is partly due to the tendency for clinics to prescribe only small quantities of injectable methadone even initially, or to prescribe methadone linctus, or to refuse opiate prescriptions altogether. This is likely to be especially the case when the supply of powdered heroin on the black market is such that there is little net advantage in resorting to the clinics for supplies of opiates. Certainly our data suggest that powdered heroin was readily available. This is not to deny of course that a proportion of addicts do approach clinics in order to come off drugs, or that there may be some price advantage in getting opiates on prescription, or that people prescribed opiates by clinics may suffer fewer complications, or that they may receive less attention from the police.

To suggest, however, that the black market would be curtailed if more heroin were prescribed by the clinics is simplistic since other considerations than the availability of clinic-prescribed heroin dictate the activities of this market. It is not completely clear that increased prescriptions of English heroin would lead to a decrease in the amount of Chinese heroin on the black market nor that a sufficient supply of prescribed English heroin and injectable methadone to users would appreciably diminish the overall black market. However, given that there may be more than an element of truth in the assertion that a policy of diminishing prescription of heroin may have contributed to an expansion of the black market in powdered heroin, it would be unfortunate if a similar parsimony in the prescription of methadone had a comparable effect on powdered heroin.

Notes

[1] During the year about 150 people, at least, had merely requested an appointment but for one reason or another never got to the point of actually consulting with a doctor. At one clinic, moreover, assessments are carried out by the nursing and social work staff in co-operation with the doctor, but the person does not get to see the doctor at this stage. Such people have not been included in the sample during the first year of the study if they did not finally speak with the doctor.

[2] In fact interviews have also recently been secured with some of the 20 people who are counted as non-respondents in the present report.

[3] If one adds to the 210 total the 20 non-respondents whom we wanted to interview and the 77 people in the uninterviewed control group, the overall total is 307. Every person number evenly divisible by 4 was allocated to the uninterviewed control group; otherwise, when the middle digit of a person number was odd, the respondent was allocated to the odd subsample; when the middle digit was even, the respondent was in the even subsample. Thus in every cycle of 20 person numbers, five were assigned to the Control Group, eight were in the odd subsample, and seven in the even subsample. This cycle has nothing to do with the six different forms of the schedule, which each interviewer used in his/her individual rotation.

[4] This finding is, however, based on American norms since we have not yet compiled British ones, but it is encouraging to note that the factor structure of the test does appear to come out properly in the present data, and that scores were not due to acquiescence (cf. Blumberg, 1973).

[5] 'Cluster' here has the following meaning: it is a subgroup of items such that most of the correlations between items within the subgroup are significantly greater than zero, while most of the correlations between (a) items in the subgroup and (b) other items in the group are not of significant magnitude.

[6] One must be cautious about concluding that, out of the overall number of people in Britain who have used opiates, about half have come to a clinic. However, one would have to be equally cautious about estimates of the non-clinic opiate using population made in more traditional ways (proportion of clinic patients among opiate users admitted to hospital or prison : cf. Holahan, 1972, pp. 285–8), since – compared with people given an opiate

script at clinic – rates of illegal activities, physical complications, and probably mortality appear to be *higher* among those refused an opiate script by a clinic (see Blumberg et al., 1974b) and may well be *lower* (but perhaps higher per injection!) among casual users who do not approach a clinic at all.

11 British opiate users: II Differences between those given an opiate script, and those not given one*

HERBERT H. BLUMBERG, S. DARYL COHEN,
B. ELIZABETH DRONFIELD, ELIZABETH A. MORDECAI,
J. COLIN ROBERTS and DAVID HAWKS.

Summary

Interview data from some of the people approaching London drug clinics during the one-year period beginning mid-November 1970 were used to compare two groups of subjects: those who were given a regular opiate script (113 people) and those who were not (61 people). The latter did not for the most part, produce an opiate-positive urine at the time. People who were given such a script were likely to have been using more illicit heroin or methadone than were people not given an opiate script, and the script given was usually a small quantity of methadone. Significantly higher rates of unemployment, illegal activities, and physical complications were demonstrated in the group who were *not* given a regular opiate script; further differences between the 'Script Group' and the 'No-Script Group' are also described.

Introduction

In the course of the analysis reported in Blumberg et al. (1974[a]) it became clear that there were important differences within the sample between those who were started off on a regular opiate script (n=113) and the 61 who were not given one. This paper is devoted to these differences and to a description of this latter, largely unresearched group.

Method

As in Blumberg et al (1974[a]) identical analyses have, in general, been carried

---

* Shortened from a paper which appeared in the *International Journal of the Addictions*, vol. 9, 1974, pp. 205–20.

out separately on 'odd numbered' and 'even numbered' respondents. The *even* group were used to attempt to replicate the findings arising from the *odd* group. Most of the findings reported in this paper have been thus replicated. But for a few of the analyses the odd and even groups were combined at the outset in order to have a sample of adequate size. All of the findings reported in this paper (unless described as trends or tendencies) were statistically significant at least at the five per cent level in *both* groups (or in the single combined group, for those few analyses that were carried out only once). The odd and even groups were each further divided into 'Script' and 'No-Script' Groups (See Table 11.1).

Table 11.1
Frequency subdivisions of the sample

Condition	Odd	Even	Total
Script Group	62	51	113
No-Script Group	34	27	61
(Script decision not yet made)	16	20	36
Total	112	98	210

A respondent was counted as being in the No-script Group if he/she did not receive from the clinic one or more prescriptions (to cover at least about eight days) for heroin and/or methadone. And, conversely, the Script Group consisted of people who were at least started off on a regular opiate script but excludes those *only* given drugs other than opiates (such as tranquillizers), and also excludes those not given any drugs. For 36 respondents (17 per cent of the sample) the script decision was unknown or had not been made at the time of the main data analyses for the present paper – these cases are excluded from comparisons between the Script and No-Script Groups.

Nearly all of the people in the Script Group had produced an opiate-positive urine specimen (as part of their assessment at clinic), while most of the people in the No-Script Group did not produce one at the time. (There were several exceptions in both directions to this rule – just under ten per cent of the sample – but they were too few to permit analysis.) These facts must be carefully borne in mind when assessing the implicatons of the differences between the Script and No-Script Groups. Thus whenever a difference is reported between the two groups, one must be careful not to infer that the difference was a contributing *cause* of the script decision. Indeed it would seem to be the case that much of the decision-making process which determines whether or not a respondent is given a regular opiate script or not, is associated with his/her ability or failure to produce a specimen of opiate-positive urine; and for the most part other factors seem to play less part in this decision process – though once the decision to give a regular script has been made, they may of course influence other components of the treatment, including the size of the script given.

It must also be borne in mind, that though for the most part the No-Script Group failed to produce an opiate-positive urine at the time of clinical assessment, this does not, of course, exclude the possibility that such respondents had been using opiates in the recent past and that they might be desirous of obtaining a legal supply of them.

Although very few people who wanted opiates, and were able to produce opiate-positive urines at clinics, were turned away without a script, this must be seen in the following perspective: approximately half of the scripts given at the commencement of treatment or maintenance were for amounts of about 30 mg. or less of opiate (median=33 mg.). This figure may be contrasted with the median amounts *claimed to be used* by the respondents in this same Script Group, which was of the order of 50 mg. Because the minority who claimed to be using relatively large amounts of heroin were not given very large scripts, the discrepancy between means is greater than that between medians; mean script was for 40 mg. (Seven mg. heroin plus 33 mg. methadone – these are means, and very few respondents received *both* heroin and methadone) while mean claimed opiate use was 111 mg.

In all of the analyses which follow in this paper, where a difference is reported between the Script and the No-Script Groups, supplementary analyses are also reported whenever the difference is a possible artifact of other variables. In addition, all of the results reported in the first paper of this series apply about equally to both the Script and No-Script Groups except where differences are specified in the present paper, in the results and discussion sections (which follow).

Procedural variables

The ratio of respondents given opiate scripts to those not given them differed from clinic to clinic and from doctor to doctor but – contrary to the opinions of some respondents and clinic staff – the differences were not significant ones.

Personal background

Family and demographic variables

Sex. Women were proportionately more likely than men to be with script group though the difference is not quite statistically significant. It is not the case that women, *per se* are more likely to be given an opiate script than men, but rather that *anyone* who is 'going with' someone who fixes is more likely to be in the Script Group, and as women are more likely than men to be going with someone who fixes (according to our findings) they are therefore only circumstantially more likely to be given an opiate script.
Age. A trend was observed in which older aged respondents were more likely to be in the Script Group than younger respondents. 'Age of first fix' is not substantially related, however, to whether a respondent is in the Script or the No-Script Group.
Employment. People in the Script Group had worked an average of 31 weeks in the year preceding the interview and those in the No-Script Group an average of 22 weeks.

Attitudes

Included in the interviews were a variety of attitude items which had been found to be related to key items in the data collected by Stimson and Ogborne (1970b). Those items which yielded consistent significant differences between

Table 11.2
Attitude items differentiating between the Script and the No-Script Groups

1 Heroin/Physeptone makes me better able to concentrate (Script Group).
2 Most people who fix regularly are unable to face up to difficulties (No-Script Group).
3 Heroin/Physeptone makes me less aware of my feelings (No-Script Group).
4 Most people who fix regularly would be happy doing nothing for the rest of their lives (No-Script Group).
5 Most people who fix regularly find the world almost too bewildering (No-Script Group).
6 I find the world almost too bewildering (No-Script Group).
7 I suffer from feelings of inferiority (No-Script Group).

Note: The Group whose members were more likely to endorse a particular item is indicated in parentheses.

the Script and No-Script Groups are listed in Table 11.2. The last four items (in Table 11.2) yielded successive positive intercorrelations.

These attitude items paint a picture of the No-Script Group as tending to take a negative and passive view of things (compared with the Script Group). Is it possible that some of those in the No-Script Group who wanted an opiate script might have 'forgotten' to fix in time for their urine tests?

Although the No-Script Group tended (more than the Script Group) to be interviewed before the script decision was made, we cannot rule out the possibility that in some cases this 'negative passive view' might be a response to the script decision itself.

The Script Group also reported being acquainted with more people who had fixed than did the No-Script Group (a rough index of involvement with other opiate users). This at least indicates that the clinics are especially likely to be serving those who are more central in the social network of opiate users.

While the largest number of respondents in both the Script and No-Script Groups were living with their families (place occupied longest in the 12 months prior to interview) the remainder of the Script Group tended to be especially likely to live with a cohabitee, while the No-Script Group tended more to live only with other non-relatives – perhaps suggesting that they are relatively distant from other people.

Illegal activities

Of those with no drug convictions in the past years, 63 per cent were in the Script Group, while only 46 per cent of those with at least one such conviction were in this group.

Drugs

Early use

There were no differences between the Script and No-Script Groups on the variables relating to early drug experience.

Recent use

Frequency of use. Members of the No-Script Group claimed to make *more* frequent use of amphetamines (both orally and intravenously), 'sleepers' and tranquillizers (orally and intravenously), and psychedelics than did the Script Group, and *less* frequent use of methadone. (Some respondents might not have understood that these questions applied to the four weeks *prior* to coming to clinic; the more frequent use of methadone by the Script Group may partly reflect the clinic prescriptions, so one should treat this finding with caution.)

The Script Group were also more likely than the No-Script Group to indicate that they were using more methadone at the time of the interview than at the time 12 months prior to the interview. Members of the No-Script Group were more likely to be *currently* fixing barbiturates than were members of the Script Group. Respondents were asked about their most recent fix, and even for this one fix the No-Script Group were more likely to have fixed barbiturates (one out of 99 in the Script Group, eight out of 43 in the No-Script Group).

Among respondents in the Script Group, 80 claimed to have been spending more than £10 per week on drugs (excluding tobacco and alcohol); while only 45 per cent of those in the No-Script Group were spending over £10.

Liking, need, obtainability and intent. A number of items yielded significant differences between the Script and No-Script Groups, and these differences are summarised in Table 11.3.

Table 11.3

Characteristics of drug use: differences between the Script and No-Script Groups

Characteristics and drug	Script	No-Script
Frequency, amphetamines[a]	1.2	1.8
Frequency, methadone ampoules	3.8	2.8
Frequency, sleepers and tranquillizers[b]	1.4	1.8
Frequency, psychedelics	1.1	1.6
Liking, heroin[c]	4.7	4.1
Need, amphetamines[a]	1.2	1.6
Need, methadone ampoules	2.9	2.3
Need, opiates other than heroin and methadone	2.0	1.4
Need, sleepers and tranquillizers	1.4	1.8
Obtainability, heroin[c]	4.1	3.6
Obtainability, methedrine ampoules	1.3	1.8

Note: frequency is measured on a scale ranging from 1 (not taken in the past four weeks) to 5 (taken daily). The liking scale ranges from 1 (dislike) to 5 (like a lot). The need scale ranges from 1 (no need) to 4 (strong need). The obtainability scale ranges from 1 (very difficult to obtain) to 5 (very easy). All entries are mean values for these respondents who have at least tried the drug in question.

[a] The means refer to oral amphetamines. Figures for injected amphetamines are similar, except that frequency is even greater for the No-Script Group (who also have significantly greater liking than the Script Group).

[b] Means refer to injected sleepers and tranquillizers, oral being used more frequently and disliked less by both groups.

[c] Means refer to English heroin, but the figures for Chinese heroin are similar except as follows: Chinese heroin was used more frequently and was needed more by the Script Group than by the No-Script Group; and both groups found it easier to obtain than English heroin.

Indeed, a number of these distinguishing items are significantly inter-correlated in such a way that it is meaningful to talk about *clusters* of items that distinguish the Script and No-Script Groups. The grouping of items into clusters was based on the entire list of variables that significantly and consistently distinguished between the Script and No-Script Groups, and was carried out in such a way that for both the odd and even subsamples, all or most of the correlations *within* clusters are statistically significant, and (except as noted) none of the correlations *between* clusters are. All of the main clusters are, in fact, represented in the present section, except for two which already have been discussed – those dealing with degree of employment and those dealing with sex differences. This is an appropriate place, then, to consider all of the other main clusters that distinguish the two groups.

In part because of the questions we chose to include in the surveys, the main clusters of items that separate the Script and the No-Script Groups correspond to the main drugs asked about. One cluster of five items has to do with Chinese heroin: those given an opiate script have, on average, a greater need, liking, and frequency of use of Chinese heroin. They also spend more on drugs and 'go to the Dilly' more often (i.e., buy drugs near Piccadilly Circus).

Another cluster of items has to do with methadone ampoules. On average, for those in the Script Group there was: greater frequency of use, greater need, greater actual claimed use, greater use at the time of interview than at the point of time a year prior to interview, greater likelihood of getting a methadone script, and a greater likelihood for the doctor to indicate that the respondent asked for methadone. Moreover respondents who were high on the cluster of methadone items were more likely to be still under treatment at the clinic two months later (than were the No-Script Group).

As a third cluster of items, those in the No-Script Group had a greater frequency of fixing amphetamines, as well as having both more liking and a greater need for doing so. They were also more likely to be given a prescription for tranquillizers.

A fourth cluster of items concerns the fixing of sleepers. Those in the No-Script Group have a greater frequency of fixing sleepers and also of using psychedelics. Frequency of fixing sleepers is significantly correlated with need to fix sleepers, which in turn had significant positive correlations with need for oral amphetamines and average need for all drugs. (The foregoing correlations notwithstanding claimed average drug need was higher for the Script Group than for the No-Script Group).

To complete the picture, there are yet more distinguishing features between the two groups, the most important of which are that those in the Script Group have had fewer court convictions and fewer physical complications.

Physical complications

The results of a number of questions dealing with physical complications, in the preceding year and prior to that, are shown in Table 11.4. The definition of each complication was left to the respondent. In most cases, except for hepatitis, claimed incidence was *greater* in the No-Script Group than in the Script Group, but because of the small frequencies many of the differences were not statistically significant. Reported hospitalisations in the past year were more frequent in the No-Script Group, and there was a tendency for the no-Script Group to say that they had had more overdoses in the 12 months prior to interview (than did the Script Group). Both hospitalisations and overdoses in the year prior to interview were significantly related to the respondent's stated need to fix sleepers. Also, these and other physical complication variables were, in some cases, significantly correlated with one another. For example, as one would expect, hospitalisations and overdoses were significantly correlated.

It may be that those who most resort to fixing sleepers are people who on occasion cannot obtain opiates or cannot afford the price. Such people might be likely to come to the clinic when they need but cannot get opiates, would possibly produce opiate-negative urine, and might therefore find themselves in the No-Script Group.

Contact with clinic

A series of questions was asked separately of the respondent and the doctor about the initial consultations up until the time the doctor conveyed to the respondent a final decision about his/her preparedness, or otherwise, to prescribe opiates or other drugs.

Respondents in the Script Group were more likely to have their overall

Table 11.4
Frequencies of physical complications

Complication	Past year No-Script %	Past year Script %	Prior No-Script %	Prior Script %
Septicaemia	10 (17)	6 (5)	8 (13)	8 (8)
Hepatitis	6 (10)	21 (19)	9 (15)	29 (26)
Abscesses	23 (39)	22[a] (20)	12 (20)	30 (29)
Overdose	25 (43)	38 (34)	28 (47)	40 (36)
Other injury or disease	17 (30)	15[b] (14)	31 (54)	35[c] (32)
Drug-related hospitalisations	25 (42)	28[d] (25)	21 (35)	27 (24)
Non-drug hospitalisations[e]	5 (9)	8 (8)	16 (27)	53[f] (48)

Note: Frequencies refer to the number of respondents who have had a particular complication at least once in the relevant time period. Percentages are based on the total number in the No-Script or Script Group for whom there was a clear positive or negative response. The following significance tests are based on differences in incidence between the Script and No-Script Groups.

[a] $\chi^2 = 6.12, p < .02$
[b] $\chi^2 = 5.87, p < .02$
[c] $\chi^2 = 7.77, p < .01$
[d] $\chi^2 = 4.35, p < .02$
[e] Excluding respondents who had any drug-related hospitalisation in the particular time period.
[f] $\chi^2 = 6.32, p < .02$

doctor/patient ralationship rated by both the respondent and the doctor as a good one, compared with those in the No-Script Group.

While most respondents in both groups said there was no 'pressure' from family, GP, or friends to come to a clinic, there was a significantly higher proportion of respondents in the No-Script, as compared with the Script Group, who did in fact say that there had been pressure from their GPs.

It seems essential to discuss, however speculatively, the possible reasons why the No-Script Group produced opiate-negative urine at the clinic. A sizeable minority of the group did not claim to be using opiates currently and came to the clinic for some other purpose (e.g., wanting sedatives or amphetamines or supportive treatment); in these cases, the reason for opiate-negative urine is self-evident. For the remainder of the No-Script Group, seven possible reasons – which are not to be taken as mutually exclusive – come to mind: (a) *Non-constant use:* opiates may have been used currently, but not recently enough to appear in urine; (b) *false negatives:* imperfections in the test procedure itself, such as opiates being masked or diluted (cf. Montalvo, et al., 1972); (c) *good intentions:* some respondents may have thought that to appear at a clinic 'drug-free' would recommend their case for being given a gradually diminished opiate prescription; (d) *ambivalence:* some might not want to be recognised as 'drug dependent,' and might thus have avoided opiate use in the period immediately before coming to clinic; (e) *unobtainability:* subjects may have come to clinic *because* they needed opiates and (perhaps temporarily) lacked a source of supply or could not afford to obtain them – in support of this one notes that the No-Script group were more likely to have been fixing barbiturates at the times of their appointments; (f) *bad deals:* although there is no documentation that this had occurred in Britain, a person may have unknowingly purchased a supply of 'Chinese heroin' consisting solely of impurities, and the resulting side effects or opiate withdrawal symptoms could have *led* to his coming to clinic. In each of these six situations a person may be a regular user of opiates and still not produce an opiate-positive urine at clinic. As a seventh reason one cannot rule out the possibility that (g) some subjects were trying to 'con' the clinics into prescribing drugs which could then be sold illicitly; however, one might reasonably think that the majority of such people would know to fix opiates before coming to clinic. Although urine analysis may be an unreliable index of a person's regular use of opiates, it is probably preferable to any more subjective assessment in decisions involving the issuing of scripts.

Conclusions

The salient characteristics of the No-Script Group, relative to the Script Group, are summarised in Table 11.5.

Most studies of opiate users have concentrated on those in receipt of a prescription from one of the drug treatment centres. The particular contribution of the present study is that it provides information on that little studied group of people who, while notified by the clinics, are not prescribed opiates by the clinics and who, in some cases, because of the dissatisfaction they express with the clinic system, are unlikely to stay in contact with the clinics. While the present study does not allow us to discern whether this sub-group will, at some time in the future, receive opiate prescriptions, at least some of the implications of their present refusal can be surmised. One of the ways that the No-Script Group was differentiated from the Script Group was in terms of their use of barbiturates; it appeared that the No-Script Group's lack of access to opiates (or less recourse to opiates) was associated with a higher incidence of physical complications in the past and can presumably be expected to result in more complications in the immediate future. The No-Script Group was also more often unemployed and engaged more in illegal activities. It might be argued, although the data available do not unequivocally demonstrate this, that the fact that the No-Script Group do not receive a prescription for opiates may be partly a result of – and partly cause of furthering – their illegal activities, their unemployment, and also their injection of barbiturates.

Table 11.5

Relative reported characteristics of the No-Script Group, as compared with the Script Group (partial list)

Item	Characteristic
Sex	Tend to be male
Age	Tend to be younger
Employment	Worked fewer weeks in preceding year
Attitude	'Negative passive'
Friends	Fewer acquaintances who had fixed
Court convictions	More with drug conviction(s) in preceding year
Drug use	Greater frequency for amphetamines-oral, amphetamines-fixed, sleepers-oral, sleepers-fixed, psychedelics; less frequent use of methadone and Chinese heroin
Complications	More abscesses and hospitalisations; trends toward more septicaemia and overdoses, less hepatitis.

The decision to prescribe opiates was closely associated with the results of urinary analysis. Despite the fact that the majority of those who did not receive a script claimed to have used opiates in the recent past, most did not have a positive urine. While in some cases attendance at a clinic may have been motivated by the desire to receive opiates which might then be sold, in others the user may have felt that refraining from using opiates immediately before attending the clinic would have recommended his case, whereas in fact it served to deny him a prescription for opiates. In other cases the person giving a negative specimen may have approached the clinic precisely because he was unable to obtain opiates; the fact of his not having used opiates in the immediate past need not however attest to his not having used them at all.

As yet we are unable to say whether the decision not to prescribe opiates is more often associated with long term abstinence than is the receipt of a prescription. In the meantime one can only wonder whether the decision not to prescribe in all cases where a negative urine is found is functional. It may be, of course, that the alternative of prescribing opiates to some individuals who have no opiates in their urine is an even less desirable alternative. Clearly, more research is needed regarding the identification of opiate use among those who would under present circumstances be refused an opiate script.

Whatever the implications of not prescribing opiates for the No-Script Group may be, comfort can be taken from the fact that those given a prescription are the people who tended to have more often used powdered heroin in the recent past and to be more integrated into a heroin-using scene. To the extent that their receiving a script results in their using less powdered heroin, the policy of prescribing followed by the clinics would appear to have beneficial consequences.

12 A comparison of Canadian narcotic addicts in Great Britain and in Canada*

JIM ZACUNE

Summary

A study based on interviews with 25 Canadian narcotic addicts, who have lived in both Canada and Great Britain while addicted, is reported. Because the two countries have different medical and legal approaches to the control of drug addiction, comparative data are presented for the sample as regards social functioning, work history, drug use and criminal involvement. Differential adjustment of individuals to living in Great Britain is evident. Social consequences that may follow from a particular national response to drug addiction are discussed.

Introduction

How is the impact of a total national response to narcotic addiction to be measured? Prospective cross-cultural studies are obviously much needed. However, an 'experiment of nature' does appear to offer a small but interesting research possibility. A group of Canadian addicts have, during the last decade or so, come to live in England and it is possible to compare their addiction and their general life adjustment in the two countries.

This paper describes an interview study on this group. It should be stressed that the insights gained from a retrospective study of a small sample is limited and that the sample is not representative of either the Canadian or British addict population. It would be entirely inappropriate to use the data as a basis for support or condemnation of the national response of either country. The data does, however, offer a comparison of the possible social consequences of living under two different medical and legal approaches to the problem of addiction.

---

* Condensed from a paper which appeared in the *Bulletin on Narcotics*, vol. 23, no. 4, 1971, pp. 41–9.

Method

Sample

The survey attempted to interview persons who had become addicted to narcotics in Canada and were now living in Great Britain. The interview sample, therefore, included two subjects who were born in England but whose addiction career began and continued for more than ten years in Canada. It did not include addicts from other countries who had made temporary visits to Canada, or Canadians who had wholly acquired their addiction in Great Britain.

Findings

Canadian addicts known in Great Britain

A search of Home Office records indicated that Canadians with a history of addiction were not known to have come to England with the specific intent of being able to obtain opiate drugs legally until 1959. In the next ten years some 91 addicts came to Great Britain, with the largest surge of migration being between 1959 and 1964 when some 70 Canadian addicts migrated. However, by 1961 the idea of coming to England for heroin maintenance or the treatment of addiction seems to have become widespread. Respondents in the sample reported hearing of the 'virtues' of the 'British system' from other addicts in Canadian prisons or on the streets of Vancouver. The migration was further encouraged by the privileged immigration status Canadians held as Commonwealth citizens, and the publicity given to the visit of a well known private British physician to Canada in 1963, who claimed success in treating addicts (Frankau and Stanwell, 1961).

The exact fate of all known Canadian addicts to have come to Britain is difficult to ascertain and only the barest details can be recovered from official records. Their length of stay varied from approximately one month up to ten years, with an estimated average of just over 18 months. Table 12.1 below indicates the probable fate of the Canadians who came to Great Britain.

Of the 36 individuals who were not reported to have left England in 1969, 24 were interviewed or, if the interview was refused, case notes and all other sources of information gathered (one case). An additional four subjects were thought to be still in England. Two were reported to be off drugs but unwilling to be interviewed, and two others could not be interviewed although several attempts were made. A further seven subjects were untraced. None of the subjects who had not been interviewed appeared in official records as receiving a prescription for narcotic drugs. Thirty-five Canadians left Great

Table 12.1

Location of Canadian addicts known to have come to Great Britain (1969)

In England	
Interviewed	25
Known, but not interviewed	4
Possibly in England but unlocated	7
Died in England	10
Deported	10
Assumed to be in Canada or elsewhere	35
Total	91

Britain without direct compulsion and little evidence that they were cured at the time of departure.

The interview sample: basic characteristics

There were 20 male subjects and five females. All but two were Canadian born. Their average age was 40.8 years with a range from 22 to 53 years. The sample had been in Great Britain for an average of 5.8 years with a range from six months to ten years. All but five persons had been here between four and eight years.

Work status

Of the 20 male subjects only one claimed to have worked steadily in Canada while addicted. Two males were musicians working various engagements and the remaining 17 had only intermittent employment. Before becoming addicted 15 males held jobs of manual sort such as shipyard worker, labourer, sawmill hand, plumber, gas-fitter and traveller with a carnival. Of the five females in the sample, two had worked briefly as secretaries, one as a telephone operator, one as a student and one was a housewife. The present work status of the sample in Great Britain is set out below.

Those employed full time held their present job between six months and seven years. Six subjects have been employed at the same job for three years or more. Seven subjects have semi-skilled or skilled manual jobs such as welder, or gas-fitter, two are employed in offices, one has a sales job, and those remaining are a croupier, a housewife and a student.

Table 12.2
Present work status in Great Britain

Full time employment	13
Part time employment	4
No, or irregular, employment	8
Total	25

Criminal records

While in Canada, the sample had a long record of convictions. The average number of offences for which a conviction was obtained was 7.3 with a range of 0–25 convictions. Only two subjects had no convictions in Canada.
The total number of offences committed by this sample in Canada was 182. These are broken down in Table 12.3.

Table 12.3
Type of criminal offence in Canada

	Offences	Subjects
Theft (including breaking and entering, safe-breaking tools, attempted theft, robbery with violence, receiving)	88	16
Possession of narcotics (including trafficking)	59	22
Vagrancy	6	6
Violation of immigration laws	4	3
Forgery and false pretences	4	3
Motoring offences (including motor manslaughter)	4	3
Drinking offences (including breaking of Liquor Act)	4	3
Damage to property	2	2
Miscellaneous	11	1
Total	182	59

By comparison only 13 of the sample have had convictions in England. The total number of convictions is 27. Details of these convictions are set out in Table 12.4.

Table 12.4
Type of criminal offence in Great Britain

	Offences	Subjects
Theft (including larceny, receiving)	8	5
Possession of opiates (including supply)	8	7
Forgery and false pretences to obtain drugs	4	3
Possession cannabis or methylamphetamine	2	2
Fraudulent use of electricity	1	1
Smuggling heroin into a prison	1	1
Grievous bodily harm	1	1
Offensive weapon	1	1
Indecent exposure	1	1
Total	27	22

Prison

The sample spent a total of 141 years and two months in prison in Canada, which is an average of 6.75 years (including the two subjects who served no time at all). Of the total number of years spent in Canada since becoming addicted, 24.6 per cent of that time was spent in prison by the sample.

While in England six subjects had been to prison for a combined total of two years and five months with a range of one day to one year. The proportion of time spent in prison is less than two per cent of the total of addicted years spent in England.

History of addiction

The average span since first addicted was $19\frac{1}{4}$ years, with a range of four to 32 years. All but two had been addicted more than ten years. While not all this time was spent physically addicted to heroin, only one subject claimed more than one year abstinence outside hospital or prison since being addicted.

Sources of supply

While in Canada, the sample obtained their supplies wholly illicitly, as there were no experimental methadone maintenance programmes at that time. When they were not in prison, the subjects always bought heroin from criminal sources.

Since arriving in England all the Canadians in the sample have had a nearly constant legal supply deriving first from individual physicians and later, after 1968, from the special treatment centres.

Dosage

A comparison of heroin dosage that the individuals received in Canada and England is nearly impossible, as the Canadian heroin is variable in purity and in quantity for given price. In contrast, the British prescribed heroin is pure and supplied in the form of 10 mg. tablets. While it seems probable that the sample has built up a heavy dosage in Canada, it is unlikely they could afford the equivalent high dosage often prescribed. While it was difficult to ascertain the exact dosage all members of the sample received in England, because of changes of physician or faulty memory, prescriptions for as high as 1,800 mg./day (30 grains) of heroin were known, and 600 mg./day (10 grains) were not uncommon.

At the time of interview all subjects were receiving opiates from a clinic. The prescribed drugs were as follows: 18 subjects were receiving heroin with an average dose of 597 mg./day (9.65 grains) and five received cocaine as well, with an average of 480 mg./day (8 grains); four were receiving only methadone (physeptone) in ampoule or linctus form; and one was receiving morphine, 480 mg./day (8 grains).

Hospital treatment

All subjects denied having hospital treatment for drug withdrawal in Canada. In England, ten subjects have had treatment in mental hospitals for their drug addiction. They accounted for a total of 31 separate admissions with a range of one to nine admissions for individuals. In addiction, three subjects were in private nursing homes while under the care of a private physician. None of the hospitalised remained abstinent for more than six months after treatment.

Contact with Canadians in England

All subjects were asked to estimate the total number of Canadians who might have come to England. The estimates were intended as a check on the official Home Office figures. All but one subject underestimated the number of Canadians officially known, and this one exception gave a figure of 1,000! The other subjects all estimated less than 80, with the mode being between 30–40 addicts (56 per cent).

Reasons for coming to England

When asked why they had originally come to England, the most common answer by the subjects was that they had spent too much time in gaol, or were frightened they would soon be sent there (76 per cent); that drugs could be legally obtained in the United Kingdom or that addicts had heard a lot about the way addicts were treated in England, were the next most common reasons (68 per cent and 60 per cent). The most common reason for preferring to live in England was that they could 'lead normal lives' (64 per cent) and this was followed by drugs being legal (60 per cent). In addition, subjects said there was less trouble from the police.

Discussion

Selection

The Canadians in this sample are a product of many selection processes. All the Canadian addicts known to have come to Great Britain represent less than three per cent of the Canadian addict population. Of the Canadians who did come, those that remain have neither died, nor been deported, nor left the country – the fate of the majority of addicted Canadians who came to Great Britain. The introduction of the Commonwealth Immigrants Act meant that those who had parents born in England found it easier to remain here than those who did not, and it is possible that the pressure of obtaining work permits and similar difficulties led some to return, although they were not compelled by law to do so. Further, the sample may be self-selected by being more experienced at avoiding legal trouble or, perhaps more positively, by being the most stable. In either case, these Canadians might be different from any other section of the Canadian addict population.

Social functioning in Canada and Great Britain

Within the limits of the selection factors above, there does seem to have been a difference in social functioning for this sample in the two countries. Schur (1966) has drawn several implications for the differing legal systems of America and Great Britain (Canada's legal system is similar to that of America), which find some limited support in this study. The Canadian system imposes criminal status upon the opiate user through strict enforcement of laws on possession and trafficking in opiates, and although it is possible for opiates to be prescribed as 'good medical practice' this was rare when these subjects were in Canada. With virtually no legal source of heroin available, the organised 'black market' has infiltrated Canada quite completely. The Canadian addict must necessarily make a double commitment – to be an addict and to support his habit by some means of theft, trickery or by trafficking in narcotics himself.

The findings on convictions and imprisonment in Canada as well as the inability of subjects to hold a legitimate job in Canada support this view. When not in prison all but two subjects were involved in some criminal 'hustling', that is stealing or confidence trickery to get money for drugs, finding supplies and suppliers, and all the time avoiding detection and arrest. The life history data taken as a whole indicates that most Canadian addicts were involved in a 'full time career' seeking out drugs from illicit sources and obtaining means of support.

In Great Britain the availability of a legal supply of heroin from a physician means that criminal activity is not a *necessary* consequence of addiction. However, this only means that an alternative of 'leading a useful and fairly normal life' exists and does not mean that all people will function in this way. For those who remained there has been less frequent prosecution and imprisonment, a greater ability to work, more opportunity for stable accommodation, no necessary involvement in the illicit drugs market and more willingness to have voluntary hospital treatment.

Differences within the sample

The social functioning of individuals varied within the sample. Differences were found between those subjects who were employed full time and those part time employed or unemployed. The employed subjects were younger, addicted a shorter time, on a lower dose of heroin in Great Britain, more often living with their spouse, and had fewer convictions in Canada. It would seem that individuals with extremely long histories of addiction and imprisonment cannot lead stable lives under a favourable legal system though their lives are certainly more stable than in Canada.

The context of the Canadians' opiate use in Great Britain

This sample is a small and special group in the context of opiate use in Great Britain. Stimson and Ogborne (1970[b]) studied a random sample of 111 addicts being prescribed heroin at London treatment clinics with emphasis on current social functioning. In comparison to their sample, on average the Canadian sample is more than 15 years older, addicted nearly four times longer, receiving three and a half times more heroin daily and had more convictions and imprisonment over-all. The differences emphasise the relative recency of an opiate problem in Great Britain and the young age of most addicts. Despite the disparity in age and length of addiction, on four crude measures of social functioning – employment, length of time at current address, convictions in England and imprisonment in England – the present sample does not appear to be more unstable than the London clinic population.

13 Treatment of methylamphetamine users during the 1968 epidemic*

MARTIN MITCHESON, GRIFFITH EDWARDS, DAVID HAWKS and ALAN OGBORNE

Summary

The treatment of a limited number of methylamphetamine users illustrated the difficulties which will arise when a drug is freely available on the illicit market. Contact was difficult to maintain and outcome in most cases was poor.

It is emphasised that drug abuse in Britain is only arbitrarily described as involving heroin: poly drug use is more often the pattern. To base explanations of dependence or frame preventive and treatment policies on any one drug is short sighted.

While the present series provides only an uncertain basis for extrapolation, the rudiments of the necessary total response are identified as follows: concern with prevention, control of manufacture and commercial distribution of drugs, the restricted prescribing of certain drugs, the offer of accessible and meaningful alternatives and the careful monitoring of trends and policies.

Introduction

Although sporadic cases had occurred earlier, the summer of 1968 saw in London the occurrence of methylamphetamine abuse reach epidemic proportions (Hawks et al., 1969). Several doctors were grossly over-prescribing and the surplus was freely available on the black market. During these months methylamphetamine takers started to be referred to us from a number of agencies and we had to make a decision as to whether we were able to offer help, and whether help should mean we ourselves prescribing the drug. We faced a dilemma for on the one hand it could be argued that there was no sense in our further adding to the quantity of methylamphetamine circulating in London, while on the other hand a case could be made for suggesting that these young people could best be helped by temporarily offering them the drug and thus involving them in a treatment situation – treatment would then have as its aim both weaning them from the

---

* Addiction Research Unit internal paper not previously published.

dependence and also aiding them with more basic problem lying behind the presenting symptom.

Our final decision was therefore to take on a limited number of patients so that we could give time to anyone we were trying to help and also offer some social work care, and in the setting of this treatment to prescribe in certain circumstances methylamphetamine on a fairly rapidly reducing basis with it from the start being made absolutely clear to our patients that they should not come to us if they were simply seeking a drug supply. The drug was only prescribed when the following criteria had been fulfilled:

1 Full inquiry had been made from other agencies who had had contact with the patient.

2 Urine testing – or in its absence, strong clinical evidence – showed that the patient had indeed been taking methylamphetamine by injection.

3 The patient was willing to give at least lip service to the idea of regular attendance and co-operation in treatment.

4 The patient claimed to be taking methylamphetamine in a regular dose of not less than four ampoules per day.

During the course of this experiment the scene suddenly changed when in October 1968 methylamphetamine was withdrawn from supply to retail chemists. We are therefore able to give not only some account of what happens when an attempt is made to treat addicts in an environment where the drug is very freely available from black market sources, but also to give some impressions as to the immediate impact of measures which curb the supply. A more systematic account of the effect of this voluntary agreement is given by Alarcon (1972). With two exceptions (October 1967 and January 1968) all the patients reported on here were first seen between May and September 1968. The total sample consists of 23 patients – 21 male and two female.

Characteristics of patients

The average age of patients when first seen was 20.8 years (range 17 to 26) with half being aged 20 or less.

Personal background

All the patients seen were British born. Even without paying regard to frequently reported subjective experience of unhappiness in the childhood home, there were ample objective pointers to this being a group which had been exceptionally exposed to disturbing early experience. In only ten instances had mother and father been together up to the patient's 16th birthday with neither parent being criminal, alcoholic, or mentally ill; in four of these 'normal' homes a sibling had been involved in drug taking.

Assessment of the basic personality was made difficult by past and present drug use. We again, therefore, looked first particularly for gross pointers of prior disturbance rather than paying attention to minor but suggestive evidence, and found that 14 subjects had manifested either gross neurotic disturbance in childhood, or had a severe history of repeated truanting from secondary school, or admitted homosexual experience. Not only the 16 subjects who were unemployed, but also those who were working, seemed to be fully involved in the drug subculture and to be spending a lot of time searching for drugs. And our patients were nearly all involved in a whole time or part time way of life likely to reinforce deviancy. Only two had not at some time been on a criminal charge although only nine had been on overtly a 'drug charge'.

Drug history

These patients in the past had all used many different drugs, typically starting at the age of 16 or so with 'pills', that is to say, amphetamine preparations or amphetamine/barbiturate mixtures, and going on to use an astonishing variety of other substances during the next few years. Two had at one time been physiologically dependent on heroin while 16 others had used heroin intermittently and bore witness to the reality of the 'chipping' phenomenon – desultory use might occur over even as long a period as two years without the patient becoming dependent.

The story of methylamphetamine use showed a number of different patterns but typically the drug had first been taken sometime during the previous 12 months, had most usually been taken even on the first occasion by injection, and had first been obtained either from black market sources of from one of two well known prescribing doctors. When first seen in the clinic every patient was taking the drug by injection either intravenously or subcutaneously, in a daily dose which was stated to range from 1 ampoule (30 mg.) to 16 ampoules (480 mg.) per day. Amphatemine psychosis (Connell 1958) was experienced so frequently as almost to be accepted as normal and in this small sample all the phenomena which have been described as occurring in methedrine psychosis were recounted.

Treatment

For 12 patients ampoules of methylamphetamine were prescribed, the average dose being four ampoules per day for this sub-group which claimed previously to have been taking an average of 7.5 ampoules a day. Of the 11 patients who were not prescribed ampoules of methylamphetamine one asked not to be given any, three broke contact after one visit and before full enquiries were completed, and seven were considered to be taking so little of the drug or to be taking it so irregularly as to make initial prescribing unnecessary. Six of these latter seven patients were given a variety of drugs orally as substitute e.g., diazepan methylamphetamine tablets, or barbiturate/amphetamine mixtures.

(a) *Maintenance of contact.* Excluding the three patients who were not seen again after the first visit, the remaining 20 patients made an average of 8.5 outpatient clinic attendences at roughly weekly intervals. The subgroup of eight patients who were not prescribed methedrine made an average of eight visits. Three patients, two of whom had originally been prescribed methedrine, remained in contact with the clinic after six months although not attending regularly; in each instance a useful therapeutic contact seemed to have been made and worthwhile social work had been possible. The remaining 17 patients who had come for more than the initial interview had all broken contact within three months; four of those who had originally been prescribed methedrine broke contact immediately when in October 1968 the drug was no longer given them.

(b) *Treatment Outcome.* Any claim as to instances of 'successful outcome' is fairly meaningless when dealing with young people who are going through a very difficult period of adjustment, and who even when off drugs may relapse any day. We feel however that with two patients something considerable was attained – although originally prescribed methedrine they are now off all drugs as confirmed by urine tests. A third patient who is in contact appears to be making slow progress and is working regularly. As for the other patients it would probably be none too pessimistic to say that we achieved nothing evident – there was for these remaining 17 no change in work status, no change in life style, and as regards drugs, very largely just the switching from one drug to another. It has not been possible to trace all these 17 failures as regards their current drug taking but at the point of breaking contact we were frequently told by them that they were obtaining other drugs from black market sources.

Despite systematic individual follow-up being impossible, we were nevertheless, with the co-operation of the Home Office, able to check whether these patients had after leaving us become registered at a drug treatment centre for the prescription of heroin. We were informed that seven had been registered at some time previous to their contact with our clinic. But only one of the 23 was attending a centre approximately six months after methedrine had been restricted and this patient's claim to be methadone and heroin dependent was being investigated.

Discussion

The problem of poly drug use

Although it is heroin which has hit the headlines the real problem which Britain at present faces is poly drug use. This statement is unlikely to be disputed by anyone having clinical acquaintance with the patients who are today seeking help. In 1964 Connell noted that amphetamine users often had experience of barbiturate and cannabis and sometimes solvent abuse; he also commented on the availability in the same *milieu* of opiates and cocaine, but the full implications of this truth so far as the framing of policy is concerned have not been openly faced. People who are in trouble with drug use tend to be using several drugs, to have used many drugs, and probably to be on the way to using many other drugs. To focus explanations, preventive policy, or treatment on any one drug is tunnel vision. As far as patients are concerned a switch from one drug to another means little. The habit of injecting barbiturates or amphetamines – dissolved amphetamine tablets since the supply of methedrine ceased – is now rife in London, and carries probably as grave risks as heroin dependence or perhaps even greater risk of death by overdose, so that the suggestion that this problem demands urgent attention is no mere academic point. To describe the patients reported in this paper as 'methedrine users' would be as inaccurate and incomplete as designating the bulk of patients who attend the new treatment centres as 'heroin users'.

The clinics set up in April 1968 were of course specifically concerned with the problems of heroin and cocaine and although coherent policy and agreement between clinics regarding prescription of those drugs seems gradually to be emerging, there is no similar consensus on how best to deal medically with the essentially poly drug problem of which heroin and cocaine taking are but particular manifestations. We need to look closely at the rationale that dictates that heroin and cocaine should be given such a very special status – an emphasis based perhaps on our over-evaluation of the importance of the physiological element in dependence. The fact that narcotics are the only drug which an adolescent can be reasonably hopeful of finding a clinic willing to prescribe for him, is a policy which inadvertently has written into it the invitation to escalate to narcotic taking. Why then is it our present policy to offer maintenance or graduated withdrawal treatment to heroin takers and not generally to 'pill' takers? Why was methedrine withdrawn while heroin continues to be prescribed?

Therapeutic failure

The report we have given of these 23 patients is largely a record of therapeutic failure: it does not need a controlled trial to underline the fact that the help being given in our clinic was mostly ineffectual. The two or three successes which we are able to instance suggest, as might be expected, that the occasional person who is well motivated, socially stable and of relatively intact personality, may respond to the type of treatment on offer, but he is the exception who proves the rule. If one were to look at the forces arrayed against treatment success and measure them up against the therapeutic forces, it would seem that the anti-therapeutic factors were usually overwhelmingly more potent in their sum. A pathological or disruptive home environment, constant involvement in a 'scene' which reinforced deviant values, criminal involvement, the underlying and often gross personality disorder, were met by transient contact once or twice a week for an hour at the most with a psychiatrist across a desk, and by some social work help. We were not offering our patients any clear alternative role, purpose, life style, or value system, or insofar as we were offering any of these things our offer was feeble compared with the forceful and continuing restatement of deviant values which was going on for the rest of the patients' waking hours. Our patients must often have perceived us simply as inexpert participants in a game in which we were bound to be the losers – they knew that we could not accurately judge the dose which they were on, that we could not tell whether they were selling the surplus or buying extra, and constant arguing and bargaining about dosage perverted the contract.

Implications for policy

The pessimistic conclusion from this small case series would be that it hints that no 'treatment' in the medical sense offers any effective answer to the problem of poly drug abuse. This would be a sad and cruel answer, for patients were certainly on occasion turning to us for help. To interpret their failure to continue in treatment as 'lack of motivation' may be quite unfairly to project the blame – we should perhaps be willing to interpret such behaviour as much due to our own failure to offer apt help as to the patients' lack of sincerity. What positive and constructive lessons can then be got from this small treatment series? One thing seems certain – the type of clinic required and its function can only be defined in the context of the country's total policy on poly drug use – a policy including purely medical interests but also reflecting basic penal, social and commercial policies. Very tentatively we would outline the rudiments of the necessary total response to this problem as follows.

1 *Prevention*

(a) One useful consequence of the drug problem may be that it forces us back to look at much more basic ills in society and to ask what measures – practical and economic – can be proposed to right these ills. A possible focus might be on the kind of experience we are offering adolescents in the last year at school and on the type of special care and counselling which could be given to the obviously troubled young person at the time when he is trying to settle in his first job. Without any criticism of teachers who are attempting much in old buildings and crowded class rooms, one may suspect that in many of our schools the last year offers little sense of direction for the adolescent who is already beginning to feel lost and who looks on the open world as a wilderness.

(b) Any attempt at treatment in a city where amphetamines are as easily obtainable as cigarettes is handicapped. The control of manufacture and commercial distribution is too lax, and over-prescribing by doctors is something which needs urgently to be dealt with.

(c) There may be a case for preventing the prescribing of certain drugs, except perhaps by hospitals or in other exceptional circumstances. The impact of any particular piece of legislation is difficult to predict, but withdrawing methedrine did not, it seems, drive large numbers of people on to heroin – although on the other hand it did not, on our evidence, succeed in stopping their drug taking. An attempt to control the prescription of barbiturate or amphetamine tablets in injectable form would obviously require much discussion with manufacturers, and any such measure should be introduced only as a carefully observed experiment.

2 *Treatment*

(a) The client has to be reached. There is need for a front line clinic, a kind of sorting office, to which patients could be referred or could refer themselves very readily and without formality, and one could envisage such clinics advertising in much the say way as, for instance, mass X-ray facilities. Our impression was that many potential referring agencies are often at present frustrated by difficulty in finding help.

(b) There is a need for development of treatment which offers the addict an immediate alternative to his present way of life and this may imply treatment which is day-long rather than an hour a week. Day centres such as the Community Drug Project, the Chelsea Centre (Chappel et al., 1969) and St. Clement's Day Hospital are experiments which need to be fostered, and the place of hostels (Home Office, 1969) needs to be explored.

(c) In the setting of support from day hospitals and hostels the treatment clinic would have more to offer and there may be a place for very carefully considered prescribing.

(d) The size of the problem and the inevitable limitation on available medical man power underline the need for prevention. As with alcoholism (Bacon,

1969) one may question whether a medical response, however humane its intentions, will ever provide other than a very small part of the total answer. The medical profession should perhaps be resistant to the notion that the addict is a 'sick person' if the implication of this is that the doctor has total responsibility for dealing with this sickness, while society itself does little to prevent the endless production of new patients.

Research

Rational policy can only be based on information which permits informed decision making. We need to know the true size of the problem, and we need some approximate method of monitoring change in the problems, size and changes in drug fashion. The natural history of poly drug use is still totally obscure. More needs to be known of the sources of illicit supply and the relative importance of thefts and of over-prescribing. The need for controlled clinical experiment is very apparent and in the absence of any such work, over-confident championing of particular methods of treatment must be avoided.

14 The evaluation of measures to deal with drug dependence in the United Kingdom*

DAVID HAWKS

Summary

Multiple dimensions are identified along which the success or failure of British measures to deal with heroin and cocaine misuse might be judged, and the relevant evidence then considered. In several instances data on which to make any properly informed judgement are lacking. That there can be no single answer to the question 'does the system work?' is particularly stressed, and success in one regard may indeed be contradicted by failure in another. For instance, a decrease in the amont of drugs prescribed by the clinics may not be unconnected with significant upward changes in black market activity. But even a conservative interpretation of the facts would suggest that an epidemic has not burgeoned in the manner which was feared, and it seems more than likely that the administrative measures which were taken influenced this result.

Introduction

The problem of drug dependence in the United Kingdom, has largely been construed as one involving the misuse of heroin and cocaine. In considering the effectiveness of measures taken to control drug dependence in the United Kingdom this definition of the problem will be accepted though it will become apparent it results in a certain myopia.

The effectiveness of any intervention can only very rarely be measured on a single dimension. Criteria which might be employed in assessing the success of the measures taken in the United Kingdom to deal with drug dependence include the number of new notifications, the total number under treatment, the number 'cured', the 'retention' of those under treatment, age of first use, time elapsing between first use and notification, number of offences involving drugs, the quantity and nature of drugs prescribed, the quantity and nature of the drugs taken, the number treated for drug overdose and the number dying

---

* Condensed from a paper presented to the Anglo-American Conference on Drug Abuse (Society's Reaction – Medicine's Responsibility) Royal Society of Medicine, London, April 1973.

from drug related causes. Other less accessible criteria include the extent of illicit buying and selling, the price of illicit drugs, the number using drugs who are not in contact with treatment centres, the extent of their criminal involvement, employment and association with other addicts; the degree to which patients and doctors express satisfaction with the measures evolved. Nor is this list, though long, complete. Reference might also be made to the quality of life of patients under treatment and the social usefulness of rehabilitated addicts.

The number of such criteria, the variability of their source, subjectivity and the time span covered, is illustrated in Table 14.1.

Not only do such criteria vary in their accessibility they differ in their orientation, some deriving from statutory sources others from informal enquiry. Some economy might be effected if it could be agreed that certain criteria of effectiveness were more important than others – that to reduce the number of notifications is of more importance than to ensure patient satisfaction with the doses prescribed. On the other hand the number of new notifications may as much reflect patient's satisfaction with the prescribing policy pursued by the clinics as it provides indication of the numbers dependent on drugs in the community. The number of new notifications is not a sufficient criterion of effectiveness. Almost certainly some criteria will be shown to be more seminal than others with change on their continua guaranteeing commensurate change on others. It may be doubted, however, whether we are yet in a position to identify these crucial outcome variables. Lacking such assurance it behoves us to monitor as many of these dimensions as possible allowing that apparently beneficial change on one may be associated with adverse change on others. The exercise of evaluation might be likened to that of trying to descern the overall direction of movement in multi-dimensional space.

There can be no singular answer to the question 'Does the system work?'. It must first be asked by what *combination of criteria* is the system to be judged to work. Nor does the necessary subtlety end with the specification of the criteria to be employed; the relationship between these criteria are such that changes on one dimension do not guarantee comparable changes on others.

The relationships between outcomes are likely to be complex, variable over time and not altogether predictable. The formulation of policy in this area is likely, therefore, to resemble much more closely the logic of 'muddling through' (Maddox, 1971) than any more rational or Utopian form. It must content itself with the realisation of part objectives by a process of careful and tentative 'trial and error' – tentative in the sense that it expresses a less than unconditional commitment to these objectives; it must be ever ready to

Table 14.1

Possible criteria of effectiveness

'Official' data, relatively accessible	*Incidence and prevalence*	Number of valid first notifications (incidence).
		Number known to be cured (from which prevalence can be determined) – social usefulness of rehabilitated users.
	Chronological	Age first use of those notified.
		Age on notification.
		Time elapsing between first use and notification.
	Drug related	Drugs prescribed.
		Quantities of drugs prescribed.
		Number treated for drug overdose or other complications of drug use.
		Number dying from drug related causes.
	Criminality and unemployment	Number of convictions involving drugs.
		Employment of those notified.
'Unofficial' data, relatively inaccessible	*Drug related (illicit)*	Drugs used (including illicit).
		Quantities used (including illicit).
		Price of illicit drugs.
		Sources of illicit drugs.
	Involvement in illegal activities	Involvement with other addicts.
		Illegal involvements.
	Inclusiveness of system	Number of users not in contact with official agencies, including those who were at one time under treatment and those never under treatment.
	Subjective	Doctor satisfaction.
		Patient satisfaction – quality of life under treatment – satisfaction in terms of drug preference.

retrace its steps, institute new measures and modify old ones. It will be obvious that such a process requires constant monitoring – it can never be a once and for all affair or subject to review only after five years. Moreover the process of monitoring will need to occur at a number of points, some inside the system and others external to it. The independent follow up of patients in treatment, the assessment of those who have at one time been in treatment but are no longer attending clinics, for whatever reason, together with those who have never been officially notified, are minimal requirements of any evaluative strategy.

The policy pursued in the United Kingdom has many of these formal and informal characteristics and it is these which in some part explain the partial success of the measures adopted.

Before concentrating on the extent to which it could be claimed that the approach adopted in the United Kingdom has been effective a brief chronological summary of its development since April 1968 will be sketched.

Following the enactment in early 1968 of the regulations affecting the treatment and notification of addicts there was a considerable and entirely predictable increase in the number of persons known to be dependent on opiates (1,306 in 1968 compared to 745 in 1967) – predictable since the previous system of notification was in no way obligatory. The vast majority of those notified in the first few months of the clinics' operation were using heroin and a substantial proportion were subsequently prescribed heroin by the treatment centres. While over 500 licences to prescribe heroin and cocaine were issued, 71 per cent of those notified in 1968 were listed with clinics in the Greater London area. While the number of new notifications did not again approximate the influx of the first few months of the clinics' operation, it was not until February 1970 that it abated. The number is now of the order of 60 per month, having recently risen slightly. The interpretation of this recent increase is contentious in the absence of information which would allow the exclusion of a number of possibilities. It may merely follow changes in the conventions affecting notification (an increasing number of new notifications derive from prison medical sources) or reflect a change in the age composition of the population which resulted in a greater number in the vulnerable age categories being exposed to the possibility of drug use. By 1970 methadone was as frequently reported to be the drug of primary dependence, reflecting the policy of the clinics increasingly to substitute methadone for heroin and the initial scarcity of heroin on the illicit market.[1]

The fact that the vast majority of addicts are polymorphous drug users, combined with the fact that the prescribing of other drugs is less stringently controlled than is the case for heroin and cocaine, has meant that changes in the supply of these latter drugs has had consequences for the use of others.

The injection of methylamphetamine assumed brief, though devastating vogue until a voluntary restriction on its prescription resulted in its at least temporary demise (Alarcon, 1972). The intravenous injection of barbiturates continues to be a cause for concern (Mitcheson et al., 1970).

With the passage of time the number prescribed heroin alone by the clinics has decreased and the number prescribed methadone alone increased. While general practitioners retain the right to prescribe methadone, in fact few have availed themselves of this dubious privilege and the principal licit source of both drugs are the drug treatment centres.

Both the total quantity of heroin prescribed and the average prescription per patient have fallen, in part reflecting the better opportunities for assessment available now and in part the tailoring of initially discrepant clinic practices by the administrative strategy of publishing for internal circulation the total and average amounts prescribed by each of the centres.

The decrease in the total amount of heroin prescribed was initially compensated for by an increase in the amount of methadone prescribed, though individual patients may not have been compensated. However, in time both have been provided in diminishing amounts. The present situation is that approximately one third of patients notified for the first time do not receive any prescription for opiates at all at least initially (Blumberg et al., 1974[a,b]) and of those who receive a prescription only 16 per cent are for heroin. The amounts presently prescribed most new patients are such that the system can probably no longer justifiably be regarded as a maintenance orientated system but rather must be thought of as an abstinence orientated system.

Data from a prospective study of patients attending a clinic for treatment for the first time (Blumberg et al., 1974[a,b]) indicates that over a twelve month period the size of the initial prescription decreased, though there was no evidence that the characteristics of patients, including their stated drug use, seen over that period of time, showed any variation. While these initial prescriptions may be modified in time it seems likely that the majority of newly notified addicts are being prescribed less than they claim to need. While these comparatively low doses may be 'maintained' for some time it is doubtful that they qualify as maintenance dosages.

It has already been stated that for a system to be evaluated it must be monitored. The monitoring of the British system from within is reasonably adequate. It can be stated at any time what numbers are receiving treatment as inpatients, what numbers are being seen as outpatients, what drugs and quantities are prescribed, what numbers are newly identified in any month, their gross characteristics, source of referral and geographic distribution. There is, however, no routine provision for the independent follow-up of patients currently under treatment or of patients who were at one time under treatment.

Monitoring the system from without is less complete. There is no routine attempt to follow-up patients who come to a clinic once and not again (estimated to be approximately 30 per cent of those attending for the first time). Nor does the peculiar relationship pertaining between the addict and those treating him permit a frank examination of what other drugs patients are using additional to those prescribed. Some measure of an addict's illegal involvement and work status is obtained by recourse to criminal and Social Security records but these provide only minimal estimates.

However, it is in the area of assessing those users of opiates who have not been in touch with the clinics at all that the present system of monitoring is most deficient. Very little is known about such people except that their number is not insignificant. Newly notified cases have on average been using opiates for three years prior to their notification and one estimate suggests that 50 per cent of their opiate using associates have not yet been notified (Blumberg et al., 1974[a,b]). Both Bransby et al. (1973) and Blumberg et al. (1974[a,b]) found that 50 per cent of those newly notified in 1970–71 had been usng opiates for at least two years prior to their first clinic attendance. Blumberg et al. report regular use of this duration while the Bransby et al. data relate to first use. If the Bransby et al. data are adopted as illustrative (and they pertain to 83 per cent of all new notifications from hospitals in the period in question), it means that approximately 400 addicts had first used opiates in 1968 without being notified. This group constitutes 14 per cent of the total then known. If it is assumed that similar circumstances pertain now (and there can be no guarantee that this is the case) it would mean that in addition to those known in 1971 (2,769) there were approximately 400 who were using opiates but who were unknown to any authority. The existence of this penumbra of unknown users obviously compromises any attempt to depict the success of the measures adopted.

No attempt will be made to present data which bear on each of the criteria listed in Table 14.1. since neither space nor the data available permit this. Rather some illustrative examples will be given which serve to emphasise the complexities involved.

There are a number of inferences which can be made on the basis of the data which are routinely collected.

Age of first use and notification

In the absence of data which suggest that addicts are notifying themselves earlier in their drug career, information which suggested that the average age of addicts on notification was dropping would reflect adversely on the effectiveness of the system adopted. No such tendency has been manifest since 1968. While there was a marked tendency for addicts to be notified at younger ages prior to the introduction of the new legislation there has been no further reduction nor does age of first use appear to have declined significantly.

Ethnicity

Nor does ethnicity appear ever to have been a significant correlate of narcotic dependence in the United Kingdom. Most studies of known narcotic users confirm that the vast majority were born in the United Kingdom (Bransby 1971[a], 1973). While it has been suggested that the Canadians who came to England between 1959–69 under the privileged status accorded British citizens from Commonwealth countries, played a significant role in the development of narcotic addiction in the United Kingdom, in fact there is little evidence to suggest that they were instrumental in creating the 'epidemic' observed in 1967–68 (Spear and Glatt, 1971). On the contrary they appear to have been a relatively self contained group, known to one another but largely atypical of the average British born addict having both a longer history of addiction and imprisonment and usually being in receipt of much larger prescriptions of narcotics. In a survey conducted in 1969 Zacune (1971) found that of the 91 Canadians known to have come to Britain 50 per cent had either returned to Canada or been deported while those who remained tended to differ from the average British addict in being more often employed and less involved in the drug scene.

Whether it can be claimed that the measures adopted in the United Kingdom have been effective in preventing the spread of narcotic addiction in those ethnic minorities which in the United States have been especially vulnerable is arguable; the relative immunity of these groups undoubtedly reflects a variety of influences, including the more selective immigration policy pursued in the United Kingdom, and cannot be attributed solely to differences in the drug control policies pursued by the two countries.

Variety of drugs used

The fact that a significant percentage of newly notified addicts has used both powdered heroin and barbiturates prior to their notification, when the use of these drugs is most likely to be declared, reflects on the success on the system, since it is reasonable to expect that the policy if successful should reduce the total number of drugs abused.

Morbidity and mortality

Death from overdose reflects a number of considerations in addition to the effectiveness or otherwise of the system of prescribing. Nevertheless it is reasonable to expect that if the policy followed is controlling the quantity and quality of drugs used, the number of deaths from overdose or other drug related causes should not increase disproportionately. In fact, with the exception of one year (1969) the number of addicts known to die from drug related causes has not varied greatly. The fact that complications are a frequent experience and hospitalisation a repetitive event indicate, however, that the system of prescribing adopted has not greatly reduced the morbidity associated with drug dependence.

Offences involving drugs

The number of offences involving drugs provides another index of the system's effectiveness. Those involving heroin have increased 121 per cent over 1970 which, together with the evidence that the amount of heroin prescribed has diminished, indicates that the increase in trafficking principally involves 'Chinese' or other heroin whose origin is wholly illicit.

Criminal involvement

Studies which have compared the criminal record of addicts before and after their notification (Mahon, 1971) suggest that fewer addicts are convicted following their notification. On the other hand Gordon (1973) has purported to demonstrate that the proportion of patients attending a London clinic convicted of crimes of violence increased following their first use of opiates, whereas the proportion convicted of larceny fell.[2] In that for most of the post drug period addicts were not attending the clinic in question, their criminal tendencies cannot be attributed to the treatment policy of the clinic.

It has been a basic tenet of the British approach that addicts, if given a regular legal prescription, would have no need or incentive to engage in illegal activities; nor was it supposed, except in so far as their use of drugs was an illegal activity, would addicts have predominantly criminal backgrounds. For addicts to have no need to engage in illegal activities assumes of course that such activities were not part of their life-style before they became addicted and that they receive sufficient amounts of the drug of their choice to have no need to supplement if from illicit sources. In actuality neither assumption has proved to be well founded. A significant proportion, (approximately 50 per cent) of notified addicts have criminal records which pre-date their drug use and a significant proportion (again approximately 50 per cent) continue to engage in illegal pursuits of a kind not closely related to their drug dependence though they are at the time in receipt of a prescription (Bewley et al., 1972: Bransby, 1971[b]). While it can be argued that no activity engaged in by an addict is irrelevant to his addiction, all that is being asserted here is that these offences are not classified as drug offences.

Blumberg et al. (1974[a,b]) found that although the amount of narcotics said to be needed by addicts on first attendance did not decrease over the 12 months of the intake, the amounts prescribed did. Given that the amount said to be needed and the amount said to be used in fact both exceeded the amounts prescribed, it is obvious that the balance must be made up from illicit sources. Even in the more 'permissive' climate described by Stimson and Ogborne (1970), when all the patients surveyed had received prescriptions for heroin for an average period of 12 months, 84 per cent were also using drugs obtained illicitly in the month prior to interview.

It must be concluded, therefore, that the somewhat naive assumption that British addicts would not have any need to engage in illegal activities has not provided an insurance against the probability of their engaging in criminal activities. What does appear to be the case, at least until recently, is that the supply of illicit heroin has not been as organised as is the case in the United States. Most of the heroin available on the black market before 1968 derived from the over-generous prescribing of a few doctors (DHSS, 1965). Following the implementation of the new regulations the chief sources of supply were almost certainly treatment centres whose lack of experience and means of assessment contributed to surplus prescribing. More recently the clinics' policy of substituting methadone for heroin and prescribing both in diminishing quantities has meant that very little English heroin has found its way on to the black market (the black market price of English heroin has increased significantly). On the other hand contaminated (Chinese) heroin has become a prevalent commodity indicating that the market has become more organised and that initially legal sources are no longer the principal sources of supply.

Illicit use by patients attending clinics

Enquiries which are independent of the treatment clinics provide another indication of the system's effectiveness. Such studies (Stimson and Ogborne, 1970[a,b]; Blumberg et al., 1974[a,b]) have consistently shown that addicts attending clinics associate with others who while using opiates are not known to clinics. They also reveal that addicts may be a long time coming to the notice of clinics. Fifty per cent of those in the Blumberg et al. study were as long as three years on average between their first injection and notification and for a little more than a third a gap of two years elapsed between first regular opiate use and eventual notification (with no abstentions of longer than two weeks intervening). Taken together these two findings suggest that at any point a significant number of people using opiates may not be known to the clinics and may not become known for some considerable time. Nor do such studies offer any assurance that following the receipt of a legal prescription most addicts abandon the use of other illicitly obtained drugs.

Whether or not addicts have recourse to other drugs appears moreover to be related to the amount of heroin they receive on prescription with those receiving larger prescriptions having less recourse to illicit drugs, suggesting that the two events may not be unrelated.

Abstinence

The number abstinent at any one time provides yet another index of effectiveness. Those studies which have followed up patients over varying lengths of time (Bewley and Ben Arie, 1968; Mahon, 1971; Chapple, et al., 1972) indicate that approximately 25 per cent are 'not known to be drug dependent at follow-up', while another 20 per cent appear to be drug free.

'Not known to be drug dependent' is not of course an absolute guarantee of an ex-addict's abstinent status and these percentages must be regarded as maximal estimates. None of the studies quoted has re-contacted all patients under circumstances calculated to reveal the true extent of their present drug involvement. The evidence available from studies of clinic populations suggests that at least some of those 'not known to official sources' will still be misusing drugs.

Other indices of rehabilitation

While an ex-addict's present involvement with drugs is an important aspect of his adjustment, it is properly regarded as only one index of his rehabilitation. Other indices less accessible to investigation but nevertheless of some significance include his level of employability, and the quality of his social relationships. Studies of addicts suggest that a significant proportion have shown only tenuous adjustment prior to becoming dependent and it must be admitted that few treatment programmes have claimed or shown themselves to be successful in the matter of improving addicts' coping skills. Except in the end an addict's adjustment potential is improved his decreased use of drugs must be regarded as a significant though temporary benefit.

Controlled comparison of treatment outcomes

The delegation of responsibility for treating addicts to the consultants in charge of clinics has not resulted in the control conditions necessary for the valid comparison of treatment programmes. Doctors treating addicts have understandably employed those means which appeared to them best suited to the individual requirements of patients and the number treated in identical ways has never been sufficient to allow a strict comparison of outcomes. While a number of studies have reported differential outcomes for different programmes (Chapple and Gray, 1968) the fact that patients were allocated to these programmes in discretionary ways has meant that no valid conclusions can be drawn as to the efficacy of different programmes. Even so critical an issue as the differential effectiveness of prescribing heroin or methadone has only very recently received investigation. The stringent criteria which must ethically prevail before patients can be randomised between heroin and oral methadone programmes are such, however, that only a minority of patients can be included in such a trial so that the generalisation of any results to the population of addicts under treatment is to some extent dubious. The interim results of such a comparison suggest that there are no significant differences in terms of outcome between the two régimes (personal communication).

Possible contradictory developments

It has already been observed that the number of criteria according to which success might be reasonably judged and the uncertain relationship between these criteria is such that success in one regard may be contradicted by failure in another. Change in one part of the causal complex may have unsolicited implications for other parts. In at least one sense this would appear to have transpired. The total amount of opiates prescribed by the clinics has gradually declined to the point where only a minority are prescribed heroin. Most of those questioned independently claim to receive less opiates than they require or were taking prior to coming to the clinic. In one regard then the policy pursued has been successful. It would seem, however, that the reduction in the amount of drugs legally prescribed has not been attended by a consequent reduction in the total amount of drugs used. It follows, therefore, that those under treatment have increasingly had recourse to illicit sources. Most observers would agree that powdered heroin is readily available on the black market. While there can be no doubt that the increased activity of the black market reflects influences additional to official prescribing policy the latter is certainly one factor in the complex equation.

It is one thing to diagnose, even accurately, the derivation of the present situation and another entirely to recommend appropriate corrective action. A retrospective analysis of the development of the present situation, however astute, does not necessarily lead logically to recommendations for future policy since the situation itself will have changed in the meantime. The effect of making heroin and methadone more readily available to those under treatment may be just to increase the total amount of opiates in circulation. The black market in powdered heroin having developed to its present stage is unlikely to be curtailed by an influx of more legally prescribed opiates, it may merely distribute these legal supplies more effectively. It is naive to imagine that the total drug situation can be controlled through the policy of prescribing adopted by the clinics any more than the present abuse of drugs can be controlled by the rigid prescription of only certain substances. The clinics are only one element, though an important one, in the equation which, without the successful curtailment of illicit sources of drugs and the provision of legitimate and accessible alternatives to addicts, is unlikely to be successful in the long run.

Conclusion

It has to be admitted that we currently lack data which bears on all the dimensions outlined in Table 14.1, and moreover that we lack even the basic prerequisite of evaluation, namely the existence of a matched group who have not been subjected to the measures described.

We lack even the comfort of studies which have directly assessed the adjustment shown by opiate users before and after they enter treatment. Those studies which have been carried out involving addicts entering treatment have tended to concentrate on the immediate past and to have relied on the retrospective account of the addict himself (Stimson and Ogborne, 1970[b], Blumberg et al., 1974[a,b], Mahon, 1971).

On the other hand it would be unnecessarily pedantic to suggest that we have no evidence of the measure's success – the number of new notifications has de-escalated markedly over the last five years, even if they show some slight evidence of reviving of late, and the total number of known addicts has not increased over the same period. While it cannot be confidently asserted that events would have been otherwise had the present measures not been enacted it is inconceivable that they have not in some way been instrumental in effecting this development. It is perhaps instructive to remember that had the Vera Institute's extrapolation proved correct we could have expected a total of 11,000 addicts in 1972. Not even the harshest critic of the British approach would assert that there were 8,000 unidentified narcotic addicts in the United Kingdom in 1972.

The anxiety which was felt in 1967–68 in relation to the escalating numbers of new notifications was not conducive to the establishment of those conditions which would have permitted a controlled trial, if, indeed such conditions could have been implemented; that we have been somewhat complacent in the evaluation of these measures undoubtedly reflects in large part the diminution of that anxiety.

Notes

[1] There is some evidence to suggest that the number of cases of methadone dependence may have been exaggerated in 1970 by the tendency of some doctors to report as methadone dependent patients, who, though presenting as cases of heroin dependence, were immediately transferrred to methadone (DHSS, 1971).

[2] Blumberg (1974[a,b]) has pointed out that if the crime rate *per year* of exposure is calculated the violent crime rate is in fact roughly constant over the two periods.

15 Appraisal

Investigations of the process of treatment are difficult if only because, in psychiatry at least, so much is undefined. The treatment of drug addiction, where it is not the mere prescribing of drugs, is perhaps the most unspecified aspect of the 'British system'. Certainly none of the papers included in this section can be construed as a study of the treatment *process* with the possible exception of that on methylamphetamine.

As Hawks (1973) has observed, the conditions prevailing in 1967–68 were not conducive to the setting up of controlled trials, so that even so crucial a question as the relative efficacy of heroin and methadone prescriptions has not been resolved. Nor has there been any systematic attempt to treat addicts according to their characteristics.

While addicts are undoubtedly treated in different ways by the various clinics, the policies of these clinics are rarely made so explicit as to allow a comparison of different régimes. Nor, of course, were addicts allocated to these régimes on a random basis.

What we have in the absence of any published controlled trial is a collection of studies relating to specific clinic populations followed-up over varying lengths of time, or investigations of more representative samples whose treatment was determined by the prescribing doctors without regard to the niceties of experimental design. Nor with hindsight does the representativeness of these samples stand close scrutiny. Blumberg and his colleagues' study, while drawing its sample from all those approaching clinics for the first time and being seen by a doctor, revealed that significant numbers of opiate users had never been in touch with the clinics, despite their having used opiates for some considerable period.

The studies included in this section relate in the main to outcome, which because the treatments prescribed are so rarely documented cannot be construed as outcome contingent upon treatment. In addition to whatever treatment was prescribed in individual cases, a whole host of variables, some relating to the addict himself, can be expected to have affected outcome.

That the process of treatment should prove difficult to define and even more so to evaluate, might have been predicted from the very ambiguities inherent in the British system; to prescribe the drug of choice and at the same time motivate the individual toward abstinence, might be thought contradictory objectives productive of considerable dissonance in the prescribing doctor. The study by Blumberg at least implies that this dissonance has been reduced by progressively abandoning the principle of prescribing, or of prescribing the drug of choice, rather than addressing the more difficult question of building motivation for an alternative career. A basic tenet of the British system has as a consequence been eroded, in part, one suspects, because the difficulty of reconciling it with the need to orientate the addict toward abstinence has never been faced, or if faced at least not resolved.

Some of the assumptions in the British approach, such as that addicts would not resort to illicit drugs when prescribed their drug of choice, were always questionable. Urine analysis, as well as being an aid to the correct discernment of dependence has become, or so it would seem, the criterion of acceptance for treatment. While the exclusion from receiving opiates of those not yet dependent on opiates is a prerequisite of a conservative policy, the fact that many of those so excluded from treatment are using other illicitly obtained drugs, including barbiturates, must reflect on the comprehensiveness of the treatment policies adopted. If the treatment clinics are to interpret their role as providing only for those who present with a positive urine, many who for one reason or another do not satisfy this criterion will be denied treatment, despite their history of illicit drug use and its attendant complications.

Another key assumption of the policy adopted in the United Kingdom is the view that prescribing which is commensurate with the patient's need will obviate the development of a black market in heroin. In 1969 reports that 'Chinese heroin' was available in London had the status of rumour. Subsequent events confirm the reality. That this development has occurred reflects the difficulty in deciding an addict's 'need' for a drug. If the average amount of opiate prescribed is taken as indicating addicts' needs, the clinics have interpreted these needs as diminishing. Enquiries independent of the clinics on the other hand suggest that there has been no diminution in addicts' expressed needs. The results has been that as average prescriptions have gone down and methadone increasingly substituted for heroin, the use of black market opiates has increased commensurately.

The difficulty of implementing any treatment policy with regard to a drug which is freely available, is amply illustrated by the paper of Mitcheson et al. and hardly requires elaboration. The fact that the dispensing of methadrine has since been confined and legislation introduced which provides for a more flexible means of controlling the prescribing of other drugs, attests to a recognition of the fact that treatment cannot be pursued without regard to supply.

Many of the developments which have occurred since 1968 may be interpreted as reflecting a too mechanical application of precepts: methadone has increasingly been substituted for heroin, both have been supplied in decreasing amounts and patients not having a positive urine have been refused treatment, a no longer trivial black market in illicitly imported heroin has developed, and the clients have in some numbers turned to barbiturates or illicit heroin. The attempt to operate the system through the mechanical manipulation of the drugs is not by itself the answer and this is clearly recognised by clinic staff. Building an addict's motivation for abstinence is more difficult, as is providing him with an alternative career. Difficult though those objectives be, there is no reason to doubt their continued relevance. Their achievement in the context of the essential ambiguities of the British approach remains an unsolved mystery, but one hopefully to be investigated in further studies of the treatment system. If the 'British system' has within it anything special to commend, it is indeed perhaps its capacity for evolution.

THEORETICAL CONSIDERATIONS

16 Introduction

This section of the book is concerned with a discussion of various theoretical models of dependence. The meanings that can be given to the word 'dependence' are many and different sciences offer explanations of its nature at inherently different levels, with articulation between those levels currently most often uncertain. In the first paper Dr Michael Russell outlines the content of two seminar series on these theoretical issues which were held at the Addiction Research Unit, and he then offers a concept of dependence which widens the usual meaning – he concludes that 'a state of dependence is a normal part of human nature'. Such a formulation may perhaps make it easier to see how a spectrum of sciences as diverse as pharmacology and sociology are indeed essentially speaking to the same matter.

Dr Jim Orford develops a model of psychological dependence which he applies to objects in general, of which drugs are but one example. He draws from decision theory and dissonance theory to explain the individual's changing solutions to the conflict between taking drugs and desisting from drug use. In discussing a possible social-psychological model of dependence Dr A. N. Oppenheim applies the concept of dissonance reduction to explain how some people become dependent on such 'things' as drugs rather than on 'people'. Finally, Dr David Robinson in a paper written from a sociological perspective examines the social consequences which result from the assumption that alcoholism is to count as a disease.

17 What is dependence?*

M. A. H. RUSSELL

Summary

Limited operational definitions of dependence have to date served the purposes of descriptive studies, but the formulation of testable theory now becomes increasingly important as guide to future research design. The listed content of two seminar series exemplify both the requirements to embrace a range of scientific disciplines and the need to put drug-seeking behaviour beside a variety of other behaviours. A definition of dependence is offered which takes negative affect experienced on deprivation as crucial: degree of dependence is equated with degree of negative affect. Dependence is therefore a continuum. The individual may be dependent on any stimulus-source, and pharmacological rewards are only one of a number of classes of reinforcers. Acceptable alternative sources for reinforcement will diminish the importance of any given reinforcer. Dependence so conceived is normal, and may embrace a whole range of socially approved activities. Covert dependence only becomes manifest in the face of social disapproval. The anology with compulsive states is considered.

Introduction

A mountaineer who has slipped and dangles over a 300 ft. precipice suspended on a half-inch nylon rope may be truly said to be dependent on that rope. But everyday use of the word 'depend' is no longer confined to its strict etymological sense of 'hanging down'. It has been broadened to embrace more than mere support and protection from fatal consequences of the law of gravity. Though not literally suspended by it, the foetus is no less 'dependent' on his half-inch umbilical cord than the fallen mountaineer is on his rope. The notion of 'dependence' has come to imply support and protection from any fateful threat to our physical or psychological existence. It includes furthermore a sense of quantification. We are more or less dependent on something according to how much or how little it would threaten our existence to be without it. The fallen mountaineer would be less dependent on

* A paper written specially for this volume.

any one rope if there were two, even less if there were three, and so on. He would be less dependent in another way if the precipice was less high and he was nearer the ground.

What purpose is served by this kind of semantic reflection upon the meaning of the word 'dependence'? Is there perhaps a connection between the dangling mountaineer and the heroin addict frantically struggling to get a needle into his thrombosed veins, or the alcoholic who on waking in the morning shakily reaches for the bedside bottle to relieve his withdrawal symptoms?

Some of us in the Addiction Research Unit felt that there may be such a link and that to explore a wider unitary concept of dependence with a view to identifying this link might help us achieve a closer understanding of the various substance-specific dependence disorders. Strictly limited operational definitions have served an essential role for the data-gathering descriptive studies that form the bulk of this book. Such definitions have also sufficed for the next hypothesis-testing stage. With considerable basic information now available from a variety of sources and disciplines, we felt it was time to turn our attention towards the formulation of a theory or theories of the nature of dependence. We approached this task by setting up a series of three-hour evening seminars at which theoretical models of dependence were presented and discussed, covering the viewpoints of a wide range of disciplines. The theoretical position papers reproduced in this section are examples of these seminar presentations. Other presentations at this first series of seminars were: 'A Pharmacological Model' by Dr Mirvin Mitchard; 'A Learning Theory Model' by Dr John Teasdale; 'A Socio-Anthropological Model' by David Triesman; 'A Psychoanalytic Model' by Dr Christopher Dare; and 'A Neurophysiological Model with Special Reference to Intracranial Self-Stimulation' by Dr H. J. Campbell.

So varied were the approaches that it became essential to adopt a very wide concept of dependence, one that could embrace phenomena ranging from 'pharmacological tolerance' and 'preferred neuronal pathways' to 'labelling' and 'deviancy amplification'. As is so often the case, one exercise in concept formulation set the scene for another. It became apparent that there is a great deal of common ground between drug dependence and various non-drug compulsions. Examples of problems pertinent to both areas are the importance of 'frequency' of the behaviour, the features of 'resistance' and 'conflict', the notion of 'damage' and the degree to which the behaviour is perceived as 'deviant'. To explore this common ground a second series of seminars was held. Contributions to this second series of seminars were: 'Compulsive Hand-Washing' by Dr R. Hodgson; 'Gambling' by Dr E. Moran; 'Compulsive Sexual Disorders' by Dr G. Rooth; 'Over-Eating' by Dr

J. T. Silverstone; 'Arson' by Dr K. L. Soothill; 'Shoplifting' by Professor T. C. N. Gibbens.

A wider concept of dependence

For many years the notion of drug dependence and addiction remained narrowly focused on the florid external manifestations of the physical withdrawal syndromes of such drugs as the opiates, the barbiturates and alcohol. With growing evidence from self-injection experiments in animals and the realisation that in humans dependence could be equally strong on drugs like cocaine, amphetamines and nicotine, even though there are no dramatic physical effects on withdrawal, emphasis has shifted to the nature of the primary pharmacological reward provided by the dependence-producing drugs. But it is obviously not sufficient to remain fixated on the pharmacological effects of these drugs. Recognition of the equal or greater importance of social and psychological factors in drug dependence has been slow. This can perhaps be better appreciated if consideration is given to such syndromes as compulsive over-eating and compulsive gambling which demonstrate how behavioural syndromes almost identical to those of drug dependence can be produced without an exchange of pharmacological agents. Thus any attempt to construct a unitary theory of drug dependence is unlikely to be complete if the concept of dependence is not widened to include syndromes which do not involve the pharmacological action of drugs.

Professor W. D. M. Paton at the opening of a symposium on Drug Dependence in April 1968 (Paton, 1969) proposed as a working definition that 'drug dependence arises when as a result of giving a drug, forces – physiological, biochemical, social or environmental – are set up which predispose to continued drug use'. It is difficult to see how, in the terms of this definition, drug dependence differs from drug use. Professor Paton seems insufficiently to have stressed the essential point – it is not frequent or continued use so much as difficulty in refraining from use that denotes dependence. One may drink milk, fruit juice, alcohol or any other beverage several times a day over a period of years and not be dependent, provided the substance can be discontinued without discomfort or difficulty; yet a few drinks on occasional evenings if they are not easy to forgo would represent a degree of dependence. Thus it would seem more reasonable to define dependence in the following way:

> The notion of dependence on a drug, object, role, activity or any other stimulus-source requires the crucial feature of negative affect experienced in its absence. The degree of dependence can be equated

with the amount of this negative affect, which may range from mild discomfort to extreme distress, or it may be equated with the amount of difficulty or effort required to do without the drug, object – etc.

This definition is substantially unchanged from one proposed some years ago (Russell, 1971). To get away from the traditionally restricted view of dependence as something linked with physically and socially destructive excessive use of pharmacologically active drugs, it may be helpful to widen the concept in the following ways:

1 *Dependence as a continuum.* This view sees the more severe degrees of dependence or addictions not as discontinuous or differing from ordinary use in anything other than degree along the same dimension. How high a degree of dependence is required before it is labelled as a 'dependence disorder' or an 'addiction' is somewhat arbitrary.

2 *Pharmacological rewards as one of a number of classes of reinforcer.* Pharmacological rewards both primary (e.g., stimulant, euphoriant or anxiety-reducing actions) and acquired (relief or avoidance of physical withdrawal effects) are really no more than one class of reinforcer, just as psychological rewards or social pressures are other classes. The degree of dependence on a particular object or activity is governed by its power as a positive reinforcer rather than the class of reinforcement it provides. Thus strong psychological or social rewards will make for a higher degree of dependence than weak pharmacological ones. If the term addiction is used to denote strong dependence, it need not be restricted to refer only to strong pharmacological needs but could equally apply to strong psychological needs as in the case of addiction to television viewing.

3 *The number of sources of reinforcement.* Apart from the relative value to the subject of the positive reinforcement it provides, the degree of dependence on any one object or class of objects will be determined also by the number of other sources available which are capable of providing the same or acceptable alternative forms of reinforcement. Thus we are not so dependent on coffee if tea is available, not so dependent on success at work if other sources of self-esteem are available, not so dependent on relationships with friends if family is available and vice versa.

4 *The normality of dependence.* A state of dependence is a normal part of human nature. It is abnormal not to suffer over the loss or lack of important objects. Most people are fortunately dependent on a whole array of objects thereby reducing the degree of dependence on any single one of them. Some of the objects and activities on which people are commonly dependent are: drugs (including alcohol and nicotine), motorcars, smart clothes, antiques, animals, people, sport, hobbies, work, clubs, gardening, playing cards, gambling,

music, television, sweet foods, books, newspapers, trees and open spaces, holidays, political and religious activities.

5 *Covert dependence.* Given that we are all dependent to varying degrees on a wide variety of objects and activities, it is only some drugs, some objects and some activities that we attempt, or are *caused* to attempt, to resist or to do without. Unless there is a forced withdrawal or strong motives to desist, such as the danger of physical or social damage or strong social disapproval, a state of dependence may remain hidden. A mild degree of dependence on cannabis or certain palatable foods may be only too apparent because the illegality of the one and the undesired fattening effect of the other, expose the dependence by motivating attempts to control or desist from indulgence. But a high degree of dependence on hard work, music, or gardening may remain hidden in that social approval of such activities makes attempts to desist unlikely, and the difficulty or even impossibility of desisting are consequently seldom exposed. This kind of dependence may even remain covert when the obsessive preoccupation (with work, music, or gardening) is manifestly destructive to family life. Thus in understanding the nature of dependence it is the powerful urge, need, attraction, and the distress or discomfort at the lack of an object or activity, that merits attention. Features such as physical or social damage are epiphenomena that serve to expose the dependent state but are not otherwise part of it.

6 *Relation between dependent and compulsive states.* The generally accepted crucial features of compulsions are that they are unwanted and perceived by the subject (and sometimes by others as well) as silly and alien to his true nature, recognised as irrational, and above all resisted with varying degrees of success or failure. As with dependent states, these notions of silliness and the exercise of resistance depends on the nature of the urge. An impulse to stab or strangle someone is more likely to be successfully resisted and controlled than an equally strong impulse to touch a stranger's hair or add up the numbers on a car number plate. As with a dependent state, the crucial feature of a compulsion is the strength of the underlying urge. The features of its being silly, unwanted, alien and resisted are epiphenomena that depend on the particular compulsion. If it *is* silly, damaging or socially disapproved it will be resisted and exposed as a compulsion. If it is a 'good' or socially approved activity like playing golf, gardening, work or music, it is not resisted and therefore never exposed as a compulsion, despite the fact that the person may be quite unable to desist if called upon to do so. This is where one comes up against the fluctuations of current social values. There are some who would regard social cannabis smoking as more acceptable than an obsession for motor cars, though currently there is more mass approval of the latter. Masturbation used to be a common compulsion among schoolboys

when they were taught that it was bad and might make them mad. Now, with less reason to resist it, it is no longer so likely to be compulsive; yet it is no doubt just as frequent and strong an urge as ever.

It is in the context of this wider if still incomplete view of the nature of dependence that the specific contributions of different sciences might be seen. Only by adopting such a wide approach is it possible to begin to articulate the very different explorations ranging from those of pharmacology to sociology.

18 The alcohologist's addiction: some implications of having lost control over the disease concept of alcoholism*

DAVID ROBINSON

Summary

Acceptance of ill-defined notions may lead to false expectations about the nature of alcoholism, its treatment and prognosis. Five implications of saying that alcoholism is a disease are discussed.

1 Whether the self-defined alcoholic is accepted as such by the medical profession will depend on the congruence of conceptions of disease, and whether the parties use similar crtieria of what constitutes alcoholism.

2 A person defined as an alcoholic may have his prognosis impaired if, according to sick-role theory, the sick person is not regarded as responsible for his condition. There is however a measure of ambiguity here, for while the disease concept relieves the alcoholic of some of the responsibility for his illness, many therapists demand 'motivation' from their patients.

3 Different diseases might serve as models for different conceptions of the disease nature of alcoholism, and usefully structure a person's experience for him. An inappropriate borrowing and thus a setting up of an inappropriate type of medical model, might though be very misleading.

4 Once alcoholism is called a disease, a widening range of behaviours may be seen as related to stages of the disease process. A self-fulfilling prophecy may then invite the individual to move through the designated stages until he reaches rock bottom.

5 The medical profession will be considered as a result of the disease concept to have competence in an ever widening area, and under the heading of prevention will be invited to deal with behaviours which are only suggestive of addiction: it will be placed in a position to act beyond its legitimate area.

The nature of drinking behaviour will be understood and effective treatment provided only if the implications of differing conceptions of 'alcoholism' and 'disease' are taken into account.

* Condensed from a paper which appeared in the *Quarterly Journal of Studies on Alcohol,* vol. 33, 1972, pp. 1028–42.

. . . any label or definition is only a matter of convenience and convention . . . the essential factor is the consistency in connotation.

E. M. Jellinek, 1957

Introduction

Attempts to spell out the nature of the relationship between alcohol consumption, alcoholism and disease have formed a well-established and lively debate. However, as Edwards (1970[b]) points out, 'much of the necessary evidence on which to make a decision as to whether alcoholism is a disease is not yet available, and when all the relevant information on the causes of abnormal drinking has been gathered in, the decision as to alcoholism being a disease will still rest very much on the definition of "alcoholism" on the one hand and of "disease" on the other'. Edwards thus directs our attention to the crucial question for the sociologist, namely the question of what counts as something for particular people in particular social situations and what are the implications of those definitions for social behaviour. Ideas about what counts as alcoholism and what is the nature of its relationship to disease are constantly changing. There has been a discernible and well-documented shift over the past century from considering alcoholism as primarily a legal or moral problem to considering it primarily as one of medicine or public health. Dr Jellinek's seminal contributions to the study of alcohol-related problems have played no small part in focusing our attention upon the core question of what it means to say that alcoholism is a disease. This paper is concerned to set out certain consequences which could follow from operating with a wide-ranging disease concept of alcoholism.

Jellinek and the disease concept of alcoholism

In this much quoted 1952 article Jellinek restricted the application of the disease conception to "addictive drinking" – 'The disease concept of alcohol addiction', he said, 'does not apply to the excessive drinking, but solely to the loss of control which occurs in only one group of alcoholics and then only after many years of excessive drinking . . . the loss of control is a disease condition *per se* which results from a process that superimposes itself upon those abnormal . . . conditions of which excessive drinking is a symptom'.

Not only was Jellinek clear about the precise nature of the disease conception of alcoholism but he was also clear about the need for a restricted definition of alcoholism itself and clear about the harmful consequences which would follow from the 'unwarranted extension' of the conception to all excessive drinking. For 'sooner or later', he believed, such a misapplication would 'reflect on the legitimate use too and, more importantly, will tend to weaken the ethical basis of social sanctions against drunkenness' (Jellinek, 1952). Later, in 'The World and its Bottle' (1957) Jellinek again denied the usefulness of defining as 'alcoholism' everything which, in any culture, is given that label. 'If the term alcoholism is extended to occasional excessive drinkers, as is the case in many countries, one may say with justification that the nature of alcoholism shows marked differences throughout the world. According to the accepted ideas about alcoholism in the Anglo-Saxon countries and even in some Latin countries occasional excessive drinkers – such as weekend or Sunday drinkers who follow a cultural pattern, or "celebrators", and even the explosive occasional relief drinker – would never be regarded as alcoholics.' 'The extension of the term alcoholism to cover all froms of drinking which may occasion damage is not impossible' but 'while such a broad connotation would perhaps eliminate much conflict in international communication on this subject, *it would hardly be a useful means*' (my emphasis).

Perhaps because of his increasing involvement with organisations committeed to 'international communication', Jellinek later reneged on this position and, in 'The Disease Concept of Alcoholism' (1960) used the term alcoholism to refer to 'any use of alcoholic beverage that causes any damage to the individual or to society'. The utility of such a wide-ranging definition of alcoholism, claimed Jellinek, was that it 'forces us to single out species of alcoholism and to speak of them in stringent terms'. While such a strategy might have helped to solve some of Jellinek's problems in 'international communication' it tended to cloud rather than illuminate other related issues. For instance, the five species of the genus alcoholism which Jellinek outlined do not in fact cover the whole range of alcoholism as he defined it. 'The definition of alcoholism, namely that alcoholism is any drinking that leads to any damage, does not permit of designating as alcoholic all those who occasion some kind of damage through their use of alcoholic beverages. I would call alcoholics only those who manifest the alpha, beta, gamma, delta, and epsilon varieties of alcoholism.' Because of the wide-ranging definition of alcoholism and the concomitant fact that 'we cannot say that alcoholics are those who suffer from alcoholism' Jellinek concentrated his attention upon only certain of the alcoholisms when he addressed himself to the question of in what way alcoholism is a disease. His answer to this question was that only gamma 'loss of control' and delta 'inability to abstain' alcoholisms qualify as diseases, because only they are addictions in the pharmacological sense.

Having come to this conclusion Jellinek felt that the next challenging question should concern the pharmacological nature of addiction to which 'the newer techniques in pharmacology, physio-pathology and biochemistry' should be addressed. He considered it was the case that 'if any physiological or biochemical anomaly – which in itself may not seem grave – can strip nervous tissue of its resistance to adaptation of its metabolism to a noxious substance then that adaptation with all its concomitant behavioural changes may be designated as a disease'. This then was what Jellinek hypothesised as the disease nature of alcoholism.

Over the whole body of his writing Jellinek was quite consistent about the distinction which should be maintained between 'alcoholism' as broadly defined and 'the disease nature of alcoholism' restrictively defined as addictive alcoholism. Unfortunately, as Jellinek pointed out, a steadily increasing majority of the medical profession, governments, voluntary associations, and general public accepted 'merely that alcoholism *is* a disease'. *This is the crux of the problem.* Certain things are consequent upon the adoption of a wide-ranging definition of alcoholism and a concomitant acceptance merely that 'alcoholism *is* a disease'. The remainder of this paper is devoted to the identification and discussion of such consequences.

Consequences of accepting a wide-ranging disease concept of alcoholism

'The statement "alcoholism is a disease" is now so widely heard in scientific and lay circles that one can hardly safely begin any undertaking in reference to alcoholism without first repeating it' (Seeley, 1962).

By accepting that 'alcoholism is a disease' an increasing proportion of the general population may, in fact, be coming to operate with quite false and unhelpful expectations and beliefs about the nature of alcoholism and thus also about the nature and role of treatment and its outcome. If they also define alcoholism as as 'any use of alcoholic beverage that causes any damage to the individual or to society' then certain things are consequent. For example:

Consequence 1 A person may define himself as an alcoholic, and thus his condition and behaviour as a medical matter, when the medical profession does not define the situation in that way, and vice versa.
Consequence 2 A person defined as an alcoholic by the medical profession may not be treatable because of the way he conceptualises his responsibility for this disease.
Consequence 3 Different diseases might serve as models for different peoples' conception of the disease nature of alcoholism. Thus a disease which may appropriately serve as a model for addictive alcoholisms may be inappropriate to a wider conception of the disease nature of alcoholism, and vice versa.
Consequence 4 An ever increasing range of conditions and behaviours may

be conceptualised as related to stages in a disease process.
Consequence 5 The medical profession may be considered to have competence in an ever-widening sphere of life.

These consequences, which have clear implications for those whose concern is with prevention, education and treatment, or with the provision of medical and social services associated with alcohol-related problems, are briefly discussed below. To an extent these consequences stem from the acceptance of *any* disease concept of alcoholism, but clearly become more problematic and assume greater significance as a more wide-ranging disease conception is accepted.

Consequence 1: A person may define himself as an alcoholic, and thus his condition and behaviour as a medical matter, when the medical profession does not define the situation in that way, and vice versa

Whether the self-defined alcoholic's definition of himself is accepted as appropriate by the medical profession as a whole, or by the particular member of the profession to whom the matter is presented, will depend upon how inclusive their disease conception of alcoholism is and whether they operate with similar criteria of what counts as alcoholism. If the medical profession operate with a restricted definition of alcoholism and a stereotype of the alcoholic as a 'down and out' recognisable by appearance, manners or loss of social position then this has clear consequences for diagnosis and for their willingness to treat as legitimate the self-defined alcoholic's presented complaint. Blane et al. (1963) have demonstrated that alcoholics not conforming to the popular Skid Row stereotype are missed diagnostically, while (Pattison, 1966) reports that many doctors will not define as an alcoholic a person who is working and retaining his social and economic standards.

However, even if the medical professional's definition is less inclusive than that of a presenting 'alcoholic' certain processes are likely to operate to *in effect* widen the disease conception in any particular case. These processes are inevitable given the medical profession's ethics, the fact that doctors are human beings and thus have a commitment and a general readiness to conceive of any presented complaint as an illness to be treated, or at least as an appeal for help to them *as doctors* to be dealt with in some way. A member of the medical profession may thus be drawn as a *medical* expert into an area which he may feel 'in his bones' does not come within his competence to be expert about. However, the process does not stop here, for *any* intervention, however reluctant, will tend to reinforce an 'erroneous' lay conception of the disease nature of alcoholism. For it, as Jellinek said (1960) 'a disease is what the medical profession recognises as such' then from the lay-man's point of view it is perfectly reasonable to define as a disease 'anything which the medical profession is seen to be willing to deal with in some way'.

When the medical profession accepts a more inclusive definition of alcoholism than does the drinker this also has implications for diagnosis and treatment. In such a situation the drinker is likely to resist any attempts to persuade him that he is an alcoholic, or is exhibiting early symptoms of the disease, if his behaviour does not match up to *his* stereotype of 'an alcoholic'. Thus if, for example, the drinker's definition of the alcoholic is restricted to the Skid Row or 'down and out' stereotype then clearly a successful preventive or early treatment programme will only be initiated with extreme difficulty, while the chances of self-presentation for help at what the medical profession might see as 'an early stage in the disease process' will be remote.

Consequence 2: A person defined as an alcoholic by the medical profession may not be treatable because of the way he conceptualises his responsibility for his condition

Both the general public and the medical profession tend to share certain assumptions about the relationship between disease and individual responsibility. These are that while the individual may have intentionally exposed himself to disease conditions, or behaved in some way which increased his likelihood of contracting a disease, it is not possible once the disease is contracted to get rid of it by will power. Parsons' (1951) discussion of the sick role still informs the majority of sociological work in this field and has been shown to reflect widespread beliefs about the nature of being ill (Robinson, 1971).

On the crucial question of responsibility for the disease or illness condition Parsons has this to say in a section in which he outlines the relationship between illness and deviance: 'By institutional definition of the sick role the person is helpless and therefore in need of help. If being sick is to be regarded as 'deviant', as certainly in important respects it must, it is . . . distinguished from other deviant roles precisely by the fact that the sick person is not regarded as 'responsible' for his condition, 'he can't help it'. Such assumptions are certainly appropriate when applied to a *restricted* definition of the alcoholism 'disease'. For, implied in the notion of 'the addictive drinker' is the idea that once the 'disease' has been contracted it can only be arrested or cured by outside intervention.

However, in the situation where the disease conception has been widened to cover other 'alcoholisms' there are immediate implications for the 'alcoholic', the medical profession and, thus, for treatment. Let us assume that both the doctor and a *non-addictive* drinker accept a wide ranging definition of alcoholism along the lines of that set out by Jellinek, and also accept that alcoholism is a disease. Any attempt by the doctor to persuade 'the alcoholic' to change his drinking habits is likely to fail since he will, by definition, believe himself incapable of doing so. In fact if the medical profession suggest any course of action for 'the alcoholic' which is based upon expectations about the alcoholic's 'will power' or the alcoholic having the right 'motivation' then such a course of action is likely to be unsuccessful if 'the alcoholic' defines out of court the notion of individual responsibility for his condition. Even in the event of the doctor and an *addictive* drinker sharing a *restricted* definition of alcoholism the problems for treatment are no less acute. As well as the drinker being likely to define out of court the responsbility for his condition and drinking behaviour, the expectation of 'will power' not being enough to change drinking behaviour is essentially implied in the very notion of 'loss of control' or 'inability to abstain' addictive drinking.

Siegler, et al. (1968) in their delineation of eight 'Models of Alcoholism' stress the importance of the question of differing conceptualisations of individual responsibility for illness conditions. A belief in the individual responsibility for a condition is one of the key distinctions between the 'old' and the 'new' medical model, while a major component of the Alcoholics Anonymous model as they present it is that it 'lifts the burden of personal responsibility from the shoulders of the alcoholic by persuading him that alcoholism is bigger than he is.' Nevertheless, many of those who attempt to treat addictive drinkers appear to demand that 'the alcoholic' display the 'correct motivation' prior to being allowed to embark upon a treatment programme, while a change in 'motivation' is presented as an essential prerequisite to starting on an upward path to recovery, according to certain diagrammatic representations of alcohol addiction and recovery (e.g., Glatt, 1970).

Consequence 3: Different diseases might serve as models for different peoples' conception of the disease nature of alcoholism. Thus a disease which may appropriately serve as a model for addictive alcoholisms may be inappropriate as a model for a wider conception of the disease nature of alcoholism, and vice versa.

Just as both laymen and professionals may differ in their beliefs about individual responsibility for any illness condition and thus about the nature of appropriate treatment in any case, so they may differ also in their ideas about what other diseases alcoholism approximates to and in what ways. Some people may operate with a quite inappropriate particular disease analogy and thus prejudice the likelihood or outcome of treatment or the possibility of recovery. For example, it would be legitimate but largely unhelpful to operate with an infectious disease model of alcoholism. Expectations as to the course or outcome of alcoholism would clearly be inadequately informed by considering as analogous measles and alcoholism. The ideas which inform our behaviour in any particular situation may be particular, specific and drawn from personal experience. It is quite reasonable therefore, in relation to such an ill-defined notion as alcoholism for people to structure their experience in alcohol-related situations by reference to those diseases and disease features which they find manageable, understandable, and which have served adequately in previous experiences with illness and disease. It is not the aim of this section to set out the implications of operating with every known disease as a model for alcoholism, nor is there any attempt to identify the range of particular disease models which implicitly or explicitly underlie the main body of medical and lay thought on alcoholism. Such challenging enterprises are quite beyond the scope of this paper. However, it is possible to indicate, quite briefly, some of the incompatible notions about 'alcoholism' and 'the alcoholic' which could stem from the widespread use of specific disease models.

If, for instance, the measles model were adopted it would be reasonable to expect one self-limiting bout of 'alcoholism' to confer immunity from further attacks. If such a view were held this would have definite implications for the alcoholic's readiness to consult initially, and also his readiness to give up drinking as part of any treatment or recovery programme. For what would be the point of abstaining if immunity to 'the disease' had been obtained? If, on the other hand, 'the alcoholic' conceived of alcoholism as a disease like bronchitis then an acute attack, possibly culminating in a period of detoxification, might be thought to have weakened the tissues in some way and made the body more susceptible to subsequent acute attack. However, it is reasonable in the bronchitis case to assume that in the interval between acute attacks the person is free from the disease. This notion is strictly at variance with a basic tenet of, for example, the Alcoholics Anonymous philosophy which encourages its members, and the general public, to believe that alcoholism is a disease which once contracted can never be cured. The most that can be hoped for is that the condition is arrested. Alcoholics Anonymous would seem to operate with the conception of alcoholism as a disease rather like cancer or diabetes which it is not in the individual's power to get rid of. However, there is also the belief that if the individual acts in a particular way (takes a drink) then the disease will *inevitably* re-manifest itself. While this view is largely consistent with the diabetes model it neither accords with the cancer conception of disease nor with the evidence concerning the many 'alcoholics' who have returned to 'normal drinking' (Davies, 1962. Kendell, 1965; Pattison et al., 1968).

The only way to square this latter incompatibility is to argue that such people were not *really* alcoholics. As in the case of any problem of definition or categorisation such a tautology is hardly useful.

Consequence 4: An ever increasing range of conditions and behaviour may be conceptualised and related to stages in a disease process.

If a member of the general public accepts that alcoholism, widely defined, is a disease then it will be perfectly reasonable for him to be on the look out for signs or symptoms of early stages in an assumed disease process. Such a strategy is encouraged by charts like Jellinek's (1952) and Glatt's (1970) which foster the notion of alcoholism as a 'developmental process' (Glatt, 1970) marked by 'phases and sequences of symptoms' (Jellinek, 1952). A member of the general public, thus bolstered in his strategy, is likely to assume that one stage in the 'developmental process' follows inevitably after another. This assumption is reasonable since it is consistent with the way in which many people conceptualise disease processes; for instance, 'once you've got it, its got to run its course'. Consequently if one stage is believed to follow another and if, for example, 'heavy habitual social drinking' is felt to be a symptom of one stage of the disease process (as it might be if a wide-ranging definition of alcoholism is accepted) then it is reasonable for the drinker to believe that there is no way of preventing his progression through the subsequent stages of the process until 'rock bottom' is reached. This again is reasonable since 'it has to get worse before it gets better' is a familiar and appropriate notion when applied to certain other diseases. It is hardly surprising, therefore, that the heavy social drinker should continue to drink if, first, he has been led to believe that an alcoholic cannot stop because he is addicted, and, second, he believes that he is an alcoholic and has a disease in which stages inevitably follow one another until rock bottom is reached. There is no reason to suppose that such a self-fulfilling prophecy mechanism should not operate in respect of alcoholism in the same way as it has been so clearly demonstrated to operate in relation to streaming and scholastic attainment in the field of education (Douglas, 1964).

Consequence 5: The medical profession will be considered to have competence in an ever-widening sphere of life.

Once the disease conception of alcoholism is extended to include the behaviours concomitant with the addiction or concomitant with the physical damage caused by alcohol consumption then there will be an inevitable extension of medical competence into an ever-widening sphere of life. This will take place under the heading of 'preventive medicine'. It is implicit in such a phrase that the medical profession will *treat* not only disease entities but behaviours considered to be part of a causal chain leading to the development of disease entities. Once this position is accepted by the general population then the medical profession is obliged to advise about, or intervene in relation to, any behaviour which falls into such a category. In the case of alcoholism, the medical profession would consider themselves, and be considered by the general public, as the relevant authority to decide upon, for example, licensing laws or alcohol price policy if it was shown that alcohol price increases and shorter licensing hours were associated with a drop in alcohol consumption. The idea that a time might come when the Medical Officer of Health would decide upon the licensing hours in a particular area should not be thought of as impossible or even extremely unlikely. For the idea that anything which is considered to affect in some way the working of the body or mind is 'a medical problem' and thus within the jurisdiction of the medical profession is happily applied in other spheres. Medicine is readily seen to be a legitimate arbiter in cases of clashes of values or political principle; witness the abortion controversy and the history of the fluoridation campaigns in the United States (Zola, 1972).

It is not being suggested that the medical profession or the many other helping agencies concerned with alcohol-related problems are coolly calculating empire-builders plotting to take control over vast areas of late twentieth century life. What is being maintained is that the general public and legislators are placing these agencies, and the medical profession in particular, in a position in which they are expected to exercise their discretionary powers and perform decision-making functions, arguably, beyond their legitimate and willingly accepted brief.

Conclusion

'No area of medicine is so bedevilled by semantic confusion as is the field of alcoholism'. (Davies, 1969).

Jellinek was very clear about what he considered to be the disease nature of alcoholism. He restricted the notion of disease to the loss of control and inability to abstain aspects of excessive drinking because they were addictions in the pharmacological sense. His definition of the broader concept of 'alcoholism' was much more wide-ranging as time went on. In 'The Disease Concept of Alcoholism' (Jellinek, 1960) it became 'any use of alcoholic beverage that causes any damage to the individual or society'. In addition, more and more people were coming to accept the view that 'alcoholism *is* a disease'. Since he was certainly the world's foremost authority on alcohol-related problems Jellinek must be held partly responsible for a much more inclusive disease conception of alcohol being held by the general public than the held himself. Certain consequences have been shown to follow from accepting a definition of alcoholism such as Jellinek's and from also accepting that alcoholism is a disease. These consequences are not set out as good things or bad things, for such questions are beyond the scope of this paper, but rather as social facts of current life.

If we are to understand and predict the nature of drinking behaviour and subsequently provide effective treatment for those considered to need such help this can only be done if we take into account the implications of peoples' differing conceptions of what counts as 'alcoholism' and what counts as 'disease'. For typification, perceiving the world and structuring it by means of categorical types is the essence of social communication and interaction. Thus, the aim of this paper has been first to suggest that we have to a certain extent 'lost control' over the disease concept of alcoholism, and second to indicate some of the implications of this 'addiction' for 'the alcoholic', for the medical profession, and for the wider society.

19 Aspects of the relationship between alcohol and drug abuse*

JIM ORFORD

Summary

An attempt is made to describe the nature of psychological dependence as being something which is not specific to any one substance. Psychological dependence is said to be manifest to the extent that an individual or others acting on his behalf experience difficulty in desisting from or preventing a given behaviour, when the given object or class of objects is still available. Drug dependence can only be said to exist in so far as pressure is put on the individual or some incentive offered him to reduce his drug taking. Such pressures may have their origin in cost, interference or risk.

A conflict, decision making approach to drug dependent behaviour is proposed which depicts future drug use in terms of a pay-off decision matrix where the cell entries represent anticipated favourable and unfavourable consequences of continued drug use. Two elements needing further specification in such a matrix are the values placed on each of the expected outcomes and their probability.

It is suggested that many of the features characteristic of drug users result from their defence of the decision to continue drug use in a conflict situation (i.e. a situation of high cognitive dissonance) – a persistence which can only be effected by distorting the entries in the pay-off matrix. The processes of selective exposure, selective perception and selective recall facilitate such distortion as does the tendency either to revalue outcomes or alter the perception of their probability. Alternatively, and perhaps additionally the individual may resolve the conflict by disclaiming all responsibility for making a decision.

The treatment implications of such a model are discussed in terms of the literature on attitude change and the probability that most decisions regarding drug use are taken without resort to expert opinion. Finally a number of testable predictions from the model are outlined and some evidence bearing on them reviewed.

---

* Proceedings, 29th International Congress on Alcoholism and Drug Dependence, Sydney, Australia, Butterworth Press, 1971

Introduction

The rationale for discussing both alcoholism and the abuse of other drugs together at the same congress clearly lies in the concept of drug dependence. The value of focusing attention upon drug dependence in general rather than upon dependence on any one drug is that it may help us to investigate, and therefore to understand, the underlying process of becoming dependent on a drug rather than continuing to pursue the more limited concern with the alcoholic or the heroin addict stereotypes. Already, being forced to look at the wider issue has resulted in the decreasing popularity of the term addiction and the increasing popularity of the word dependence. The decision of the World Health Organisation and others to shift its terminology in this way was presumably due to an increasing awareness of the great variation in the addictive properties of different drugs.

It seems that there is a convergence of opinion towards the idea that the essence of our concern with drugs as different as the opiates, the barbiturates, the amphetamines, alcohol, cannabis and nicotine, is the idea of psychological dependence. If this is so, then it follows that it should be of higher priority to study the general phenomenon of psychological dependence than specific dependences. This is particularly important now that we recognise that psychological dependence may develop to a large and increasing number of drugs and that as fashions and laws change so patterns of dependence may change also.

Attempting a definition of psychological dependence

In attempting to define psychological dependence I believe that it is important to avoide setting an arbitrary cut-off point between dependent behaviour and non-dependent behaviour. Often, in labelling behaviour as dependent behaviour, we insist that the behaviour must be of at least a certain frequency or that the object of the behaviour must be consumed in at least certain quantities or, more commonly, that the behaviour must cause harm or damage of at least a certain degree. It may be preferable to say that whenever an organism continues to consume, or approach frequently, an 'object' or class of 'objects', including any drug or drugs, then that organism is to some degree psychologically dependent on that object or class of objects. In other words, we are all to some extent dependent upon all the substances we continue to consume and are to some extent dependent upon all the people or objects that we continue to approach or make use of. To clinicians this definition may not seem very useful but on the other hand it may be more useful to have a definition which enables us to recognise all manner of patterns of dependence, rather than to attempt to define a clinical syndrome in terms of the presence or absence of signs and symptoms that may be seen not to exist at all once one looks beyond the immediate preoccupations with a limited subclass of dependence on a particular drug.

The argument here is that psychological dependence is not an all-or-none thing; there are degrees of it. Furthermore it is suggested that the degree of psychological dependence is shown by the amount of difficulty experienced by the individual himself, or by others, in getting the individual to desist from this behaviour when the object or class of objects that he is consuming or approaching is still available to him. In other words, although we are dependent on many things, some are more dependent on some things than others and the degree of dependence is shown by the amount of pressure which must be applied against the behaviour in order for it to stop. Another way of putting the same thing is to ask how high the incentive for stopping the consumption of a particular drug need be in order to persuade an individual to stop. Someone who drinks 20 cups of tea a day is dependent on tea but we might persuade him to give up his tea drinking by offering him a lower incentive than would be necessary to persuade the smoker who smokes 20 cigarettes a day to give that up; the degree of psychological dependence in the latter case would then have been shown to be greater than in the former.

It must be admitted that this definition is in the behaviouristic rather than the mentalistic tradition (Keehn, 1968) based as it is upon the interaction of, on the one hand, readily observable approaching and consuming behaviour and, on the other hand, readily observable reinforcements and incentives. A popular alternative is to define psychological dependence in terms of the subjective experience of compulsion or lack of control over behaviour. This not only has the disadvantage of reliance upon an experience which is subjective and not directly observable but in addition it could be argued that this experience of feeling 'hooked' is a function of many complex and little understood mental processes, quite apart from the behaviour to which the feeling refers.

The central role of pressures against drug taking for a definition of drug dependence

It follows from the definition being offered here that drug dependence can only be seen to exist to the degree that pressure is put upon individual, or some incentive offered him to reduce his drug taking.

The major sources of such pressure could probably be categorised in many different ways; two such methods of classification will be suggested here. First, pressures or incentives to reduce drug use may have their source in cost, interference or risk.

(a) The cost of resources spent in acquiring and consuming the drug. These resources may be time or money or less tangible resources such as the individual's conformity to his own or others' moral or legal code.

(b) Interference with other activities of the individual or of others, due to the consumption or the effects of consumption of the drug. The regular consumption in large quantities of certain drugs is incompatible with the carrying out of activities necessary to the fulfilling of certain role obligations which society may expect the individual to fulfil. The amount of pressure upon the individual to modify his drug-taking behaviour which comes from this source depends very much on the particular roles which any particular individual is required to fulfil.

(c) The perception of a risk of future discomfort due to the effects of the drug. For example, pressure will be applied to an individual to modify his drug-taking behaviour if he perceives or if others perceive, that by continuing his drug use he runs the risk of future illness.

An alternative classification might be in terms of whether the pressures to reduce drug use are self-generated or generated by others.

The exact sources of pressure put upon an individual to modify his drug use depend not only upon his social role, such as whether he is married or not, the job he does and the values and goals of his peers, but also upon the particular drug which he is using. A large alcohol consumption, for example, may result in pressures of the interference type, both self- and other-generated; due to the depressant effect of alcohol such a large consumption would be incompatible with other activities which the individual would like to perform and which others expect him to perform. Failure to perform these activities results in pressure being put upon the individual to alter his drinking habits. Smoking of tobacco may result in pressures of the risk type predominantly; the smoker himself or his close relatives and friends may be increasingly aware of the risk to health of continuing to consume this particular drug in this particular way. It seems that the consumption of opiates may result in pressures of all types, although it is by no means clear to what extent these pressures are the result of legal systems which make the acquiring of the drug a very costly business or to what extent the risks to health are due to currently fashionable ways of consuming the drug and to what extent the pressures which arise against continuing opiate use are a consequence of the intrinsic properties of the drug.

The major point here is that these pressures to modify drug use, whatever their source, are not merely secondary to the primary process of dependence but are in fact essential to our understanding of dependence itself. We can only speak of a person's drug-using behaviour as being dependent, to the degree that the behaviour remains unchanged despite a certain degree of pressure. If the pressures so far brought to bear upon an individual's drug-taking behaviour are only slight then we may only speak of slight dependence; if pressures brought to bear have been moderate and still the behaviour is unmodified then we may speak of moderate dependence. We may not speak of severe dependence until it can be seen that the behaviour remained unchanged despite great pressure.

A conflict, decision-making theoretical approach to drug-dependent behaviour

The situation in which the drug-dependent individual finds himself is one of conflict between opposing motivational forces, his motivation towards continued use of the drug being opposed by the pressures against it. The situation can be thought of as one in which the individual is required to make a decision about which of these opposing motivations he is to respond to. An appropriate representation of the position is that in Fig. 19.1 which shows the four cells of a two by two pay-off decision matrix.

	Discontinue Use	Continue Use
Positive	Respect from non-users 1	2 Relief of anxiety
Negative	3 Disrespect from users	4 Premature death

Fig. 19.1 Hypothetical pay-off decision matrix concerning future drug use

Entries in the four cells of the matrix represent anticipated favourable consequences of discontinuing use of the drug (such as an increase in the respect which non-users of the drug have for the individual), favourable consequences of continuing (such as relief of anxiety or withdrawal symptoms), negative consequences of discontinuing (such as increasing disrespect from other users) and negative consequences of continuing (such as the risk of premature death, vocational failure, etc.). Entries in the first and last cells (top left and bottom right) constitute reasons for stopping the abuse of the drug whereas entries in the second and third cells (top right and bottom-left) constitute reasons for carrying on. The individual himself may be unable to give complete verbal expression to all the entries in the matrix; in particular he may be unable to verbalise all the entries in the cell that represents the positive consequences of continuing the abuse. The model depicted in Fig. 19.1 is probably over-simplified in that it assumes only two alternative solutions.

Janis and Mann (1968) have proposed a similar decision-making model which they illustrate with what they describe as a balance sheet of conflicting outcomes or pay-offs verbalised by a smoker whose complacent attitude has been challenged by publicity about the American Surgeon-General's report on smoking and lung cancer.

A more precise picture of the elements in the decision-making of an individual faced with a decision whether to carry on with his drug taking or not, might be obtained by determining for each item in the pay-off matrix two parameters which form an essential part of most decision-making theories (Feather, 1959). First, can we be more precise about the value that the individual puts upon each expected outcome? So far, each expected outcome has been categorised merely as positive or negative. Certain expected outcomes will surely be more important to the person than others and those that are more highly valued, either positively or negatively, will have a proportionately greater influence upon decision-making and hence should be given greater weight. To what extent does the individual value the approval of non-users of his drug, the approval which he is losing as a result of his continued drug use and the approval which he expects to regain if he chooses to discontinue his drug use? How important is it to him that he avoids the unpleasant feeling of anxiety or depression which he expects to avoid by continuing his drug use and which he expects to experience if his drug use were to stop?

The second thing which we should know about each item appearing on the balance sheet is just how probable the individual perceives this outcome to be if he adopts the solution to this problem which he expects will lead to that outcome. What exactly is the perceived probability of the drug user's wife leaving him if he continues with his drug use; what exactly is the perceived probability of dying within a specific period of time through an overdose? If we could assign a number to both the value of an outcome and the perceived probability of an outcome then perhaps we might be in a position to predict what solution an individual would make in the conflict situation created by these opposing motives. Decision-making theorists have suggested that the importance of an expected outcome in determining a decision is proportional to its value multiplied by its perceived probability. This means that the eventual decision will depend particularly on items on the balance sheet which have high value to the individual and which he perceives to be much more probable following one decision than another.

The importance of defending decisions

At any one time, the ongoing behaviour of a drug user will correspond to one or other of the possible solutions to his decision-making problem, although the amount of commitment to that solution will vary. The individual will either be carrying on as before or he will have stopped or he will be carrying on but in some modified way. I would suggest that many of the features which we believe to be characteristic of drug users are in fact the results of defending the decision to continue with drug use in the situation of conflict represented by the pay-off decision matrix or balance sheet. In a situation of intense conflict, whatever decision is made, it must have been made in the face of considerable oppositional pressure. If the individual continues with his drug use, then he must do this knowing that there are some highly positively valued and highly probable outcomes which he is jeopardising and some highly negatively valued and probable outcomes of which he runs the risk. The situation is one of high cognitive dissonance, that is, a situation in which any individual has behaved in a way that he knows to be contrary to ideas or beliefs he holds about such behaviour. The theory of cognitive dissonance (Festinger, 1957) suggests that in itself cognitive dissonance is a source of discomfort to the individual who is thus motivated to reduce this state of discomfort in some way. Having made the decision to behave in a particular way, the individual has no option but to reduce this uncomfortable state of dissonance by altering his ideas, beliefs or notions concerning this behaviour. The greater the commitment which the individual has made to his behavioural choice, the greater the need for modification of his attitudes. This can only mean that the individual must in some way distort the evidence provided by the composition of the pay-off decision matrix or balance sheet. In other words, he must falsify the evidence. It is the contention of this paper that much of the behaviour of drug-dependent persons is a direct result of their attempt to falsify the evidence in an effort to reduce the discomfort which arises when they commit themselves to continue with drug use despite the evidence against doing so. Rational men would stop using the drug, presented with this evidence; they have not stopped. The discomfort engendered by an awareness of this discrepancy can only be reduced by distorting the evidence.

This distortion may be brought about by any one or more of at least three processes. It will be apparent that these processes are in many ways similar to the defence mechanisms with which clinicians will be only too familiar.

1 First, the processes of *selective exposure, selective perception* and *selective recall* may be used in order to deny or to minimise the reality of harmful consequences of continued drug use. By exposing himself to people or literature that minimise the harmful consequences of continued drug use and

by avoiding exposure to people and literature that maximise the same and by selectively perceiving and recalling those parts of all communications on the subject that the individual receives which support continued drug use, the individual concerned may construct his own balance sheet or pay-off matrix which would look very different from the one constructed by a dispassionate observer. A special form of selective perception and selective recall is provided by the use of fantasy or cognitive rehearsal. A person intent on continued drug use may repeatedly fantasise situations in which use of his favourite drug has led to relief of unpleasant feelings and hence perhaps to more effective social behaviour. On the other hand he may be less likely to fantasise the possible harmful consequences. This may be a particularly powerful way of distorting the evidence and hence providing support for the decision to continue using the drug.

2 Secondly it may be possible to detract from the importance of certain selected items on the balance sheet by arguing either that they are less highly valued than they really are or by maintaining that they are more or less probable than they really are. These mechanisms can perhaps all be described as *rationalisations,* and it is possible, for every pay-off decision matrix, to construct a complementary rationalisation matrix as in Fig. 19.2, each item of which is a rationalisation of the equivalent item in the pay-off decision matrix.

	Discontinue Use	Continue Use
Positive	Non-users will fail to respect 1	2 Anxiety is created by drug use
Negative	3 Respect from users not important	4 Premature death unlikely

Fig. 19.2 Hypothetical rationalisation matrix concerning future drug use

So far all the processes of selective exposure, perception or recall and rationalisation may be thought of as altering either the perceived value or the perceived probability of items in the pay-off matrix.

3 A third mechanism used in support of the decision to continue is of a rather different kind. The person who has chosen to continue his use of a drug despite pressures against continued use may accept all the items in the pay-off matrix that represent reasons for discontinuing his use and may accept the values and probabilities a dispassionate observer would place upon them but may justify his continued use on the grounds that his behaviour is outside the

realm of decision-making altogether. The individual may opt out of responsibility for making a decision on the grounds that he is subject to forces beyond his control. He may project blame on to others and say that he is driven to behave in the way he does by other people or perhaps, more commonly, he may claim to be driven by an inner compulsion whose source he is unaware of and which he cannot understand. This particular mechanism for supporting continued drug use is one in which professional workers are particularly likely to collude and which is made readily available for the individual drug user's needs by clinical notions of dependent behaviour as a sickness or as something qualitatively different from non-dependent consuming behaviour.

So far the operation of the mechanisms for distorting the pay-off decision matrix have been illustrated with the example of an individual who has committed himself to continue with his drug use. However, there is no reason why the process should be in any way different in kind for the individual who has committed himself to stopping his drug use; selective exposure, recall and perception and rationalisation should operate so as to minimise or deny those elements of the decision matrix which constitute reasons for carrying on with drug use, whilst maximising or bolstering those elements which constitute reasons for discontinuing use.

So far suggestions have been made about what happens to drug-dependent individuals who make a firm decision one way or the other about their drug use. What happens to individuals who are unable to come to any such firm decision, who are unable to make a firm commitment? Most drug-dependent people who become the concern of treatment agencies are probably at this stage. The only difference may be that commitments made by people at this stage do not last very long; decisions arrived at are quickly reversed. None the less, the processes of defensive distortion may be much the same in support of a decision that lasts only 24 hours as they are in support of a decision which lasts for years. The person at this stage of ambivalence may support those elements of the decision matrix that constitute reasons for carrying on his drug use at one minute and at the next he may minimise those same elements but support instead those clements which favour discontinuing. The decision made at any one time by an individual in this ambivalent stage will depend very much upon circumstances. It will presumably depend, among other things, upon whether he is experiencing withdrawal symptoms at the time or whether he is experiencing particular anxieties which he has learnt are relieved by his drug of choice. Presumably it will also depend upon the company he finds himself in; in the company of other users of the same drug a decision to go on using and hence to support his decision by defensive distortion will be more likely than when the individual is in the company of non-users such as perhaps his family, his counsellor or his psychiatrist. The result will be extreme unreliability and unpredictability of behaviour and expressed attitudes. This is to be understood as a direct consequence of the conflict engendered when behaviour of a highly dependent nature is opposed and the dependent individual is unable to come to any long-term decision.

Implications for the modification of drug-dependent behaviour

One advantage of considering drug-dependent behaviour as a problem in decision-making, is that it may help us to see our efforts at modification or treatment in proper perspective. It follows from the previous arguments that we are really in business to help people make decisions about their future conduct; maybe the essence of what we try to do with drug-dependent people is that we try to persuade them to see their balance sheet in our way. Indeed, when we diagnose or label an individual as alcoholic or drug-dependent what we are doing is making an interpretation or a summary of the individual's pay-off matrix or balance sheet. What we mean when we say someone is drug-dependent is that after talking and listening carefully to the individual concerned and perhaps to other people who know him well, we have drawn up what we see as being the balance sheet of his life in relationship to his particular drug and, having done that, we have come to the conclusion that he would be better off if he were to adopt the solution of giving up his drug. We may choose to convey the idea that we have spotted the signs and symptoms of an illness syndrome, that we have made a medical diagnosis, but that does not alter the fact that what we have really done is to offer assistance with the individual's decision-making problem.

This should surely make us all think very carefully about the interpretations of other people's pay-off matrices that we are inclined to make after only very brief acquaintance. Why is it that drug-dependent people so frequently disagree with the interpretation of their balance sheet that we offer? In most cases, it may be because of the processes of defensive distortion outlined above; in such cases an assessment should clearly be made of the particular distortions being used, so that a rational attack upon these defences may be made. In other cases the dependent individual may genuinely disagree with us about the values and probabilities to be assigned to the various possible outcomes. In that case perhaps we should consider whether the solution to the decision problem which we are offering is the only one available. Maybe there are certain categories of drug-dependent people for whom total abstinence from their drug of choice is not the best solution. As our notions of dependence broaden, this category of people, for whom the obvious solution may not be the simplest, may increase.

A further implication for modification concerns the nature of our attempt at persuading a person to see things our way. Much theoretical work on attitude change has concerned itself with the question of whether one-sided or two-sided communications are the more effective in changing people's attitudes. By a two-sided communication is meant a form of persuasion which brings up arguments against the point of view being advocated and in the course of the communication attempts to deal with them rationally. A one-sided communication, on the other hand, makes no attempt to deal with opposing arguments and merely puts forward as persuasively as possible the point of view being advocated. The findings are that more intelligent people are persuaded to the point of view advocatd after hearing two-sided communications and that, quite apart from intelligence, people who have themselves some prior knowledge of the issue concerned are more persuaded again by two-sided communications. It is a strong impression that, in general, professional communications on the subject of drug dependence and the solution to it tend to be one-sided. The decision-making model of drug dependence suggests that a drug-dependent person is extremely familiar with all sides of the arguments concerning the solutions which he might adopt towards his drug-taking, even though he may for some considerable time perceive certain aspects of the arguments in only a distorted way. None the less, it seems reasonable to argue that the drug-dependent person himself is the one most familiar with all the arguments in his particular case; he himself is the expert. This suggests that once we have decided what solution to the problem we think the drug-dependent person should adopt, we should attempt to persuade him of this by communicating in a two-sided fashion. This means we should not try to present a picture of a pay-off matrix as distorted as the one perceived by the person himself but in the opposite direction, but that we should admit recognition of the positive value of drug use for the individual. For if our interpretation of the matrix is correct then the evidence is on our side.

The final implication for treatment or modification is that we, as the professional decision-makers, should not overvalue our own role in the decision-making process. Most people do not need expert help when taking decisions about their future conduct; logically, the same applies to decisions made about the use or non-use of drugs. However the model presented here suggests that there must be many people who decide to change their drug-using habits without resort to expert assistance. Strangely enough, the model suggests that this might happen particularly when drug use is progressive – progressive in the sense that the negative or harmful consequences of continued drug use increase cumulatively as time goes on. In such cases, the solution of stopping drug use should become more obviously the rational solution as time passes. We are not in a position to know how frequently it occurs that a person stops his drug use spontaneously as time goes on and as the harmful consequences of his continued use increase, although Winick (1962), in proposing the notion of 'maturing out' in relation to opiate dependence, has suggested that it may be very frequently and the same has recently been hinted at by Drew (1968) in relation to alcoholism. Even if the drug-dependent person makes a commitment to continue with his drug use and distortion of his perceived pay-off matrix occurs, there must be a limit to the amount of distortion of reality of which each individual is capable. Depending on his degree of dependence upon the drug and his individual capacity for defensive distortion, if harmful consequences continue to accumulate, the time must come when cognitive dissonance can no longer be adequately reduced and the individual becomes susceptible to attitude and behaviour change and receptive to communications that advocate new solutions to his problem. If dissonance reduction by distortion produces some sort of strain analogous to the strain in an extended spring, then we might suppose that when this method of dissonance reduction finally fails the change might be dramatic. Certainly in the case of alcoholism, dramatic and unpredicted changes in behaviour seem frequently to occur, not uncommonly in association with some change in religious belief or observance. Again we are not in a position to know the frequency of conversions which occur spontaneously without our assistance accompanied by a change in drug-using habits.

Testable predictions from the model

Finally a number of predictions can be made on the basis of the model presented in this paper. It is a truism that theoretical models should not be thought of as necessarily representing the whole truth but should rather be thought of as useful aids to investigation. The ultimate test of a theory is whether it can make fairly precise predictions which can be tested. The following predictions might be made from the conflict, decision-making model of drug dependence.

1 The probability of change in an individual's drug-using behaviour will depend upon the balance of incentives in the pay-off decision matrix as perceived by the individual at that time. It will not depend on the absolute size of any one component of the matrix. To be more precise, looking at Fig. 19.3 where the probability of each outcome is represented by p and the value of each outcome by v, the probability of change will be proportional to the sum of the products of p and v in the top left and bottom right quadrants minus the

	Discontinue	Continue
+	$p_1^1 \times v_1^1 = (pv)_1^1$ $p_1^2 \times v_1^2 = (pv)_1^2$	$p_2^1 \times v_2^1 = (pv)_2^1$ $p_2^2 \times v_2^2 = (pv)_2^2$
−	$p_3^1 \times v_3^1 = (pv)_3^1$ $p_3^2 \times v_3^2 = (pv)_3^2$	$p_4^1 \times v_4^1 = (pv)_4^1$ $p_4^2 \times v_4^2 = (pv)_4^2$

Probability of discontinuing use

$$= (pv)_1^1 + (pv)_1^2 \ldots + (pv)_4^1 + (pv)_4^2 \ldots - (pv)_2^1 - (pv)_2^2 \ldots - (pv)_3^1 - (pv)_3^2$$

Fig. 19.3 Predictions from the conflict, decision-making model concerning the probability of change in drug use

sum of the products of p and v in the top right and bottom left quadrants. In other words, the probability of a change in drug-taking behaviour depends on the strength of the incentive for changing minus the strength of the incentive for carrying on without change. A study by Keutzer (1968) concerning the prediction of success in a smoking treatment programme has gone some way towards the use of a measure based upon the balance of motivational forces as a possible predictor of behavioural change. Keutzer asked her cigarette smokers to estimate the age at which they expected to die, firstly if they continued to smoke and secondly if they stopped smoking; by subtracting the two she obtained smokers' own estimates of the number of years of their lives they expected to lose as a result of continuing to smoke. In addition she presented her smokers with 18 statements which she described as rationalisations. Three examples were 'I have to smoke to relieve my nerves'; 'everybody's entitled to one weakness'; 'the emotional effects of going without cigarettes are more hazardous to me than smoking'. Keutzer subtracted the number of rationalisations which the smokers agreed to from the number of years they expected to lose as a result of continuing to smoke and related the resulting index to eventual change in smoking habits. Of 22 predictor variables this index was the only one significantly related to reduction in cigarette smoking as a result of the treatment programme offered.

2 It follows from the first prediction that, if the incentive for carrying on the drug use is held constant, then the more harm that is being caused by drug use, the greater the probability of change. In other words, as the consequences of an individual's drug use get worse and worse, so long as there is not a corresponding increase in the incentives for continuing to use the drug, the probability of the individual's drug use changing will increase. This may be in

line with Winick's theory of the maturing out of opiate dependence and might go some way towards explaining why, in alcoholism treatment studies, youthfulness and recency of onset have not been found to be good prognostic indicators (Edwards and Guthrie, 1967). It may also help to explain the popularity of the alcoholism folklore idea of reaching 'rock bottom'.

3 If drug use continues unchanged despite increasing harm to the individual or to others, then there will be an increasing probability of the use of mechanisms of defensive distortion of the pay-off decision matrix in support of the decision to continue with drug use. This should be reflected in the individual's under-estimation of the quantity and frequency of his own drug use, an under-estimation of the cost of his drug use in terms of money, time, unfulfilled role obligations and other types of damage. In addition it should be reflected in a tendency for over-estimation of the positive consequences of drug use such as the adequacy of the drug-user's social performance after ingestion of the drug. These tendencies towards under- or over-estimation might be demonstrated by comparing the report of drug use and its consequences given by the drug-user himelf with objective observations or with reports given by family or others who might be expected to be in a position to report on certain aspects of drug use and its consequences.

4 The probability of drug use continuing unchanged, despite increasing negative consequences, will be related to the drug-user's capacity for this sort of defensive distortion. If continued drug use is in any way related to personality then the important personality characteristics might be expected to be concerned with the ability to adopt the processes of defensive distortion outlined above. This might help to explain why one of the most striking findings on personality in the field of alcoholism for example, is that of Witkin (1965), who demonstrated that various groups of alcoholic patients score highly on a test of something he calls 'field dependence' which is a characteristic which he considers to be highly related to capacity for using the defensive mechanism of denial. It may be that, in the past, in looking for personality correlates of drug abuse, we have looked too much in the direction of unpleasant feelings, such as anxiety, which might be relieved by drug use, not realising that the groups of drug users we see are not only drug-users but people who have continued with drug use despite the harm it has caused them and that the characteristics which distinguish them from other people may therefore be the characteristics which have allowed them to continue with behaviour which is maladaptive.

5 The closer the balance of incentives as seen by the drug user himself the greater the variability of drug use and the greater the unreliability of expressed opinion and attitude. In more precise terms, variation in one person's drug use from occasion to occasion, from day to day, or from week to week, and

unreliability of the opinions he expresses about the consequences of his drug use, will be related to the closeness with which the sum of the products of p and v in the top left and bottom right quadrants of the pay-off matrix equals in size the sum of the products of p and v in the other two quadrants. In other words, the more ambivalent a person is about his drug use, the more variable his drug use will be and the greater the unpredictability of what he says from time to time about his drug use.

6 When change in a person's drug use does occur, distortion of the pay-off matrix will occur in the opposite direction, that is, there will be a tendency to minimise the positive value of the drug and a tendency to maximise the harm it has caused. The amount of this distortion will be related to the amount of distortion defending drug use which took place before change occurred. In plain terms, the more defensive an individual has been about his drug use before he changed the more defensive he will be about his behaviour after he has changed.

7 When attempting to influence the drug-using behaviour of an individual, the content of the communication directed towards that individual which will be most efficacious in producing change will be related to the form and content of the pay-off decision matrix concerning drug use as perceived and expressed by the individual. This means that in individual cases an analysis should be made of the mechanisms of defence being used. One suggestion here is that two-sided communications might be more efficacious than one-sided communications particularly when the individual concerned is of higher educational achievement and has not distorted his balance sheet beyond the point at which he ceases to be aware of conflicting incentives.

20 Towards a Social Psychology of Dependence*

A. N. OPPENHEIM

Summary

This paper applies some theories from within the field of social psychology (in particular dissonance theory) to a consideration of dependence. In the general sense dependence is seen as the common human condition: we strive for the myth of independence. Drug takers will be disapproved of particularly because they mock at society's honoured myths. Drug taking may however be seen as a functional, even if disapproved, approach to dissonance reduction. The varied manners in which drugs might achieve this end are set out in a diagram and contrasted with the socially legitimate solutions. Implications for treatment and prevention are discussed.

Introduction

The problem of dependency on drugs or other substances has not so far attracted wide attention among social psychologists. There is no psychological theory of dependency and the present paper does no more than apply some selected general theories within the field of social psychology (in particular, dissonance theory) to the particular problem area of dependence.

Given the present state of knowledge, it would seem premature to try to produce an over-arching model or theory of the dependence process. The possible requirements of such a model would have to include at least the following:

(a) conceptualisation of dependency phenomena
(b) initial development of dependency
(c) continued dependency, tolerance and escalation, and loss of control
(d) substitute objects
(e) withdrawal syndromes
(f) reduced and intermittent dependencies.

Obviously we need a mix of models from several disciplines. For example, a

* Based on a paper originally presented at the WHO Conference on the Epidemiology of Drug Dependence, London, September 1972.

pharmacological model can account for some of (c) continued dependency, tolerance and escalation, and loss of control; some of (d) substitute objects, and (e) withdrawal syndromes – but it cannot account for the development of initial dependence.

This paper will deal mainly with (a) conceptualisation of dependency phenomena, and (b) initial development of dependency.

A Conceptualisation of dependency phenomena

1 Societal expectations

The term 'dependence', which has been substituted for the earlier term 'addiction', denotes a state or condition of the individual in relation to some class or classes of 'objects'. While it requires scientific elucidation, it also indicates societal disapproval. We regard a state of 'dependence' as deviant and possibly as one which requires help or treatment. In recent years, states of dependency on psychotoxic drugs have come in for much social, as well as medical, criticism. Why is this so?

We can distinguish between dependency on *people* (individuals, groups, institutions, families) and dependency on *things* (objects, substances, machines). In our culture, we seem to disapprove of dependency on things (smokers, alcoholics, junkies, hedonists, gamblers, etc.) but not of dependency on people (babies, adolescents, the old, the sick, disabled, housewives, the mentally subnormal, etc). But there are exceptions: diabetics, mongols and renal failure cases depend on drugs and machines, but of this we do not disapprove.

We note that dependency on 'things' is often easier; they are usually more dependable, available, and demand less effort than people – though there are exceptions.

Dependency on people is often institutionalised (through roles and norms, rights and obligations). A rough and ready *exchange theory* could apply; it is acceptable to be dependent, so long as the individual is contributing, or will contribute, or has contributed, to society. (Points of exchange can be separated in time.)

Perhaps the basic dependency role is the child–mother relationship leading from dependency to independence-striving (adolescence) to interdependence (so-called mature human relationships).

Dependency on 'things' can be seen as a striving towards apparent independence (of people) and difficulty in sustaining interdependent relationships. The 'things' may become substitutes for people.

However, in seeking to free himself, with the aid of substances, from the bonds of personal dependence, the individual may become dependent on those substances.

2 *Cult of realism*

In our culture we socialise individuals to conform to, and believe in, the existence of 'reality' and become 'realistic'. This may be difficult at times because it can be painful but we disapprove of attempts to escape into 'unreality' or fantasy. What reality *is,* is established consensually – it varies from time to time and from culture to culture, but society depends on common agreement about what is 'real'. We are suspicious of subjective beliefs and percepts, and therefore often treat artists, psychotics, or people under the influence of drugs, or mystical or emotional experiences as deviant. We note that we accept a good deal of 'unrealism' in everyday life.

Almost anything can be mind-altering or mood-altering (sunshine, a blow of a hammer, opium, a letter). Personal relationships (such as bereavement, falling in love, hatred) can lead to 'distortions of reality' but of these we rarely disapprove; we reserve our disapproval for distortions which are due to 'things' – even painkillers (e.g., in childbirth) and sleeping pills. Alcohol, gambling and hallucinogens are subject to even more marked disapproval.

These changes of reality can be of three kinds:

(a) *perceptual* – altered picture of self, of the world (hallicinogens);
(b) *attitudinal/emotional* – mood altering, stimulating, abreactive, depressant, etc.; reduced awareness of reality, increased pleasure;
(c) *behavioural* – where the substance is used as a symbolic passport of belonging to a group/subculture, process of identification and role-taking, analogous to hair styles, dress and music.

To some extent these attempts to change inner or perceived 'reality' can be regarded as coping mechanisms, as devices to come to terms with a disturbing or painful situation. A set of conditions becomes particularly disturbing when it consistently produces negative feedback about the Self. The self-concept depends on feedback – hopefully, realistic feedback – but there is a limit to the amount of negative feedback which an individual can sustain. Beyond a certain point he will turn more and more to those feedback sources that give him the most favourable picture of himself (i.e. he becomes prone to source-selective feedback), or he will tend to withdraw from many aspects of communication altogether.

Could we perhaps regard drug-taking as providing a continuous positive feedback loop, producing a positive image of the Self and of the world, and reducing the awareness of pain and disapproval?

3 Myth of independence

Our culture expects most of us to make the transition from childhood dependence to adult interdependence, and to forget the painful fact that we can never be independent, especially in a mass society. We are expected to learn to ignore feelings of powerlessness, meaninglessness, self-estrangement, and control by 'the System'; those who either cannot find interdependence or cannot ignore these dissonances will try to cope by seeking to alter 'reality', internal or external, in the face of the myth of independence.

Added to these general problems is the fact that some people like to *create* dependence: over-protective mothers and wives, some animal lovers, some people in positions of power. Such people cannot allow emancipation and independence training; thus they create in others a low sense of self-esteem and inadequate self-percept. It may be worth enquiring into the background of many drug-takers with this point of view in mind; are they seeking to escape from this kind of dependency-lock? Are they, in fact, unable both to conform to the myth of independence and to develop interdependent relationships because they are still involved with powerful dependency-creating figures?

Dependency need not necessarily generate problems and disapproval. For example, dependency can be acceptable for the young, the weak, the ill, and for those who are only too happy to let others cope and look after them; sometimes we have cultural roles which have an implied condition of such dependency. However, beyond a certain point dependency becomes resented and is felt as limiting, exploitative or tyrannising.

Thus resentment is probably less if the dependent state is (a) temporary, or (b) part of a mutually desired exchange relationship or (c) seen as an unalterable common condition, e.g. dependence on the State or the System. To some extent both resentment of dependence and independence-striving are seen as virtuous, e.g. in adolescence, and are socially approved as transition processes in the young or the convalescent. This is seen as consistent with greater realism and with the myth of independence. On the other hand, to relinquish 'control' or 'self control' to another agent or substance is seen as wrong or deviant, as a failure to engage reality and as an unwillingness or inability to fulfil the social expectations of independent adulthood.

4 Summary

We have seen that dependency is a very common condition. We all start life as dependents, and most likely will become dependent again in old age. In between times we strive for the myth of independence, and form interdependent relationships; we disapprove of those who are dependent because they deviate from the norms of 'realism' and of 'independence'.

This disapproval is less if the person contributes to society now or in the future, or has done so in the past; if he depends not on things or substances but on people; if he has a role which includes a dependency component; if he does not reject 'reality'; if he tries to overcome his dependency; and if he does not try to create dependency in others.

Drug-takers attract every one of these forms of disapproval; they reject reality, they contribute little to society, they have no approved social role, they depend not on people but on things, they deliberately create dependency in themselves and in others, and they mock the cultural myths.

B Initial development of dependency

1 A dissonance-reduction model

The basic postulate of dissonance theory is that an individual will experience dissonance as unpleasant, and will try to reduce it or avoid it – though there are exceptions to this, e.g. curiosity and the exploratory drive. Mild degrees of dissonance can lead to socially adaptive cognitive, emotional or behavioural changes; high degress of dissonance may lead to less culturally-approved solutions.

Most dissonance situations have three components.

(A) *Norms or expectations* set by some external agent, such as a reference group, a socialising agent, society. Their impact will depend on the individual's awareness and acceptance of such expectations, on mediating agents (e.g., the mass media), and on subcultural and personality factors.
(B) *The Self, or future Self* as seen by the individual. He may see himself in terms of roles, in terms of character and personality, in terms of achieved 'success'.
(C) *Dissonance* which is essentially the discrepancy between A and B: the feelings of anxiety, guilt, failure, deprivation, disapproval, and so on that are experienced when differences are noted between self and expectations.

Much of ordinary socialisation practice is based on an implied dissonance model; the young person is presented with a model of himself as he '*ought*' to be, he is made to see his shortcomings and is expected to feel dissonance; he is then shown ways in which he can hope to reduce this dissonance by hard work, conformity, developing the 'right attitudes' and eventually he may reach a state of consonance.

Some forms of health education use deliberate dissonance arousal techniques: thus we offer powerful evidence about the link between cancer and smoking in the hope that the individual will stop smoking in order to reduce the feeling of dissonance which our message has aroused. However, he may choose otherwise. A person has three basic strategies for dealing with dissonance: he may change himself; he may reject the expectations offered to him and seek others to which he *can* conform; or he may deal with the dissonance directly, by sustaining or repressing it, by using drugs, or in other ways.

2 *Application to drug-taking*

Fig. 20.1 contrasts the socially accepted and the drug-taking approach to dissonance reduction. Both approaches are, in a sense, 'functional' to the individual and behaviour can only be understood, predicted and modified when we know which mode of dissonance reduction the person is using.

Thus, in their efforts to reduce dissonance, people may deny the validity of societal norms and expectations, pointing to hypocrisies and seeking new norms by joining deviant subcultures (Mode A).

Alternatively, they may accept societal expectations but despair of ever being able to change their Self sufficiently, thus feeling that 'success' is denied them. Drugs offer ways of altering the Self, and of achieving the positive feedback of apparent 'success' – at least temporarily (Mode B).

A third mode would be to attack the dissonance directly, by escapist, thrill seeking behaviour, sprees on alcohol or amphetamines, or by seeking continuous mild states of euphoria (Mode C).

More than one method of dissonance reduction may be used by any individual. Correlation between mode of dissonance reduction and drug-of-choice will vary a good deal, depending on cultural factors. Also it should be noted that the diagram deals with *initial* drug-taking, not with habituation or tolerance. The drug-taking solution is not the only alternative; delinquency (Mode A), schizophrenia (Mode B), and suicide (Mode C) are among several other possibilities.

Rapid social change and break-up of traditional values increase the probability that culturally approved methods of dissonance reduction will be rejected. Thus the model points to vulnerable high risk subgroups, who may also be among the first to try *new drugs or different methods of taking drugs.*

3 *Comments*

Where levels of experienced dissonance become intolerable, we note that some individuals shift from interdependence on others to dependence on substances. One of the problems raised by the proposed model is the need to predict or explain why and when this shift occurs and at what level dissonance becomes 'intolerable' to different people.

	Socially accepted approach to dissonance reduction	Drug-taking approach to dissonance reduction
A *Social expectations* (As perceived; as mediated; different cultures and personality factors: may be stable or changing).	*Mode A* 1 Choose reference group and conform. 2 Try to change the expectations (active rebellion). 3 Exploratory behaviour; testing the limits.	*Mode A* 1 *Alter expectations* by joining deviant subculture; drug taken (e.g., cannabis) more for symbolic value than for psychic effect. 2 *Deny expectations* seek normlessness and oblivion (e.g., opiates).
B *Self, or future Self* (Personality; school achievement; job success, etc).	*Mode B* 1 Alter Self through identification, maturation, social learning. 2 Hard work and achievement.	*Mode B* 1 *Re-make Self* with the aid of hallucinogens, seek omnipotence, etc. 2 Use drugs for greater self-actualisation, artistic insight and creativity; 'cult of the present'. 3 Refuse to take responsibility for Self.
C *Dissonance* (Guilt, depression, deprivation).	*Mode C* 1 Learn to tolerate mild degrees of dissonance as spurs to achievement. 2 In some cultures: accept life-long dissonance, cult of acceptance and religious absolution. 3 Explosive release through carnivals and festivals.	*Mode C* 1 *Attack dissonance* directly, get rid of depression (alcohol, amphetamines, cocaine), seek thrills, sprees. 2 Seek continuous, mild euphoria.

Fig. 20.1 Diagrammatic presentation of dissonance reduction.

The model illustrates how psychological dependence can develop because the continuous need for dissonance reduction sets up a 'feedback loop effect' which acts as reinforcement. In the socially approved modes this effect makes the person dependent on praise, achievement, 'success' and other forms of reinforcement. In the drug-taking approach the psycho-active substances act as such dependency-producing reinforcers, offering the individual a way of coping with dissonance which for him is functional.

We should bear in mind that in many cultures the drugtaking individual is surrounded by pressures which continue to threaten him with dissonance, and these pressures in turn help to make him *more* dependent on his chosen style of dissonance reduction.

The model has implications for *treatment*. The cultural percept of the chosen drug may gives us an indication of the individual's underlying problem and dissonance reduction mode. We may also find that drug-takers have dependency problems in the family. The model also makes it clear that treatment is unlikely to succeed unless the individual is offered an alternative and effective (for him) method of dissonance reduction which ultimately improves his self-esteem and gives him a continuous series of success experiences. Another treatment implication is that in some cases it may be necessary – in the early stages of treatment – *to increase* dissonance deliberately, followed by the teaching of different coping methods which do not involve drugs.

Finally, the model has implications for *prevention*. Instead of being concerned with the spread of psycho-active substances, it points to high-risk groups or situations. These might include subcultures that are undergoing rapid social change, and others that have defined their success avenues so narrowly that many people are doomed to life-long failure. Under such conditions we may expect a proportion of the population to experience intolerable levels of dissonance, and to turn to drug-taking as one way of achieving dissonance reduction. The choice of drug, and the level of acceptance of any new drug, will depend on its cultural image and on the mode of dissonance reduction in which it is used (as indicated under A, B or C in the diagram). We must be careful, however, not simply to equate dissonance with material disadvantage and not to assume high levels of dissonance where they *may* not exist, e.g., in working-class subcultures, or in minority groups. The concept is subtler than this, and its assessment will require careful survey research. We would also expect to find that much depends on subjective, individual differences in feelings and expectations, on relative deprivation, and on the strength of the cultural norms.

21 Appraisal

These four papers do not represent the whole range of disciplines which today have something to say about the study of dependence, but even within the relatively narrow spectrum of their social/psychological focus they bring to notice a number of the fundamental perplexities (and challenges) which now confront anyone, whatever his discipline, who enters this broad area of drug studies.

The first question which becomes evident is that there is at present a lack of agreement even in the most general terms as to the delimitation of what is to be studied – of what is to count as 'it'. Before any theoretical discussion can be got under way as to the nature of 'it', there would be advantages in first setting up an agreed nomenclature. At present there is haziness as to whether by dependence is meant some unspecified state of the total man in society, a change in habit strength or drive state or some other postulated psychological variable, a change in observed behaviour without recourse to intervening postulates (e.g., drug-seeking behaviour), or an alteration in neurophysiological functioning. Such conceptual clarification might also throw light on the extent to which dependence studies are properly and profitably inter-disciplinary. With some tighter definitions it might be possible to distinguish those circumstances where different sciences are in fact addressing themselves to aspects of the same question, as opposed to the situation where different people merely think they are talking about the same thing because they have all been lured into the use of the same mushy word, 'dependence'. In passing one might enter a plea for some agreement as to whether the word (however mushy) is to be 'dependence' or 'dependency'.

One particular conceptual problem which is today coming to the fore is the extent to which drugs are special – the question of whether drug dependence is anything of a special kind, or whether alternatively a drug is just one of a broad range of objects which may act as reinforcer and excite dependence. In the present set of essays it is the latter view which seems to find favour. That drugs as a class of objects do however have rather special properties should not be forgotten: any ordinary model of stimulus/response becomes much complicated when varieties of drug tolerance are brought into play, or when reinstatement of tolerance complicates any ordinary expectation of a reminiscence effect.

There is then a general feeling coming across from these papers that theories are not only fun, but that they are also badly needed for the guidance of further research. Such a position is of course no different from that which is likely to pertain in any other area of scientific endeavour. What may at present distinguish the drug field is a feeling that there are indeed ideas waiting very fruitfully to be brought together but that meanwhile we are in something of a muddle. The way out of that muddle will not be found simply by replacing the word dependence (which replaced the word addiction) by some other word recommended by some other committee. The way forward will only come from much review and debate and experiment. The message of this section of the book should finally perhaps be that the business to which the present papers in small measure contribute, is a busness which much needs to be carried forward.

List of Contributors

Blumberg, H. H., AB, MA, PhD, research worker and lecturer, Addiction Research Unit.

Cohen, S. D., MB, BCh., *formerly* research worker, Addiction Research Unit.

Davidson, J., B.Soc.Sc., Graduate School, London School of Economics, *formerly* research worker, Addiction Research Unit.

Dronfield, B., BA, Dip.Crim., *formerly* research worker, Addiction Research Unit.

Edwards, G., MA, DM, MRCP, MRC Psych., Hon. Director, Addiction Research Unit; Reader in Drug Dependence, Institute of Psychiatry; Hon. Consultant Psychiatrist, Bethlem Royal and Maudsley Hospitals.

Hawks, D. V., BA, Postgrad. Dip. Psychol., PhD, Senior Clinical Psychologist, Dept. of Clinical Psychology, Whitchurch Hospital, Wales; *formerly* Deputy Director and Senior Lecturer, Addiction Research Unit.

Hitchins, L., BA, Community Development Project, London Borough of Southwark, *formerly* research worker, Addiction Research Unit.

Kosviner, A., BA, MSc., research worker, Addiction Research Unit.

Mitcheson, M., BA, MB, BCh., DPM, MRC Psych., Consultant-in-Charge, Drug Dependence Clinic, University College Hospital, London; *formerly* research worker, Addiction Research Unit.

Mordecai, E. A., BA, *formerly* research worker, Addiction Research Unit.

Oppenheim, A. N., BA, PhD, Reader in Social Psychology, London School of Economics; Consultant to Addiction Research Unit.

Orford, J., MA, PhD, Lecturer, Addiction Research Unit.

Roberts, J. C., BA, *formerly* research worker, Addiction Research Unit.

Robinson, D. A., BA, PhD, Lecturer, Addiction Research Unit.

Russell, M. A. H., BM, MRCP, MRC Psych., Hon. Consultant Psychiatrist, Maudsley Hospital; Senior Lecturer, Addiction Research Unit.

Stimson, G. V., PhD., Medical Sociology Research Centre, University College of Swansea, Glamorgan, Wales; *formerly* research worker, Addiction Research Unit.

Webb, M., MB, MPhil., MRCPI, MRC Psych., Consultant Psychiatrist, Dept. of Psychiatry, Trinity College, Dublin.

Zacune, J., BA MSc., Lecturer in Social Psychology, North Staffordshire Polytechnic, Stoke-on-Trent, Staffordshire; *formerly* research worker, Addiction Research Unit.

References

Adams, B. G., Horder, E. J., Horder, J. P., Modell, M., Steen, C. A. and Wigg, J. W., 'Patients receiving barbiturates in an urban general practice', *Journal of the College of General Practitioners,* vol. 12 (1966), pp. 24–31.

de Alarcon, R., 'An epidemiological evaluation of a public health measure aimed at reducing the availability of methylamphetamine', *Psychological Medicine,* vol. 2 (1972), pp. 293–300.

de Alarcon, R., 'Methaqualone', *British Medical Journal,* vol. 1 (1969[b]), p. 122.

de Alarcon, R., 'The spread of heroin abuse in a community', *Bulletin on Narcotics,* vol. 21 (1969[a]), pp. 17–22.

American Medical Association: 'Narcotics addiction: official actions of the American Medical Association, 1963'.

Backhouse, C. I., and James, I. P., 'The relationship and prevalence of smoking, drinking and drug taking in (delinquent) adolescent boys', *British Journal of Addiction,* vol. 64 (1969), pp. 75–9.

Bacon, S. D., 'The Dent Lecture, 1969', Society for the Study of Addiction (1970).

Ball, J. C., 'Reliability and validity of interview data obtained from 59 narcotic drug addicts', *American Journal of Sociology,* vol. 72, 6 (1967), pp. 650–4.

Bestic, A. *Turn Me on Man,* Tandem Books, London (1966).

Bewley, T. H., 'Adverse reactions from illicit use of lysergide', *British Medical Journal,* vol. 3 (1967), pp. 28–30.

Bewley, T. H., 'Heroin and cocaine addiction', *Lancet,* vol. 1 (1965), pp. 808–10.

Bewley, T. H., 'Recent changes in the pattern of drug abuse in the United Kingdom', *Bulletin on Narcotics,* vol. 28 (1966), pp. 1–9.

Bewley, T. H. and Ben-Arie, O., 'A study of 100 consecutive in-patients', *British Medical Journal,* vol. 1 (1968), pp. 727–30.

Bewley, T. H., Ben-Arie, O. and James, I. P., 'Survey of heroin addicts known to the Home Office', *British Medical Journal,* vol. 1 (1968[a]), pp. 725–6.

Bewley, T. H., Ben-Arie, O. and Marks, V., 'Relation of hepatitis to self injection techniques', *British Medical Journal,* vol. 1 (1968[b]), pp. 730–2.

Bewley, T. H., James, I. P. and Mahon, T., 'The evaluation of the effectiveness of prescribing clinics for narcotic addicts in the United Kingdom', in C. T. D. Zarajonetis (ed.), *Drug abuse: Proceedings of the*

International Conference, Philadelphia (1972), pp. 73–92.
Binnie, H. L. and Murdock, G., 'The attitudes to drugs and drug takers of students at the University and Colleges of Higher Education in an English Midland City,' unpublished report (1969).
Birtchnell, J., 'Early parent death and mental illness', *British Journal of Psychiatry,* vol. 116 (1970), pp. 281–2.
Birtchnell, J., 'Parent death in relation to age and parental age at birth in psychiatric patients and general population controls', *British Journal of Preventive and Social Medicine,* vol. 23 (1969), pp. 244–50.
Blane, H. T., Overton W. F. and Chafetz, M. E., 'Social factors in the diagnosis of alcoholism', *Quarterly Journal of Studies on Alcohol,* vol. 24 (1963), pp. 640–63.
Blumberg, H. H., 'Letter to editor: Violence among attenders at a London drug clinic', *British Journal of Psychiatry,* vol. 122 (1973), p. 570.
Blumberg, H. H., 'Specificity of acquiescence', *Journal of Personality Assessment,* vol. 37 (1973) pp. 479–85.
Blumberg, H. H., Cohen, S. D., Dronfield, B. E., Mordecai, E. A., Roberts, J. C. and Hawks, D., 'British opiate users: I People approaching London drug treatment centres', *International Journal of the Addictions,* vol. 9 (1974[a]), pp. 1–23.
Blumberg, H. H., Cohen, S. D., Dronfield, B. E., Mordecai, E. A., Roberts, J. C. and Hawks, D., 'British opiate users: II Differences between those given an opiate script and those not given one', *International Journal of the Addictions,* vol. 9 (1974[b]), pp. 205–20.
Bowlby, J., 'Disruption of affectional bonds and its effects on behaviour', *Journal of Contemporary Psychotherapy,* vol. 2 (1970), pp. 75–86.
Brain Committee, Inter-Departmental Committee on Drug Addiction, HMSO, London (1961).
Brandon, S. and Smith, D., 'Amphetamines in general practice', *Journal of the College of General Practitioners,* vol. 5 (1962), pp. 603–6.
Bransby, E. R., 'Note for discussion: DHSS study of drug dependent patients', Interdepartmental Memo, CCDD/(71)3 (1971[b]).
Bransby, E. R., 'A study of patients notified by hospitals as addicted to drugs: first report', *Health Trends,* vol. 3 (1971), pp. 75–9.
Bransby, E. R., Curley, G. O. and Kotulanska, M. T., 'A study of patients notified by hospitals as addicted to drugs: second report', *Health Trends,* vol. 5 (1973), pp. 17–20.
British Medical Journal: 'Down and out', vol. 2 (1966), p. 1546.
Brooke, E. M. and Glatt, M. M., 'More and more barbiturates', *Medicine, Science and Law,* vol. 4 (1964), pp. 277–82.
Burroughs, W., *Junkie,* Olympia Press, London (1966).

Campbell, H. J., *The Pleasure Areas,* Eyre Methuen, London (1973).

Central Statistical Office: *Annual abstract of statistics,* no. 108, HMSO, London (1971).

Chambers, C. D., 'Barbiturate – sedative abuse: a study of prevalence among narcotic abusers', *International Journal of the Addictions,* vol. 4 (1969), pp. 45–57.

Chapple, P. A. L., 'Dangers of mandrax for patients on oral methadone', *Medical News,* vol. 21 (Feb. 1969).

Chapple, P. A. L. and Gray, G., 'One year's work at a centre for treatment of addicted patients', *Lancet,* vol. 1 (1968), pp. 908–11.

Chapple, P. A. L., Gray, G. and Marks, V., 'Treatment of heroin addiction', *Lancet,* vol. 1 (1969), p. 940.

Chapple, P. A. L., Somekh, D. F. and Taylor, M. E., 'A five year follow-up of 108 cases of opiate addiction; general findings and a suggested method of staging', *British Journal of Addiction,* vol. 67 (1972), pp. 33–8.

Chein, I., Gerard, D. L., Lee, R. S. and Rosenfield, E., *Narcotics, delinquency and social policy: the road to H,* Tavistock Publications, London (1964).

Clark, J. A., 'The prognosis in drug addiction', *Journal of Mental Science,* vol. 108 (1962), pp. 411–18.

Connell, P. H., 'Adolescent drug taking', *Proceedings of the Royal Society of Medicine,* vol. 58 (1965[b]), pp. 409–12.

Connell, P. H., 'Amphetamine misuse', *British Journal of Addiction,* vol. 60 (1964), pp. 9–27.

Connell, P. H., *Amphetamine Psychosis,* Maudsley Monograph, No. 5, Chapman and Hall, London (1958).

Connell, P. H., *'The assessment and treatment of adolescent drug takers with special reference to the amphetamines',* Proceedings Leeds Symposium on Behavioural Disorders, May and Baker, Dagenham (1965[a]), pp. 3–10.

Connell, P. H., *'The impact of the new approach to the problem of drug dependence in Great Britain',* paper presented to 29th International Congress on Alcoholism and Drug Dependence, Melbourne, Australia, February 1970; Butterworth, London (1971).

Couch, A. S., 'Psychological determinants of interpersonal behaviour', unpublished doctoral dissertation, Harvard University (1960).

Crockett, R. and Marks, V., 'Amphetamine taking among young offenders', *British Journal of Psychiatry,* vol. 115 (1969), pp. 1203–4.

Cumberlidge, M. C., 'The abuse of barbiturates by heroin addicts', *Canadian Medical Association Journal,* Vol. 98, (1968), pp. 1045–9.

Davies, D. L., 'The concept of alcoholism', in R. Scott Bodley and R. Walker Milnes (eds), *The Medical Annual,* Wright, Bristol (1969).

Davies, D. L., 'Normal drinking in recovered alcohol addicts', *Quarterly*

Journal of Studies on Alcohol, vol. 23 (1962), pp. 94–104.
Department of Health and Social Security: 'On the state of public health', Annual Report of the Chief Medical Officer, HMSO, London (1971).
Dole, V. P., 'In the course of professional practice', *New York Journal of Medicine*, vol. 65 (1965), pp. 927–31.
Douglas, W. J. B., *The home and the School*, MacGibbon and Kee, London (1964).
Drew, L. R. H., 'Alcoholism as a self-limiting disease', *Quarterly Journal of Studies on Alcohol*, vol. 29 (1968), pp. 956–67.
Edwards, G., 'The British approach to the treatment of heroin addiction', *Lancet*, vol. 1 (1969), pp. 768–72.
Edwards, G., 'The status of alcoholism as a disease' in R. V. Phillipson (ed.), *Modern trends in Drug Dependence and Alcoholism*, Butterworths, London (1970[b]), pp. 140–61.
Edwards, G. and Guthrie, S., 'A controlled trial of inpatient and outpatient treatment of alcohol dependency', a slightly shortened version of a paper of the same title originally appearing in *Lancet*, vol. 1 (1967), pp. 555–9.
Everitt, B. S., *Cluster Analysis*, Heinemann (in press, 1974).
Feather, N. T., 'Subjective probability and decision under uncertainty', *Psychological Review*, vol. 66 (1959), pp. 150–64.
Festinger, L., *A Theory of Cognitive Dissonance*, Row, Peterson, Evanston, Ill. (1957).
Finney, D. J., 'The Fisher–Yates test of significance in 2 x 2 contingency tables', *Biometrika* (1 and 2), vol. 35 (1948), pp. 145–56.
Frankau, I. and Stanwell, P., 'The treatment of drug addiction', *Lancet*, vol. 2 (1961), pp. 1377–9.
Gardner, R. and Connell, P. H., 'One year's experience in a drug dependence clinic', *Lancet*, vol. 2 (1970), pp. 455–8.
General Register Office: *Census 1961*, 'England and Wales: Socio-Economic Group Tables', HMSO, London (1966[b]).
General Register Office: *Classification of Occupations, 1960*, HMSO, London (1960).
General Register Office: *Classification of Occupations, 1966*, HMSO, London (1966[a]).
General Register Office: *Sample Census, 1966*, 'England and Wales, County Report: Greater London', HMSO, London (1967).
Glatt, M. M. 'The abuse of barbiturates in the United States', *Bulletin on Narcotics*, vol. 14 (1962), pp. 19–38.
Glatt, M. M., 'Abuse of methylamphetamine', *Lancet*, vol. 2 (1968), pp. 215–6.
Glatt, M. M., The Alcoholic and the Help He Needs, Priory Press, Royston

(1970).
Glatt, M. M., Pittman, D. J., Gillespie, D. G. and Hills, D. R., *The Drug Scene in Great Britain; Journey into Loneliness,* Arnold, London (1967).
Gobius, J. du S. and Hawks, D. V., 'A retrospective study of heroin addicts known to the Home Office in 1965; interim analysis 1968', unpublished report (1970).
Gordon, A. M., 'Patterns of delinquency in drug addiction', *British Journal of Psychiatry,* vol. 122 (1973), pp. 205–10.
Hamburger, E., 'Barbiturate use in narcotic addicts', *Journal of the American Medical Association,* vol. 189 (1964), pp. 366–8.
Hawks, D. V., 'The dimensions of drug dependence in the United Kingdom', *International Journal of the Addictions,* vol. 6 (1971), pp. 135–60.
Hawks, D. V., 'The epidemiology of drug dependence: Priorities for future research', paper delivered to the Royal Society of Medicine, 1970; *Bulletin on Narcotics,* vol. 3 (1970), XXII, pp. 15–24.
Hawks, D. V., 'Evaluation of measures to deal with drug dependence in the United Kingdom', *Proceedings of the Royal Society of Medicine,* vol. 66 (1973), pp. 113–9.
Hawks., D. V., Ogborne, A. and Mitcheson, M. C., 'The strategy of epidemiological research in drug dependence', *British Journal of Addiction,* vol. 65 (1970), pp. 363–8.
Hawks, D. V., Mitcheson, M., Ogborne, A. and Edwards, G., 'Abuse of methylamphetamine', *British Medical Journal,* vol. 2 (1969), pp. 715–21.
Hewetson, J. and Ollendorf, R., 'Preliminary survey of 100 London heroin and cocaine addicts', *British Journal of Addiction,* vol. 59 (1964), pp. 109–14.
Holahan, J. F., 'The economics of heroin', in *Dealing with drug abuse: a report to the Ford Foundation,* Macmillan, London (1972), pp. 255–99.
Home Office: *The Rehabilitation of Drug addicts,* HMSO, London (1969).
Hore, B. D., 'Factors in alcoholic relapse', *British Journal of Addcition,* vol. 66 (1971), pp. 83–8.
James, I. P., 'A methylamphetamine epidemic?', *Lancet,* vol. 1 (1968), p. 916.
James, I. P., 'Suicide and mortality amongst heroin addicts', *British Journal of Addiction,* vol. 62 (1967), pp. 391–8.
James, I. P. and d'Orban, P. T., 'Patterns of delinquency among British heroin addicts', *Bulletin on Narcotics,* vol. 22 (1970), pp. 13–19.
Janis, I. L. and Mann, L., 'A conflict theory approach to attitude change and decision making' in A. C. Greenwald, T. C. Brock, and T. M. Ostrom, (eds.), *Psychological Foundation of Attitudes,* ch. 13, Academic Press, New York (1968).
Jellinek, E. M., *The Disease Concept of Alcoholism,* Hillhouse Press, New

Haven (1960).
Jellinek, E. M., 'Phases of alcohol addiction', *Quarterly Journal of Studies on Alcohol,* vol. 13 (1952), pp. 673–84.
Jellinek, E. M., 'The world and its bottle', *World Health,* Geneva, vol. 10, no. 4 (1957), pp. 4–6.
Jossor, R., Graves, T. D., Hanson, R. C. and Jessop, S. L., *Society, personality and deviant behaviour,* Holt, Rinehart and Winston, New York (1968).
Johnson, J. and Clift, A. D., 'Dependence on hypnotic drugs in general practice', *British Medical Journal,* vol. 4 (1968), pp. 613–17.
Jones, T., *Drugs and the Police,* Butterworth, London (1968).
Keehn, J. D., 'Alcohol and drug dependence: Comparisons and Interactions', paper read to the International Conference on Drug Dependence, Quebec, September 1968, Government of Quebec, Canada (1968), p. A1.
Kendell, R. E., 'Normal drinking by former alcohol addicts', *Quarterly Journal of Studies on Alcohol,* vol. 26 (1965), pp. 247–57.
Kessell, N., 'Self-poisoning', *British Medical Journal,* vol. 2 (1965), pp. 1265–70.
Keutzer, C. S., 'A measure of cognitive dissonance as a predictor of smoking treatment outcome', *Psychological Report,* vol. 22 (1968), pp. 655–8.
Kiloh, L. G. and Brandon, S., 'Habituation and addiction to amphetamines', *British Medical Journal,* vol. 2 (1962), pp. 40–3.
Kohn, P. M. and Mercer, G. W., 'Drug use, drug-use attitudes and the authoritarianism–rebellion dimension', *Journal of Health and Social Behaviour,* vol. 12 (1971), pp. 125–31.
Kosviner, A., Mitcheson, M., Myers, K., Ogborne, A., Stimson, G. V., Zacune, J. and Edwards, G., 'Heroin use in a provincial town', *Lancet,* vol. 1 (1968), pp. 1189–92.
Kramer, J. C., Fischman, V. S. and Littlefield, D. C., 'Amphetamine abuse. Pattern and effects of high doses taken intravenously', *Journal of the American Medical Association,* vol. 201 (1967), pp. 305–9.
Lancet: 'Abuse of methylamphetamine', vol. 2 (1968), p. 818.
Latscha, R., 'Tests of significance in a 2 x 2 contingency table: Extension of Finney's table', *Biometrika,* vol. 40 (1 & 2), (1953), pp. 74–5.
Laurie, P., *Drugs: Medical, Psychological, and Social Facts,* Penguin, London (1967).
Lemert, E. M., 'The behaviour of the systemic check forger' in H. S. Becker (ed.), *The other side. Perspectives on deviance,* Collier–Macmillan, London (1964), pp. 211–24.
Lindesmith, A. R., *'The addict and the law',* Indiana University Press, London (1966).

Linken, A., 'The social pharmacology of drugs of dependence; II The psychological aspects of student drug taking', in C. W. M. Wilson (ed.), *Adolescent drug dependence,* ch. 4, Pergamon Press, Oxford (1968[a]), pp. 159–66.

Linken, A., 'A study of drug taking among young patients attending a clinic for venereal diseases', *British Journal on Venereal Disease,* vol, 44 (1968[b]) pp. 337–41.

Linken, A., 'The young drug-takers', *Sunday Times,* 27 January 1963, p. 24.

Lodge, I. C. Patch, 'Homeless men in London: I Demographic findings in a lodging house sample', *British Journal of Psychiatry,* vol. 118 (1971), pp. 313–17.

Maddox, G. L. 'Muddling through. Planning for health care in England', *Medical Care,* vol. 4 (1971), p. 9.

Mahon, T. A., 'An exploratory study of hospitalized narcotic addicts in Great Britain', *Acta Psychiatrica Scandinavica,* Suppl. 227 (1971).

Marks, V., and Chapple, P. A. L., 'Hepatic dysfunction in heroin and cocaine users', *British Journal of Addiction,* vol. 62 (1967), pp. 189–95.

Meyer, A. S., Brotman, R. and Freedman, A. M., *'Continuities and discontinuities in the process of patient care for narcotic addicts',* mimeographed report, New York Medical College (1965).

Ministry of Health: 'Departmental Committee on morphine and heroin addiction' (Rolleston Committee), HMSO London (1926).

Mitcheson, M. C., Davidson, J., Hawks, D., Hitchins, L. and Malone, S., 'Sedative abuse by heroin addicts', *Lancet,* vol. 1 (1970), pp. 606–7.

Montalvo, J. G., Scrignar, C. B., Alderette, E., Harper, E. and Eyer, D., 'Flushing, pale-coloured urines, and false negatives urinalysis of narcotic addicts', *International Journal of the Addictions,* vol. 7 (1972), pp. 355–64.

Mott, J., 'The psychological basis of drug dependence: the intellectual and personality characteristics of opiate users', *British Journal of Addiction,* vol. 67 (1972), pp. 88–99.

Murphy, F. W. Brady, J. and Paul, S., 'Drug abuse in a London suburb', unpublished report, (1969).

Noble, P. J., 'Drug taking in delinquent boys', *British Medical Journal,* vol. 1 (1970), pp. 102–5.

O'Connell, S., 'Social and psychological characteristics of the drug-taking of homeless young persons', condensed from an unpublished thesis submitted in part fulfillment of the requirements for the M.Phil. (Psychiatry), University of London, 1970.

Ogborne, A. and Stimson, G. V., personal communication, 1969.

O'Malley, J. E., Anderson, W. H., and Lazare, A., 'Failure of outpatient treatment of drug abuse: 1 Heroin, *American Journal of Psychiatry,* vol.

128 (1972), pp. 865–72.
Orford, J., Waller, S. and Peto, J., 'Drinking behaviour and attitudes and their correlates among university students in England', *Quarterly Journal of Studies on Alcohol,* vol. 35 (1974), pp. 1316–74.
Oswald, I. 'Human brain protein, drugs and dreams', *Nature,* vol. 223 (1969), pp. 893–7.
Owens, J., 'Integrated approach', *British Medical Journal,* vol. 2 (1967), pp. 501–2.
Parsons, T., *The Social System,* Free Press, Chicago (1951).
Paton, W. D. M., p.3 in H. Steinberg (ed.), *The scientific basis of drug dependence,* Churchill, London (1969).
Pattison, E. M., 'A critique of alcoholism treatment concepts with special reference to abstinence', *Quarterly Journal of Studies on Alcohol,* vol. 27 (1966), pp. 49–71.
Pattison, E. M., Headley, E. G., Glesser, G. C. and Gottschalk, L. A., 'Abstinence and normal drinking; an assessment of changes in drinking patterns in alcoholics after treatment', *Quarterly Journal of Studies on Alcohol,* vol. 29 (1968), pp. 610–33.
Preble, E. and Casey, J. J., 'Taking care of business – the heroin user's life on the street', *International Journal of the Addictions,* vol. 4 (1969), pp. 1–24.
Rathod, N. H., 'The use of heroin and methadone by injection in a new town', *British Journal of Addiction,* vol. 67 (1972), pp. 113–21.
Robinson, D., *The Process of Becoming Ill,* Routledge & Kegan Paul, London (1971).
Rubington, E., 'Two types of drug use', *International Journal of the Addictions,* vol. 3 (1968), pp. 301–18.
Sapira, J. D., Jasinsky, D. R. and Goredetsky, C. W., 'Liver disease in narcotic addicts: II The role of the needle', *Clinical Pharmacology and Therapeutics,* vol. 9, 6 (1968), pp. 725–39.
Schofield, M., *The Strange Case of Pot,* Penguin, Harmondsworth (1971).
Schur, E. M., *Narcotic Addiction in Britain and America,* Associated Book Publishers, London (1966).
Seeley, J. R., 'Alcoholism is a disease: Implications for social policy', in D. J. Pittman and C. R. Snyder (eds.), *Society, Culture and Drinking Patterns,* Wiley, New York (1962), pp. 585–93.
Sharpley, A., *Evening Standard* (1964): 'Thousands of teenagers have just lost a weekend' (3 February), p.1; 'The non-stop world of "Pill's Paradise"' (4 February), p.7. 'Home Office moves soon on spreading of purple-hearts among teenagers' (5 February), p.1; 'Confessions of a drug-taker' (6 February), p.1. 'The first effects of legislation on purple-hearts' (1 May).

Shepherd, M., Oppenheim, A. N. and Mitchell, S., 'The definition and outcome of deviant behaviour in childhood', *Proceedings of the Royal Society of Medicine,* vol. 59 (1966), pp. 379–82.

Siegler, M. Osmond, H. and Newell, S., 'Models of alcoholism', *Quarterly Journal of Studies on Alcohol,* vol. 29 (1968), pp. 571–91.

Sington, D., Quotation on p.13 in *Drug Addiction,* Office of Health Economics, Publication No. 25, London (1967).

Spear, H. B. 'The growth of heroin addiction in the United Kingdom', *British Journal of Addiction,* vol. 64 (1969), pp. 245–55.

Spear, H. B. and Glatt, M. M., 'The influence of Canadian addicts on heroin addiction in the United Kingdom'. *British Journal of Addiction,* vol. 66 (1971), pp. 141–9.

Stimson, G. and Ogborne, A., 'Survey of addicts prescribed heroin at London clinics', *Lancet,* vol. 1 (1970[a]), pp. 1163–6.

Stimson, G. V. and Ogborne, A. C., 'A survey of a representative sample of addicts prescribed heroin at London clinics', *Bulletin on Narcotics,* vol. 22, 4 (1970[b]), pp. 13–21.

Sutter, A. G., 'The world of the righteous dope fiend', *Issues in Criminology,* vol. 2, (1966), pp. 177–222.

Teasdale, J. 'Drug dependence', in H. J. Eysenck (ed.) *Handbook of Abnormal Psychology,* 2nd edition, Pitman, London, (1973), pp. 97–130.

Webb, M. Hawks, D. V. and Kosviner, A., 'Cannabis use in a student population', unpublished M. Phil. thesis, University of London (1969).

Wiener, R. S. P., *Drugs and School Children,* Longman, London (1970).

Willis, J. H. 'Drug dependence: some demographic and psychiatric aspects in UK and US subjects', *British Journal of Addiction,* vol. 64 (1969) pp. 135–46.

Wilson, C. W. M. and Beacon, S., 'An investigation into the habituating properties of an amphetamine-barbiturate mixture', *British Journal of Addiction,* vol. 60 (1964), pp. 81–92.

Winick, C., 'Maturing out of narcotic addiction', *Bulletin on Narcotics,* vol. 14 (1962), pp. 1–7.

Witkin, H. A., 'Psychological differentiation and forms of pathology', *Journal of Abnormal Psychology,* vol. 70 (1965), pp. 317–36.

Wright, J. D., 'A survey of the knowledge and attitudes about drug misuse among fourth year pupils at three Wolverhampton schools', unpublished report, Health Department, Wolverhampton (1968).

Young, J. and Crutchley, J. B., 'Student drug use', *Drugs in Society,* vol. 2 (October 1972), pp. 11–15.

Zacune, J., 'A comparison of Canadian narcotic addicts in Great Britain and Canada', *Bulletin on Narcotics,* vol. 23 (1971), pp. 41–9.

Zacune, J. Mitcheson, M. and Malone, S., 'Heroin use in a provincial town – one year later', *International Journal of the Addictions*, vol. 4 (1969), pp. 557–70.

Zacune, J. Stimson, G., Ogborne, A., Mitcheson, M. and Kosviner, A., 'The assessment of heroin usage in a provincial community' in H. Steinberg (ed.) *Scientific Basis of Drug Dependence*, Churchill, London (1969), pp. 323–30.

Zola, I. K., 'Medicine as an institution of social control', *Sociology Review*, vol. 20 (1972), pp. 487–504.

Bibliography of the Addiction Research Unit

Blumberg, H. H., 'British users of opiate-type drugs: a follow-up study', *British Journal of Addiction* (in press).

Blumberg, H. H., 'Drug taking among children and adolescents' in M. Rutter and L. Hersov (eds.), *Recent Developments in Child Psychiatry*, Oxford (in press), ch. 23.

Blumberg, H. H., 'Professional education and training on the problems of alcohol and drugs' in J. Zacune and C. Hensman (eds.) *Drugs, Alcohol and Tobacco in Britain*, London (1971), ch. 18.

Blumberg, H. H., 'Surveys of drug use among young people', *International Journal of the Addictions* (in press).

Blumberg, H. H., Cohen, S. D., Dronfield, B. E. Mordecai, E. A., Roberts, J. C. and Hawks, D. V., 'British opiate users: I People approaching London drug treatment centres' *International Journal of the Addictions*, vol. 9 (1974), pp. 1–23.

Blumberg, H. H., Cohen, S. D., Dronfield, B. E., Mordecai, E. A., Roberts, J. C. and Hawks, D. V., 'British opiate users: II Difference between those given an opiate script and those not given one', *International Journal of the Addictions*, vol. 9 (1974), pp. 205–20.

Blumberg., H. H., Cohen, S. D., Dronfield, B. E., Mordecai, E. A., Roberts, J. C. and Hawks, D. V., 'Opiate use in London', *Journal of the American Medical Association* (in press).

Chandler, J., Hensman, C. and Edwards, G., 'Determinants of what happens to alcoholics', *Quarterly Journal of Studies on Alcohol*, vol. 32 (1971), pp. 349–63.

Crow, I., 'Two groups of cannabis users in South London', *Drugs & Society*, vol. 2 (June 1973), pp. 10–14.

Edwards, G., 'Addiction as a public health problem', *Medical Officer*, vol. 113 (1965), pp. 177–80.

Edwards, G., 'Alcoholic swamps', *New Society*, vol. 2 (September 1971), pp. 459–61.

Edwards. G., 'Alcoholism as a public health problem in the USA', *Lancet*, vol. 1 (1962), pp. 960–2.

Edwards, G., 'Alcoholism studies and the Addiction Research Unit' in *Portfolio for Health. 2 The developing programme of the DHSS in health services research*. DHSS, London (1973).

Edwards, G., 'Alternative strategies for minimizing alcohol problems: coming

out of the doldrums', *Journal of Alcoholism* (in press).
Edwards, G., 'The British approach to the treatment of heroin addiction', *Lancet*, vol. 1 (1969), pp. 768–72.
Edwards, G., 'Cannabis and the criteria for legislation of a currently prohibited recreational drug: groundwork for a debate', *Acta Psychiatrica Scandinavica*, supplementum 251 (1974), pp. 1–62.
Edwards, G., 'Cannabis and the psychiatric position' in J. D. P. Graham (ed.) *Cannabis sativa*, London (in press).
Edwards, G., 'The circulating alcoholic', *Medicine, Science and the Law* (October 1964), pp. 254–8.
Edwards, G., 'Classification of pathological drinking', paper presented at Third Symposium on Advance Medicine held at the Royal College of Physicians, London, February 1967; proceedings published by Pitman, London (1967), pp. 303–16.
Edwards, G., 'A community as case study: alcoholism treatment in antiquity and Utopia', paper, 2nd Annual Alcoholism Conference, National Institute on Alcohol Abuse and Alcoholism, Washington, DC (June 1972), pp. 1–2.
Edwards, G., 'Double-blind trial of lobeline in an anti-smoking clinic', *Medical Officer*, vol. 112 (1964), pp. 158–160.
Edwards, G., 'A doubtful prognosis', *International Journal of Psychiatry*, vol. 9, (1970–71), pp. 354–8.
Edwards, G., 'Drug dependence – putting history on the agenda', paper, Round Table Conference on Non-medical Use of Dependence – producing Drugs, Geneva (1971).
Edwards, G., 'Drug problems UK/USA', *Proceedings of the Royal Society of Medicine* (1973), pp. 2–6.
Edwards, G., 'Drugs, drug dependence and the concept of plasticity', *Quarterly Journal of Studies on Alcohol*, vol. 35 (1974), pp. 176–95.
Edwards, G., 'The early diagnosis of alcoholism', *Medical World* (November 1961), pp. 372–6.
Edwards, G., 'Encounter with the alcoholic', *Medical World* (December 1960), pp. 512–18.
Edwards, G., 'Epidemiology applied to alcoholism. A review and an examination of purposes', *Quarterly Journal of Studies on Alcohol*, vol. 34 (1973), pp. 28–56.
Edwards, G., 'Hypnosis and lobeline in an anti-smoking clinic', *Medical Officer*, vol. 111 (1964), pp. 239–43.
Edwards, G., 'Hypnosis in the treatment of alcohol addiction', *Quarterly Journal of Studies on Alcohol*, vol. 27 (1966), pp. 221–41.
Edwards, G., 'The meaning and treatment of alcohol dependence', *Hospital Medicine*, vol. 2 (1967), pp. 272–81.

Edwards, G., 'Patients with drinking problems', *British Medical Journal,* vol. 4 (1968), pp. 435–7.
Edwards G. 'Personality and addiction', *Howard League Journal,* vol. 12 (1966), pp. 136–9.
Edwards, G., 'Personal view', *British Medical Journal,* vol. 4 (1971), p. 619.
Edwards, G., 'The place of treatment professions in society's response to chemical abuse', *British Medical Journal,* vol. 2 (1970) pp. 195–9.
Edwards, G., 'Planning for the 70's. Social background to the use and abuse of alcohol and drugs; professional aspects', in *Proceedings 29th International Congress on Alcoholism and Drug Dependence,* Sydney (1971).
Edwards, G., 'The problem of cannabis dependence', *Practitioner,* vol. 200 (1968), pp. 226–33.
Edwards, G., 'Public health implications for liquor control', *Lancet,* vol. 2 (1971), pp. 424–5.
Edwards, G., 'The relevance of the American experience of narcotic addiction to the British scene', *British Medical Journal,* vol. 3 (1967), pp. 425–9.
Edwards, G., 'Research report: The Addiction Research Unit of the Institute of Psychiatry, London', *Psychological Medicine,* vol. 2 (1972), pp. 192–7.
Edwards, G., 'The status of alcoholism as a disease', in R. Phillipson (ed.) *Modern Trends in Drug Dependence and Alcoholism,* Butterworth, London (1970).
Edwards, G., 'The streets of Calcutta', *New Society* (7 May 1970), pp. 771–4.
Edwards, G., 'Unreason in the age of reason': 1 Past history and present mental state, II Internal audit; Edwin Stevens Lectures delivered to the Royal Society of Medicine 1971, Royal Society of Medicine, London (1971).
Edwards G. and Guthrie, S., 'A comparison of in-patient and out-patient treatment of alcohol dependence', *Lancet* vol. 1 (1966), pp. 467–8.
Edwards, G. and Guthrie, S., 'A controlled trial of in-patient and out-patient treatment of alcohol dependence', *Lancet,* vol. 1 (1967), pp. 555–9.
Edwards, G., Chandler, J. and Hensman, C., 'Drinking in a London suburb: I Correlates of normal drinking', *Quarterly Journal of Studies on Alcohol,* suppl. 6 (1972), pp. 69–93.
Edwards, G. Gattoni, F. and Hensman, C., 'Correlates of alcohol-dependence scores in a prison population', *Quarterly Journal of Studies on Alcohol,* vol. 33 (1972), pp. 417–29.
Edwards, G., Hawker, A. and Hensman, C., 'Setting up a therapeutic community', *Lancet,* vol. 2 (1966), pp. 1407–8.
Edwards, G., Hensman, C. and Peto, J., 'A comparison of female and male motivation for drinking', *International Journal of the Addictions,* vol. 8, 4

(1974), pp. 577–87.
Edwards, G., Hensman, C. and Peto, J., 'Drinking in a London Suburb: III Comparisons of drinking troubles, among men and women', *Quarterly Journal of Studies on Alcohol,* Supplement 6 (1972), pp. 120–8.
Edwards, G., Hensman, C. and Peto, J., 'Drinking in a London suburb: re-interview of a sub-sample and assessment of consistency in answering', *Quarterly Journal of Studies on Alcohol,* vol. 34 (1973), pp. 1244–54.
Edwards, G., Hensman, C. and Peto, J., 'Drinking problems amongst recidivist prisoners', *Psychological Medicine,* vol. 1 (1971), pp. 388–99.
Edwards, G., Kyle, E. and Nicholls, P., 'A study of alcoholics admitted to four hospitals: I Social class and the interaction of the alcoholic with the treatment system', *Quarterly Journal of Studies on Alcoholism,* vol. 35 (1974), pp. 499–522,
Edwards, G., Chandler, J., Hensman, C. and Peto, J., 'Drinking in a London suburb. II Correlates of trouble with drinking among men', *Quarterly Journal of Studies on Alcohol,* Supplement 6 (1972), pp. 94–119.
Edwards, G., Hawker, A., Williamson, V. and Hensman, C., 'London's Skid Row', *Lancet,* vol. 1 (1966), pp. 249–52.
Edwards, G., Hensman, C., Chandler, J. and Peto, J., 'Motivation for drinking among men: survey of a London suburb', *Psychological Medicine,* vol. 2 (1972), pp. 260–71.
Edwards, G., Hensman, C., Hawker, A. and Williamson, V., 'Alcoholics Anonymous: the anatomy of a self-help group', *Social Psychiatry,* vol. 1 (1967), pp. 195–204.
Edwards, G., Hensman, C., Hawker, A. and Williamson, V., 'Who goes to Alcoholics Anonymous?' *Lancet,* vol. 2 (1966), pp. 382–4.
Edwards, G., Kellog-Fisher, M., Hawker, A. and Hensman, C., 'Clients of Alcoholism Information Centres', *British Medical Journal,* vol. 4 (1967), pp. 346–9.
Edwards, G., Hawker, A., Hensman, C., Peto, J. and Williamson, V., 'Alcoholics known or unknown to agencies: epidemiological studies in a London suburb', *British Journal of Psychiatry,* vol. 123 (1973), pp. 169–83.
Edwards, G., Rathod, N. H., Thomson, I. G., Kyle, E. and Nicholls, P., 'Case note abstraction: a methodological substudy as a cautionary tale', *International Journal of the Addictions,* vol. 11, no. 3 (1976, in press).
Edwards, G., Williamson, V., Hawker, A., Hensman, C. and Postoyan, S., 'Census of a Reception Centre', *British Journal of Psychiatry,* vol. 114 (1968), pp. 1031–9.
Egert, S., 'Casework intervention with families of alcoholics', paper, International Congress on Alcoholism and Drug Dependence, Amsterdam

(1972).
Feyerabend, C., Levitt, T. and Russell, M. A. H., 'A rapid gas-liquid chromatographic estimation of nicotine in biological fluids', *Journal of Pharmacy and Pharmacology* (in press).
Gath, D., Hensman, C., Hawker, A., Kelly, M. and Edwards, G., 'The drunk in court: a survey of drunkenness offenders from two London courts', *British Medical Journal,* vol. 4 (1968), pp. 808–11.
Gelder, M. G. and Edwards, G., 'Metronidazole in the treatment of alcohol addiction: a controlled trial', *British Journal of Psychiatry,* vol. 114 (1968) pp. 437–75.
Hawker, A., Edwards, G. and Hensman, C., 'Problem drinkers on the payroll', *Medical Officer,* vol. 118 (1967), pp. 313–5.
Hawks, D., 'The dimensions of drug dependence in the United Kingdom', *International Journal of the Addictions,* vol. 6 (1971), pp. 135–60.
Hawks, D., 'Drug dependence – a case in point' in E. Vallance (ed.) *The limits of State Intervention in the Prevention of Self-destructive Behaviour,* Allen & Unwin, London (in press).
Hawks, D., 'The epidemiology of drug dependence in the United Kingdom', *Bulletin on Narcotics,* vol. 22, no. 3 (1970), pp. 15–24.
Hawks, D., 'The epidemiology of narcotic addiction in the United Kingdom' in E. Josephson and E. E. Carroll (eds), *Drug Use: Epidemiological and Sociological Approaches,* Hemisphere P. C., Washington (1974), pp. 45–63.
Hawks, D., 'The evaluation of measures to deal with drug dependence in the United Kingdom', *Proceedings of the Royal Society of Medicine,* vol. 66 (1973), pp. 113–19.
Hawks, D. V., 'Is treatment economical?' *C. C. A. Journal of Alcoholism,* vol. 2, no. 4 (1971), pp. 34–9.
Hawks, D. V., 'Social research as a determinant of social policy', Proceedings of the Second International Institute on the Prevention and Treatment of Drug Dependence, ICAA, Baden (1971).
Hawks, D., Ogborne, A. and Mitcheson, M., 'The Strategy of epidemiological research in drug dependence', *British Journal of Addiction,* vol. 65 (1970), pp. 363–8.
Hawks, D., Mitcheson, M., Ogborne, A. and Edwards, G., 'Abuse of Methylamphetamine', *British Medical Journal,* vol. 2 (1969), pp. 715–21.
Hensman, C., 'Alcoholism – psychosocial aspects', paper presented at Third Symposium on Advanced Medicine; Proceedings published by Pitman, London (1967), 317–27.
Hensman, C., 'Problems of drunkenness amongst male recidivists', Proceedings of International Symposium on the Drunkenness Offence,

Published by Pergamon, Oxford (1969), pp. 35–50.

Hensman, C., Chandler, J., Edwards, G., Hawker, A. and Williamson, V., 'Identifying abnormal drinkers: prevalence estimates by general practitioners and clergymen', *Medical Officer,* vol. 120 (1968), pp. 215–220.

Hershon, H. I., 'Alcoholsim and the concept of disease', *British Journal of Addiction,* vol. 69 (1974), pp. 123–31.

Hershon, H. I., 'Alcoholism, physical dependence and disease', comment on 'The alcohologist's addiction', *Quarterly Journal of Studies on Alcohol,* vol. 34 (1973), pp. 506–8.

Hershon, H. I., 'Alcohol withdrawal symptoms: phenomenology and implications', *British Journal of Addiction,* vol. 68 (1973), pp. 295–302.

Hershon, H. I., Cook, T. and Foldes, P., 'What shall we do with the drunkenness offender?', *British Journal of Psychiatry,* vol. 124 (1974), pp. 327–35.

Hitchins, L., Mitcheson, M., Zacune, J. and Hawks, D., 'A two-year follow-up of a cohort of opiate users for a provincial town', *British Journal of Addiction,* vol. 66 (1971), pp. 129–40.

Kosviner, A., 'Prevalence, characteristics and correlates of cannabis use in the UK student population', paper 3rd International Cannabis Conference, London (1974).

Kosviner, A., 'Psychosocial aspects of cannabis use' in J. D. P. Graham (ed.), *Cannabis sativa,* London (in press).

Kosviner, A., 'Unwanted neighbours: a report of public reaction to setting up a residential rehabilitation programme for ex-addicts', *International Journal of the Addictions,* vol. 8 (1973), pp. 801–8.

Kosviner, A. and Hawks, D., 'Cannabis use amongst British university students: II Patterns of use and attitudes to use amongst users', *British Journal of Addiction* (in press).

Kosviner, A., Hawks, D. V. and Webb, M. G. T., 'Cannabis use among British university students: I Prevalence rates and differences between students who have tried cannabis and those who have never tried it', *British Journal of Addiction,* vol. 69 (1974), pp. 35–60.

Kosviner, A., Mitcheson, M., Myers, K., Ogborne, A., Stimson, G., Zacune, J. and Edwards, G., 'Heroin use in a provincial town', *Lancet,* vol. 1 (1968) pp. 1189–92.

Kyle E. 'Patient role and staff role in a therapeutic community', *Journal of Alcoholism,* vol. 4 (1969), pp. 179–82.

Litman, G. K., 'Behavioral modification techniques in the treatment of alcoholism: a review and critique' in *Research advances in alcohol and drug problems,* Vol. 3, Toronto (in press).

Litman, G. K., 'Psychological aspects of alcoholism theory and treatment', *Journal of Alcoholism,* vol. 9 (1974), pp. 48–9.

Litman, G. K., 'Stress, affect and craving in alcoholics. The single case as a research strategy', *Quarterly Journal of Studies on Alcohol,* vol. 35 (1974), pp. 131–46.

Melotte, C. J., 'A drugs advisory centre', *Social Work Today,* vol. 5 (1974), p. 281.

Melotte, C., 'A rehabilitation hospital, for drug users: one year's admission', *British Journal of Criminology* (in press).

Melotte, C. and Ogborne, A. .C., 'Strategies for the successful follow-up of treated drug abusers', *Journal of Drug Issues,* vol. 5 (1975, in press).

Mitcheson, M., Davidson, J., Hawks, D., Hitchins, L. and Malone, S., 'Sedative abuse by heroin addicts', *Lancet,* vol. 1 (1970), pp. 606–7.

Nicholls, P., Edwards, G. and Kyle, E., 'A study of alcoholics admitted to four hospitals: II General and cause-specific mortality during follow-up', *Quarterly Journal of Studies on Alcohol,* vol. 35 (1974), pp. 841–55.

Ogborne, A. C., 'Addicts, their associations and behaviour', *Social Science and Medicine,* vol. 8 (1974), pp. 557–65.

Ogborne, A. C., 'Coffee pot pourri', *Drugs and Society,* vol. 2, no. 9 (1973), pp. 6–9.

Ogborne, A. C., 'Two types of heroin reaction', *British Journal of Addiction,* vol. 69 (1974), pp. 171–5.

Ogborne, A. C. and Stimson, G. V., 'A three-year follow-up of a representative sample of heroin addicts', *International Journal of the Addictions,* vol. 10, no. 6 (1975).

Orford, J., 'Alcoholism and marriage: the argument against specialism', *Journal of Studies in Alcoholism* (in press).

Orford, J., 'Aspects of the relationship between alcohol and drug abuse', Proceedings, 29th International Congress on Alcoholism and Drug Dependence, Sydney, Australia; Butterworth Press (1971).

Orford, J., 'A comparison of alcoholics whose drinking is totally uncontrolled and alcoholics whose drinking is mainly controlled', *Behaviour, Research and Therapy,* vol. 11 (1973), pp. 565–76.

Orford, J., 'Controlled drinking in the existing behaviour repertoires of alcohol dependent men', *Journal of Alcoholism,* vol. 9 (1974), pp. 56–8.

Orford, J. F., 'Personality factors in alcoholism: a psychological approach', *Update,* vol. 4 (1972), pp. 1371–8.

Orford, J. F., 'A prospective study of the relationship between marital factors and the outcome of treatment for alcoholism', unpublished PhD thesis, University of London (1975).

Orford, J., 'Prospects for research', Proceedings of International Symposium on the Drunkenness Offence, published by Pergamon, Oxford (1969), pp. 165–73.

Orford, J., 'Psychological approaches to alcoholism', *Update,* vol. 3 (1971), pp. 1005–13.

Orford, J., 'Simplistic thinking about other people as a predictor of early drop-out at an alcoholism halfway house', *British Journal of Medical Psychology,* vol. 47 (1974), pp. 53–63.

Orford, J. and Hawker, A., 'An investigation of an alcoholism rehabilitation halfway house: II The complex question of client motivation', *British Journal of Addiction,* vol. 69 (1974), pp. 315–23.

Orford, J. and Hawker, A., 'A note on the ordering of onset of symptoms in alcohol dependence', *Psychological Medicine,* vol. 4 (1974), pp. 281–8.

Orford, J., Hawker, A. and Nicholls, P., 'An investigation of an alcoholism rehabilitation halfway house: I Type of client and modes of discharge', *British Journal of Addiction,* vol. 69 (1974), pp. 213–24.

Orford, J., Hawker, A. and Nicholls, P., 'An investigation of an alcoholism rehabilitation halfway house: III Reciprocal staff–resident evaluation', *British Journal of Addiction,* vol. 70 (1975, in press).

Orford, J., Hawker, A. and Nicholls, P., 'An investigation of an alcoholism rehabilitation halfway house: IV Attractions of the halfway house for residents', *British Journal of Addiction,* vol. 70 (1975, in press).

Orford, J., Walker, S. and Peto, J., 'Drinking behaviour and attitudes and their correlates among university students in England: I Principal components in the drinking domain; II Personality and social influence; III Sex differences, *Quarterly Journal of Studies on Alcohol,* vol. 35 (1974), pp. 1316–74.

Orford, J., Guthrie, S., Nicholls, P., Oppenheimer, E., Egert, S. and Hensman, C., 'Self-reported coping behaviour of wives of excessive drinkers, and its association with drinking outcome', *Journal of Studies of Alcohol* (in press).

Otto, S., 'Women alcoholics. A special case for treatment', *C. C. A. Journal of Alcoholism,* vol. 3, no. 3 (1974), pp. 25–8.

Raw, M., 'Persuading people to stop smoking', *Behaviour, Research and Therapy,* vol. 13 (1975, in press).

Roberts, C., 'How treatment centres help narcotic addicts', *General Practitioner* (1973), pp. 18–19.

Roberts, J. C., 'West End types', *New Society,* (4 February 1971), pp. 195–6.

Roberts, C., 'What do narcotic addicts think of the drug dependence clinics?', *Drugs and Society,* vol. 2 (February 1973), pp. 16–19.

Robinson, D., 'Alcoholism as a social fact: notes on the sociologist's viewpoint in relation to the proposed study of referral behaviour', *British*

Journal of Addiction, vol. 68 (1973), pp. 91–7.
Robinson, D., 'The alcohologist's addiction: some implications of having lost control over the disease concept of alcoholism', *Quarterly Journal of Studies on Alcohol,* vol. 33 (1972), pp. 1028–42.
Robinson, D., 'Becoming an alcoholic: handling referrals to an outpatient department', *Japanese Journal of Studies on Alcohol,* vol. 9, no. 2 (1974), pp. 109–122.
Robinson, D., 'Becoming an alcoholic: notes on a study of procedural definitions', *Journal of Alcoholism,* vol. 8 (1973), pp. 5–12.
Robinson, D., 'Becoming ill', *Journal of Psychosomatic Research,* vol. 18, no. 3 (1974), pp. 277–81.
Robinson, D., 'The Erroll Report: key proposals and public reaction', *British Journal of Addiction,* vol. 69 (1974), pp. 99–104.
Robinson, D., *From Drinking to Alcoholism: a sociological commentary,* John Wiley & Sons, London and New York (1976).
Robinson, D., 'Illness and deviance' in A. Wertheimer and M. C. Smith (eds), *Pharmacy Practice: Social and Behavioral Aspects* (1974). University Park Press, Baltimore.
Robinson, D., 'Illness behaviour and children's hospitalization: a schema of parents' attitudes toward authority', *Social Science and Medicine,* vol. 6 (1972[b]), pp. 447–68.
Robinson, D., *Patients, Practitioners and Medical Care: Aspects of Medical Sociology,* Heinemann, London (1973).
Robinson, D., 'Please see and advise: making and handling referrals to an alcoholism outpatient clinic', in M. E. J. Wadsworth and D. Robinson (eds.), *Studies in Everyday Medical Life,* London (1976 in press).
Robinson, D., *The Process of Becoming Ill* Routledge and Kegan Paul, London (1971).
Robinson, D., 'Sociological theories of dependence: an illogical notion', in D. Hawks, (ed.) *The Epidemiology of Drug Dependence,* WHO (1973).
Robinson, D., 'To what end? Notes on the treatment of alcoholics', *Japanese Journal of Studies on Alcohol,* vol. 10, no. 1, (1974), pp. 123–139.
Robinson, D., 'Where the Erroll Committee went wrong', *Drugs and Society,* vol. 2 (March 1973), pp. 17–20.
Robinson, D., Day, I., Edwards, G., Hawks, D., Hershon, H., MacCafferty, M., Oppenheimer, E., Orford, J., Otto, S. and Taylor, C., 'Where Erroll went wrong on liquor licensing. A critique of The Report of the Departmental Committee on Liquor Licensing, Cmnd. 5154, HMSO (1972)', Camberwell Council on Alcoholism (1973).
Russell, M. A. H., 'Blood carboxyhaemoglobin changes during tobacco smoking', *Postgraduate Medical Journal,* vol. 49 (1973), pp. 684–7.

Russell, M. A. H., 'Changes in cigarette price and consumption by men in Britain, 1946–1971: a preliminary analysis', *British Journal of Preventive and Social Medicine,* vol. 27 (1973), pp. 1-7.
Russell, M. A. H., 'Cigarette Dependence: I Nature and classification', *British Medical Journal,* vol. 2 (1971), pp. 330–1.
Russell, M. A. H., 'Cigarette Dependence: II Doctor's role in management', *British Medical Journal,* vol. 2 (1971), pp. 393–5.
Russell, M. A. H., 'Cigarette smoking: natural history of a dependence disorder', *British Journal of Medical Psychology,* vol. 44 (1971), pp. 1–16.
Russell, M. A. H., 'Effect of electric aversion on cigarette smoking', *British Medical Journal,* vol. 1 (1970), pp. 82–6.
Russell, M. A. H., 'A psychiatric perspective' in E. Vallance (ed.) *The Limits of State Intervention in the Prevention of Self-destructive Behaviour,* Allen & Unwin, London (1973).
Russell, M. A. H., 'Realistic goals for smoking and health: a case for safe smoking', *Lancet* (1974), pp. 254–7.
Russell, M. A. H., 'The smoking habit and its classification', *The Practitioner,* vol. 212 (1974), pp. 791–800.
Russell, M. A. H., 'Smoking in Britain: strategy for future emancipation', *British Journal of Addiction,* vol. 66 (1971), pp. 157–66.
Russell, M. A. H., 'The smoking problem', *Nursing Times,* vol. 68 (1972), pp. 601–2 and 653–4.
Russell, M. A. H., 'Tobacco and the nation's health', in J. Zacune and C. Hensman (eds.), *Drugs, Alcohol and Tobacco in Britain: the Problems and the Response,* Heinemann, London (1971).
Russell, M. A. H., and Feyerabend, C., 'Blood and urinary nicotine in non-smokers', *Lancet,* vol. 1 (1975), pp. 179–81.
Russell, M. A. H., Armstrong, E. and Patel, U. A., 'Temporal contiguity in electric aversion therapy for cigarette smoking', *Behaviour, Research and Therapy* (in press).
Russell, M. A. H., Cole, P. V. and Brown, E., 'Absorption by non-smokers of carbon monoxide from room air polluted by tobacco smoke', *Lancet,* vol. 1 (1973), pp. 576–9.
Russell, M. A. H., Cole, P. V. and Brown, E., 'Passive smoking: absorption by non-smokers of carbon monoxide from room air polluted by tobacco smoke', *Postgraduate Medical Journal,* vol. 49 (1973), pp. 688–92.
Russell, M. A. H., Peto, J. and Patel, U. A., 'The classification of smoking by factorial structure of motives', *Journal of the Royal Statistical Society,* Series A (General) vol. 137, no. 3 (1974), pp. 313–46.
Russell, M. A. H., Wilson, C., Cole, P. V., Idle, M. and Feyerabend, C., 'Comparison of increases in carboxyhaemoglobin after smoking

"extra-mild" and "non-mild" cigarettes', *Lancet,* vol. 2 (1973), pp. 687–90.

Russell, M. A. H., Wilson, C., Patel, U. A., Cole, P. V. and Feyerabend, C., 'Comparison of the effect on tobacco consumption and carbon monoxide absorption of switching to high and low nicotine cigarettes', *British Medical Journal,* vol. 4 (1973), pp. 512–16.

Russell, M. A. H., Wilson, C., Patel, U. A., Feyerabend, C. and Cole, P. V., 'Plasma nicotine levels after smoking cigarettes with high, medium and low nicotine yields', *British Medical Journal* (in press).

Smart, R. G. and Ogborne, A., 'Losses to the addiction notification system', *British Journal of Addiction,* vol. 69 (1974), pp. 225–30.

Stimson, G. V., 'Drug-taking in the younger generation', *Ditchley Paper* no. 4 (1969), p. 32.

Stimson, G. V., 'Heroin behaviour – diversity among addicts attending London clinics', Irish University Press, London and Dublin (1973).

Stimson, G. V., 'Patterns of behaviour of heroin addicts', *International Journal of the Addictions,* vol. 7 (1972), pp. 671–91.

Stimson, G. V., 'The social background to drug addiction', Proceedings of 5th Symposium on Advanced Medicine, (ed.) R. Williams, Published by Pitman, London (1969), pp. 360–8.

Stimson, G. V. and Ogborne, A., 'Survey of Addicts Prescribed Heroin at London Clinics', *Lancet,* vol. 1 (1970), pp. 1163–6.

Stimson, G. V. and Ogborne, A., 'A survey of a representative sample of addicts prescribed heroin at London clinics', *Bulletin on Narcotics,* vol. 22, no. 4 (1970), pp. 13–22.

Teasdale, J., Segraves, R. T. and Zacune, J., ' "Psychoticism" in drug-users', *British Journal of Social and Clinical Psychology,* vol. 10 (1971), pp. 150–71.

Triesman, D., 'Logical problems in contemporary cannabis and psychedelics research', *International Journal of the Addictions,* vol. 8, (1973), pp. 667–82.

Zacune, J., 'A comparison of Canadian narcotic addicts in Great Britain & Canada', *Bulletin on Narcotics,* vol. 23, no. 4 (1971), pp. 41–9.

Zacune, J., and Hensman, C., aided by members of the Addiction Research Unit, *Drugs Alcohol and Tobacco in Britain: The Problems and the Response',* William Heinemann Medical Books (1971).

Zacune, J., Mitcheson, M. and Malone, S., 'Heroin use in a provincial town – one year later', *International Journal of the Addictions,* vol. 4 (1969), pp. 557–70.

Zacune, J., Stimson, G., Ogborne, A., Mitcheson, M. and Kosviner, A., 'The assessment of heroin usage in a provincial community', in H. Steinberg (ed.) *Scientific Basis of Drug Dependence,* Churchill, London (1969), pp. 323–30.

Index

Abcesses 142
Abstention from opiates 128, 172
Adams et al. (1966) 23
Age: of addicts 11, 37, 59, 120, 144; at first use of drug, 58, 168–9
Alarcon (1969a), 15, 27; (1969b) 22; (1972) 156, 167
Alarcon and Rathod (1968) 12
Alcohol and drugs:
relations between abuses of 199–212:
psychological dependence, definition of 200; pressure against drug taking 201–3; conflict of decision-making theoretical approach to drug behaviour 203–4; defending positions 205–8; implications 208–10; testable predictions for the model 210–13
and university students 47
Alcoholism, disease concept of 188–98: Jellinek's view 188–91; consequences 191–6
Amphetamine abuse 20–2:
oral, frequency of taking 82–3
Anumonye and McClure (1970) 31

Background: British opiate users 120–2, 137–8; methylamphetamine users 156; *see also* Family
Backhouse and James (1969) 31
Barbiturate abuses 22–3, 82–3
Behaviour pattern and university students, table of 40; *see also* Patterns of behaviour
Bestic (1966) 32, 107
Bewley (1963, 1964) 68; (1966) 22, 24; (1967) 25; (1968) 8, 22–3, 25
Bewley and Ben Arie (1968) 18, 172
Bewley et al. (1968) 17–18; (1972) 171
Binnie and Murdock (1969) 24–5, 32
Birthplace of addicts 120
Black market in heroin 97; *see also under* Sources
Blane et al. (1963) 192
Blumberg, Herbert H. 118–33, 134–45
Blumberg (1973) 132
Blumberg et al. (1973a) 31; (1974a) 134, 167–8, 171, 174–5; (1974b) 133, 167–8, 171, 174–5
Brain Committee 6, 94
Brandon and Smith (1962) 21
Bransby (1971a) 169; (1971b) 171; (1973) 169
Bransby et al. (1973) 168
British approach to heroin addiction 93–103: law 94–5; hypotheses underlying system 95; problems 96–100; ways of overcoming problems 100–2; prevention 102–3
British opiate users and the opium script 134–45
division into script and no-script groups 135
procedural variables 136
background 137–8
drugs involved 138–41
clinical contact 141–5
at London Drug Treatment Centres 118–33; backgrounds 120–2; education and employment 121; personalities 122; current life-style 122–4; illegal activities 123; drug use 124–9; clinical contact 129–30
Brooke and Glatt (1964) 22
Burroughs (1966) 116

Cannabis 23–5:
and the British university student 30–51: college surveys 32–3; prevalence survey 32–5; questionnaire 35; results of survey 37; demographic factors 37–42; attitudes, behaviour and personality factors 42–6; political activities 43; tobacco 46; alcohol 47
frequency of use 34, 36
table of prevalence of 31
Canadian narcotic practices compared with Great Britain 146–54:
sample 147, 148
findings 147–52: addicts in Great Britain 147; work status 148; criminality 149; prison 150; sources of supply 150; dosage 151; hospital treatment 151; contact with other Canadians 151; reasons for coming to England 152

Causation of drug addiction 27–8
Chambers (1969) 68
Chappel et al. (1969) 161
Chapple (1969) 22
Chapple and Gray (1968) 173
Chapple et al. (1972) 172
Characteristics of heroin addicts under treatment 110
Chein (1964) 125-6
'Chinese' heroin 98, 118, 140, 177
Chronic course of heroin usage 85
Clark (1962) 18
Clinics: and illicit obtaining of drugs 171; contact by, of British opiate users 129–30, 141–5
Cloward and Ohlin (1960) 50
Cluster analysis in patterns of behaviour 106–9
Cocaine 53, 82–3, 94
Cohen, S. Daryl 118–33, 134–45
Complications following drug use 113–14, 141–2
Compulsory treatment for heroin, should there be? 99
Connell (1958) 20, 157; (1964, 1965) 20–1; (1969) 95
Consequences of use of methylamphetamines 65–6
Contact, method of establishing: heroin addicts 74; opiate users 129–30, 141–5
Convictions, table of, amongst university students 41; *see also* Criminality; Illegal activities; Previous convictions
Couch (1960) 120, 122
Course of study and university drug users 44–5
Cramer's index 37
Criminality and drug addiction 16–17, 55, 56, 106, 123–4, 138, 144, 149, 150, 170–1; *see also* Convictions
Criteria of effectiveness in dealing with drug dependence 165
Crockett and Marks (1969) 20
Crumbaugh 45
Cultural background of student drug users 38–9; *see also* Background; Family
Cumberlidge (1968) 68
Customs and Excise 9

Dangerous Drugs Acts, 1965 and 1967 14, 94
Dangerous Drugs (Notification of Addicts) Regulations, 1968 6, 8, 94
Davidson, James 68–72
Davies (1962) 196; (1969) 197
Delinquency and drug addiction 16–17; heroin 78
Delusions 62
Demography: heroin users in provinces 75–8; methylamphetamine users 53–7; student drug users 37–42
Dependence, what is? 182–7; definition 184–5
DHSS (1965) 171; (1971) 175
Diet and methylamphetamines 54
Disease, concept of alcoholism as 188–98
Dissonance-reduction model 218–19, 220
Doctors and heroin prescriptions 98–101
Dole (1965) 72
Dosage in Canadian addicts 151
Douglas (1964) 196
Drew (1968) 210
Dronfield, B. Elizabeth 118–33, 134–45
Drug dependence: criteria of effectiveness in dealing with 165; in United Kingdom *see* Heroin users in a provincial town; *see also* Dependence, what is?; Measures to deal with drug dependence in the United Kingdom; Treatment; Social psychology of dependence
Drug: table of offences of 13–14; uses by British opiates 124–9
Drugs: characteristics of use of, tabled 126; choice of by addicts 12; illicit sources of 26, *see also* Sources; mean age at which first taken 58; (Prevention of Misuse) Act, 1964 14; variety used 169
Drug Treatment Centres *see* British opiate users

Educational background: British opiate users 121; heroin users 76; methylamphetamine users 55; university drug users 39
Edwards, Griffith 52–67, 93–103, 155–62
Edwards (1969) 104; (1970b) 189
Edwards and Guthrie (1967) 212
Effectiveness in dealing with drug dependence 165
Employment: British opiate users 121, 137, 144; Canadian drug users 148; heroin users 76; methylamphetamine users 54–5; rating and treatment of heroin addicts 105
Epidemiology *see* Cannabis and British university students; Heroin addicts,

sedative abuse by; Heroin users in a provincial town; Methylamphetamine, abuse of; United Kingdom, dimensions of drug dependence in
Ethnicity 169
Everitt (1964) 106
Extraversion and the university drug user 46
Eysenck Personality Inventory 45, 50, 122

Family:
background: British opiate users 137; heroin users 76; university drug users 38
pathology of methylamphetamine users 54
Feather (1959) 204
Female patterns of behaviour 112; *see also* Sexes of addicts
Festinger (1957) 205
Finney (1948) 109
Frankau and Stanwell (1961) 104, 147
Frequency of use of drugs: amphetamines, oral 82–3; British opiate users 126, 127–8; cannabis among university students 34, 36; heroin 69, 82–3
Friends of British opiate addicts 122–3, 128

Gardner and Connell (1970) 104
Geographic distribution of addicts 14–15
Glatt (1962) 22; (1968) 53; (1970) 194, 196
Gobius and Hawks (1970) 12, 19
Gordon (1973) 170
Great Britain *see* United Kingdom
Grouping of addicts (for this study) 106–17
Guttman Scale 106

Hallucinations 62
Hamburger (1964) 68
Hawks, David 5–29, 30–51, 52–67, 68–86, 118–33, 135–45, 155–62, 163–75
Hawks (1973) 176
Hawks et al. (1969) 11, 16, 20, 27, 68, 155; (1970) 28
Hepatitis 142
Heroin addicts:
sedative abuse by 68–72; materials and methods of research 69; frequency of use table 69; initial source table 70–1
tables of numbers of 10
who are stabilised 99
Heroin itself:
current dosages of 60
supply and pattern of use of 61
users in a provincial town 73–86:
survey and scope 74
findings: initial 75–8; after 1 year 78–80; after 2 years 80–2; after 3 years 83–4
heterogenity of users 84–86
users, table of samples of 79
see also British approach to heroin addiction; Patterns of behaviour of heroin addicts
Heterogenity of heroin users 84
Hitchens, Laura 68–72
Holahan (1972) 142
Home Office (1969) 161
Hospital treatment *see* Treatment
Hyperactivity 62
Hypnosis and drug addiction 22–3
Hypotheses in treatment of heroin addiction 95

Illegal activities of British opiate users 123, 138, 144, 170–1; *see also* Conviction; Criminality; Previous conviction
Illicit sources of drugs 26, 171; *see also under* Sources
Importation of heroin, illegal 98
Income and heroin treatment 106
Initiation into use of drugs 27
Intensity of use and methylamphetamines, table of 59
Involvement and methylamphetamine users 54
and heroin addicts 106

James (1967) 17; (1968) 53; (1969) 68
James and D'Orban (1970) 16
Janis and Man (1968) 204
Jellinek (1952) 189–90, 196; (1957) 189–90; (1960) 190–2, 197–8
Jessor et al. (1968) 50
Johnson and Clift (1968) 23
Jones (1968) 15
'Junkie' groups (for study purposes) 107–17

Keehn (968) 201
Kendell (1965) 196
Kessell (1965) 22
Keutzer (1968) 211
Key variables in heroin treatment, table of 108
Kiloh and Brandon (1962) 21
Kohn and Mercer (1971) 122
Kosviner, Adele 30–51
Kosviner et al. (1968) 12, 15, 16, 20

Kramer et al. (1967) 58

Lancet (1968) 53
Latscha (1953) 109
Laurie (1967) 107
Law and treatment of heroin addiction 94–5
Legislation to control prescribing 102
Life-style of British opium addicts 122–4
Liking for, of British opiate users 128
Lindesmith (1966) 112
Linken (1963) 20; (1968) 24; (1968a) 31; (1968b) 32
'Loner' groups (for study purposes) 108–17
LSD 23–5

Maddox (1971) 164
Mahon (1971) 170, 172, 174
Malone, Sarah 68–72
Mandrax 23
Mayer et al. (1965) 109
Measures to deal with drug dependence in United Kingdom 163–75: introduction 163–8; age of first use 168–9; ethnicity 169; variety of drugs used 169; morbidity and mortality 170; criminal offences 170–1; illicit use by clinical patients 171; abstinence 172; rehabilitation 172; controlled treatment 173
Mental Health Act, 1959 99
Merton (1957) 50
Methadone, frequency of taking 82–3
Methylamphetamine, abuse of 52–67; demography of sample 53–7; supply and pattern of use 57–61; side effects 61–3; dosages 60; who uses 63–4; choice of drug 64–5; consequences of use 65–6
Methylamphetamine users, treatment of 155–62:
 characteristics of patients 156–8: background 156; drug history 157; treatment 157–8, 161–2
 therapeutic failure 159
 poly-drug use 159
Meyer et al. (1965) 116
Misuse of Drugs Act, 1971 14
Mitcheson, Martin 52–67, 68–72, 155–62
Mitcheson et al. (1970) 16, 18, 20, 22, 26, 28, 113, 167
Morbidity and drug addiction 18, 170
Mordecai, Elizabeth A. 118–33, 134–45
Mortality and drug addiction 17–18, 170
Motivation to refuse heroin 98
Mott (1972) 122

Murphy et al. (1969) 11

Narcotic abuse *see under* United Kingdom, dimensions of drug dependence in
Narcotic addicts, prognosis of 19
Nationality of addicts 12–14
Neuroticism and the university user 46
No-script group of British opiate users 135–45

Occupation *see* Employment
O'Connell (1970) 11
Ogborne, Alan 52–67, 155–62
Ogborne and Stimson (1969) 69
O'Malley et al. (1972) 130
Opiates 81–2; *see also* British opiate users; Heroin
Oppenheim, A. N. 214–21
Orford, Jim 199–213
Orford (1974) 49
Origin of addicts 11–12; *see also* Ethnicity
Overdoses 142
Over-prescribed heroin 98, 102
Owens (1967) 15

Parsons (1951) 193
Paton (1969) 184
Patterns of behaviour of heroin addicts 104–117:
 sample and data 104–5
 findings: four scales to measure 105–6; cluster analysis 106–9; characteristics 109–13
 physical complications following drug use 113–14
 treatment policy 115–17
 see also Behaviour
Pattison (1966) 192
Pattison et al. (1968) 196
Personality: measures of student drug users 45; of British opiate users 122, 137
Physical complications following drug use 113–14, 141, 142
Political attitudes of student drug users 43
Poly-drug use, problem of 159
Poverty and drug addiction 15–16
Preble and Casey (1969) 107
Prescriptions: barbiturates 22; stimulants 21
Preventive measures and heroin drug addiction 102–3, 160, 221
Previous convictions and British opiate users 123–4, 144; *see also* Convictions; Criminality

Provinces, the *see* Heroin users in provincial town
Psychology of dependence *see* Social psychology of dependence

Questionnaires 35

Rathod (1972) 126
Realism, cult of 216
Registration as heroin addict 96
Rehabilitation 172; *see also* Treatment
Religion of student drug users 42–3
Research and heroin treatment 102, 162
Roberts, J. Colin 118–33, 134–45
Robinson, David 188–98
Robinson (1971) 193
Russell, M. A. H. 182–7
Russell (1971) 185

Schur (1966) 112
Scott and Willcox (1965) 20
Script group of British opiate users 135–45
Seeley (1962) 191
Septicaemia 142
Sexes of addicts 11, 37, 120, 137, 144
Sharpley (1964) 20
Side-effects, methylamphetamine 61–3
Siegler et al. (1968) 194
Sleep and methylamphetamines 55
Social psychology of dependence 214–21: societal expectations 215–16; cult of realism 216; myth of independence 217; dissonance-reduction model 218–20; application to drug-taking 219
Socio-economics: background to university drug users 38; grouping table 16; groups of parents of heroin users 76
Sources of drugs: illicit 26, 171; for Canadians 150; of heroin 70–1, 77, 98; of methylamphetamine 57–61; of opiates 128
Spear (1969) 8, 14
Spear and Glatt (1971) 169
Stable heroin addicts 107–17
Stimson, G.V. 104–17
Stimson and Ogborne (1970) 12, 16, 18, 20, 24, 31, 105, 119, 153, 171, 174
Substitute drugs for heroin 98
Suicide and drugs 17–18
Supply and pattern of use of methylamphetamine 57–61; *see also* Sources
Sutter (1966) 107

Theory *see* Dependence, what is?; Alcoholism, disease concept of; Alcohol and drugs, relation between abuses of; Social psychology of dependence
Therapeutic failure 159
Tobacco and university students 46
Treatment 25–6; *see also* British approach to heroin addiction; British opiate users; Canadian narcotic practices compared with Great Britain; Measures to deal with drug dependence in United Kingdom; Methylamphetamine users, treatment of; Patterns of behaviour of heroin addicts
'Two Worlder' group (of heroin addicts) 109–17

United Kingdom, dimensions of drug dependence in 5–29
  narcotic abuse by addicts 6–20: sexes 11; age 11; origin 11–12; drug choice 12; nationality 12–14; geographic distribution 14–15; poverty 15–16; delinquency and criminality 16–17; mortality 17–18; morbidity 18; prognosis 19–20
  amphetamine abuse 20–2
  barbiturate and non-barbiturate hypnotic use 22–3
  cannabis and LSD 23–5
  treatment 25–6
  illicit sources 26
  initiation 27
  causation 27–8
  see also British approach to heroin addiction; British opiate users; Canadian narcotic practices; Treatment; Measures to deal with drug dependence in United Kingdom
University students *see* Cannabis and the British university student

VD 31
Vocational orientation of student drug users 42

Webb, M. G. T. 30–51
Webb et al. (1969) 24, 27
Weiner (1970) 49
Willis (1969) 16
Wilson and Beacon (1964) 21
Winick (1962) 210
Witkin (1965) 212

Work *see* Employment
World and its Bottle, The (Jellinek) 190

Yough and Crutchley (1972) 32, 49

Zacune, Jim 146–54
Zacune (1971) 12, 15, 169
Zacune et al. (1969) 12, 15–19, 27
Zola (1972) 197

Other SAXON HOUSE Studies

Hopwood, A. G.	*An accounting system and managerial behaviour*
Black, I. G., et al	*Advanced urban transport*
Pollock, N. C.	*Animals, environment and man in Africa*
McLean, A. T.	*Business and accounting in Europe*
Rogers, S. J., B. H. Davey	*The common agricultural policy and Britain*
Hermet, G.	*The communists in Spain*
Klingen, J. S.	*Company strategy*
Chrzanowski, I.	*Concentration and centralisation of capital in shipping*
Bailey, R. V., J. Young (eds)	*Contemporary social problems in Britain*
Mack, J. A.	*The crime industry*
Sjølund, A.	*Daycare institutions and children's development*
Lewis, C.	*Demand analysis and inventory control*
Jambrek, P.	*Development and social change in Yugoslavia*
Macmillan, J.	*Deviant drivers*
Richards, M. G., M. E. Ben-Akiva	*A disaggregate travel demand model*
Teff, H.	*Drugs, society and the law*
Snickers, F. et al (eds)	*Dynamic allocation of urban space*
Ellison, A. P., E. M. Stafford	*The dynamics of the civil aviation industry*
Birnbaum, K. E.	*East and West Germany*
Masnata, A.	*East-West economic co-operation*
Ghosh, D.	*The economics of building societies*
Richardson, H. W.	*The economics of urban size*
Starkie, D. N., D. M. Johnson	*The economic value of peace and quiet*
John, I. G. (ed.)	*EEC policy towards Eastern Europe*
More, W. S. (ed.)	*Emotions and adult learning*
Grassman, S.	*Exchange reserves and the financial structure of foreign trade*
Thompson, M. S.	*Evaluation for decision in social programmes*
von Geusau, F.A.M.A. (ed.)	*The external relations of the European Community*
Bergmann, T.	*Farm policies in socialist countries*
Ash, J. C. K., D. J. Smyth	*Forecasting the U.K. economy*
Blank, S.	*Government and industry in Britain*
Buttler, F. A.	*Growth pole theory and economic development*
Richardson, H. W., et al	*Housing and urban spatial structure*
van Duijn, J. J.	*An interregional model of economic fluctuations*
Brittain, J. M., S. A. Roberts (eds)	*Inventory of information resources in the social sciences*
Fukuda, H.	*Japan and world trade*
Jackson, M. P.	*Labour relations on the docks*
Stephenson, I. S.	*The law relating to agriculture*
Hess, H.	*Mafia and Mafiosi*
Vodopivec, K.	*Maladjusted youth*
Hovell, P. J., et al	*The management of urban public transport*
Funnell, B. M., R. D. Hey (eds)	*The management of water resources in England and Wales*
Martin, M. J. C.	*Management science and urban problems*
Rhenman, E.	*Managing the community hospital*
Giddings, P. J.	*Marketing boards and ministers*
Klaassen, L. H., P. Drewe	*Migration policy in Europe*
Chapman, C. B.	*Modular decision analysis*

Hodges, M.	*Multinational corporations and national governments*
Liggins, D.	*National economic planning in France*
Friedly, P. H.	*National policy responses to urban growth*
Madelin, H.	*Oil and politics*
Tilford, R. (ed.)	*The Ostpolitik and political change in Germany*
Friedrichs, J., H. Ludtke	*Participant observation*
Fitzmaurice, J.	*The party groups in the European parliament*
Brown, J., G. Howes (eds)	*The police and the community*
Lang, R. W.	*The politics of drugs*
Denton, F. T., B. G. Spencer	*Population and the economy*
Dickinson, J. P. (ed.)	*Portfolio analysis*
Wilson, D. J.	*Power and party bureaucracy in Britain*
Wabe, J. S.	*Problems in manpower forecasting*
Willis, K. G.	*Problems in migration analysis*
Farnsworth, R. A.	*Productivity and law*
Shepherd, R. J.	*Public opinion and European integration*
Richardson, H. W.	*Regional development policy and planning in Spain*
Sant, M. (ed.)	*Regional policy and planning for Europe*
Thorpe, D. (ed.)	*Research into retailing and distribution*
Dickinson, J. P.	*Risk and uncertainty in accounting and finance*
Hey, R. D., T. D. Davies (eds)	*Science, technology and environmental management*
Britton, D. K., B. Hill	*Size and efficiency in farming*
Buchholz, E., et al	*Socialist criminology*
Paterson, W. E.	*The SPD and European integration*
Blohm, H., K. Steinbuch (eds)	*Technological forecasting in practice*
Piepe, A., et al	*Television and the working class*
Goodhardt, G. J., et al	*The television audience*
May, T. C.	*Trade unions and pressure group politics*
Labini, P. S.	*Trade unions, inflation and productivity*
Casadio, G. P.	*Transatlantic trade*
Whitehead, C. M. E.	*The U.K. housing market*
Balfour, C.	*Unions and the law*